GEORGE A. ROMERO'S INDEPENDENT CINEMA

GEORGE A. ROMERO'S INDEPENDENT CINEMA

Horror, Industry, Economics

Tom Fallows

EDINBURGH
University Press

Edinburgh University Press is one of the leading university presses in the UK. We publish academic books and journals in our selected subject areas across the humanities and social sciences, combining cutting-edge scholarship with high editorial and production values to produce academic works of lasting importance. For more information visit our website: edinburghuniversitypress.com

© Tom Fallows, 2022

Edinburgh University Press Ltd
The Tun – Holyrood Road
12 (2f) Jackson's Entry
Edinburgh EH8 8PJ

Typeset in 10/12.5 pt Sabon
by IDSUK (DataConnection) Ltd

A CIP record for this book is available from the British Library

ISBN 978 1 4744 7995 0 (hardback)
ISBN 978 1 4744 7997 4 (webready PDF)
ISBN 978 1 4744 7998 1 (epub)

The right of Tom Fallows to be identified as author of this work has been asserted in accordance with the Copyright, Designs and Patents Act 1988 and the Copyright and Related Rights Regulations 2003 (SI No. 2498).

CONTENTS

List of Figures and Tables   vi
Acknowledgements   vii

    Introduction   1

1. Latent Image(s): Revealing Industrial Alternatives, 1963–1973   27

2. A New Dawn: Cult, Risk and the Independent Film Producer, 1973–1979   55

3. 'Camelot is a State of Mind': Professional Product, Independent Spirit, 1979–1982   83

4. The Once and Future King: Agency and the Limits of Control, 1981–1985   108

5. Last Stand: Mergers, Acquisitions and the Small Business Enterprise, 1985–1994   135

Epilogue: Life After Death   165

Laurel Mediography   170
Bibliography   173
Index   197

FIGURES AND TABLES

Figures
1.1	*Night of the Living Dead* budget breakdown	33
1.2	Joan looks to escape her role as 'housewife-mother' in *Jack's Wife* (1972)	42
2.1	Laurel business wheel	70
3.1	A new direction for both Laurel and its biker-knights in *Knightriders* (1981)	103
4.1	*Pet Sematary* Memorandum of Agreement, 20 March 1985	117
4.2	The apocalypse on a scaled-down budget in *Day of the Dead* (1985)	123
5.1	The Viacom–Paramount merger, 1994	158

Tables
1.1	Four types of business orientation	49
2.1	Leading US cinema chains in 1977	76
5.1	Types of merger	144

ACKNOWLEDGEMENTS

The bitter irony of writing a book about the man who gave us the 'zombie apocalypse' during a very real global pandemic has not been lost on me. But while George A. Romero's locked-in survivors almost always turn on each other when the world outside goes to hell, I received nothing but support from a countless number of people. This work began as a Ph.D. research project at the University of Exeter and would not have been possible without the guidance and expertise of James Lyons and Helen Hanson. Thanks to Callan Davies, who gave constant encouragement and valuable feedback throughout, and Yannis Tzioumakis, whose generous advocacy helped move this project towards publication. I must also offer my sincere gratitude to the team at Edinburgh University Press, particularly Gillian Leslie, Richard Strachan and Sam Johnson, and to copy editor Fiona Screen.

I would be remiss if I did not mention the contributors and institutions that shaped this project: David Ball, Nicola Borrelli, Tony Buba, Tom Dubensky, Kate Egan, Mitchell Galin, Barney Guttman, John Harrison, Adam Hart, Ed Lammi, Debra Ramsay, John A. Russo, Jeffrey Stanley, Andrew Stein, Mark Steven, William Teitler, Linda Ruth Williams, Paul Williams and Paolo Zelati. Thanks to Suzanne Romero and the George A. Romero Foundation; Benjamin Rubin, coordinator of the Horror Studies Collection at the University of Pittsburgh; Roye Werner and Jill Chisnell at Carnegie Mellon University's Hunt Library; Michael Lillard at Columbia University's Watson Library; Phil Wickham at the Bill Douglas Cinema Museum; Kathy Baro and the staff of the University of Exeter Library; UCC Boole Library; the University of Exeter College of Humanities Graduate School; and the British Association of American Studies.

Thanks to my wonderfully courageous mum Marilyn Fallows, my ridiculously supportive American parents Charlie and Tammi Curran, John Rubanski, Silvia Berretta, Deniz Çizmeci, Andrea Gori, Stuart Green, Pamela Heard (welcome Aaron!), Alex Johns, David Kanhai, Curtis Owen, David Pickerill, Ed James, Ashley Mahlmeister, Nathan Mahlmeister, Juliette Scott-Foss, Oley Morgan, Mike, Ben, J, Sam, Jack, Emilia, Kumi, Beckie, Laura, Matilda, Otis, Josh and to my family around the world, from Stoke-on-Trent to Virginia and beyond.

Finally, I must thank George A. Romero, whose work continues to inspire me and who was the exception to the rule that you should never meet your heroes. And to my lockdown companion, proof-reader, wife and best mate Annie Curran: I couldn't survive an apocalypse without you. Nor would I want to.

For Annie Curran

INTRODUCTION

By 1973, George A. Romero's career as an independent film director appeared to be over. His debut feature *Night of the Living Dead* (1968) – a violent horror film made in Pittsburgh, PA – had generated $30 million worldwide[1] on a budget of $114,000, yet the film's success was difficult to emulate. *Night* was followed by a series of box office failures and financial disasters, leaving Romero with a personal debt of around half a million dollars and the fear that regional independent filmmaking was unsustainable in the long term. Fortuitously, that same year Romero met would-be producer Richard P. Rubinstein, a twenty-six-year-old New York business graduate with his own ideas on how to survive in the independent sector. Their subsequent partnership, Laurel Entertainment, would implement a number of practices that helped shape non-Hollywood production, including the use of multinational funding structures, skilful branding, manipulations of ancillary markets and product diversification. In the process, Romero cemented his reputation as one of the most culturally significant horror auteurs to emerge from the US.

But while Romero's status as a leading cult filmmaker is assured, the activities of the small independent production company that facilitated a substantial part of his output have been neglected. Laurel was the platform from which Romero produced his most varied and defining work: the teen vampire horror *Martin* (1977); the non-horror biker movie *Knightriders* (1981); the Stephen King anthology *Creepshow* (1982); and the instantly iconic *Dawn of the Dead* (1978). After Romero left the company in 1985, his career was less stable, best remembered for a regrettable flirtation with Hollywood in the 1990s (that failed to produce a single film in seven years) and a final, and ultimately inescapable, return to the living dead in the mid-2000s. Laurel's value, meanwhile, extended beyond Romero to regional filmmaking more widely, helping establish a base of talent that still supports 'runaway' Hollywood productions in Pittsburgh to this day. And although the firm closed in 1994, its product remains attractive to content-hungry media executives, exemplified by the recent *Creepshow* series by streaming service Shudder (2019-present) and a remake of the firm's miniseries *The Stand* (Garris, 1994) for CBS. Since its incorporation, Laurel's influence has been extensive, and worthy of closer attention.

George A. Romero's Independent Cinema offers an intricate, micro-industrial case study of a production company on the margins of both the industry and current academic frames of analysis. Delving into the real-world conduct of the firm provides a unique perspective on independent filmmaking practices and production cultures, enhancing our understanding of institutional actions and creative incentives in this sector. Laurel's remarkable longevity across three decades (four when we take into account parent company the Latent Image) traversed divergent periods of American independent cinema, enabling a consideration of the macro-industrial changes that impacted this small-sized media enterprise. As such, this book incorporates and expands upon a media industry studies framework that, in the words of Jennifer Holt and Alisa Perren, 'perceives culture and cultural production as sites of struggle, contestation, and negotiation between a broad range of stakeholders'.[2] The following pages also present new insight into the work of George Romero and, not least, the under-researched figure of the independent film producer, revealing the myriad economic, legal and institutional forces that feed into and dictate cultural objects away from Hollywood.

Sitting within this broader study of the firm, the evaluation of Romero's approach to independent filmmaking intersects with theories on auteurism and cult cinema. Although these strands were crucial to his framing as an important regional director who 'redefined the genre film',[3] this book reviews these factors in closer relation to industrial parameters, looking at their relevance to systems of corporate governance and marketplace strategies. I assess how these fields interacted and were internally arranged within the firm, charting the innovations, compromises and contradictions of this infrastructural convergence. Interrogating Laurel's corporate development expands existing critical materials to address these branches from a ground-level perspective, asking what auteurship, cult horror and independence meant to practitioners, not just artistically, but also in terms of economic and industrial permanence.

History and 'Prehistory'

The Laurel media entity was named after the official state flower of Pennsylvania – the mountain laurel (*Kalmia latifolia*) to be precise – a wildflower that conveniently symbolised the company's regional specificity and its determination to flourish without need of external cultivation. The firm started as Laurel Productions of Pennsylvania in 1970 as a subsidiary of Romero's regional advertising firm the Latent Image, itself active since 1963. Partnership with Rubinstein in 1973 initially moved the company towards television production under the moniker Laurel Tape & Film, before breaking away from its parent to produce a series of iconic cult films in the 1970s and 1980s. Speaking on the set of *Dawn of the Dead* in 1978, Rubinstein stated that the then-titled Laurel Group operated in

> a 'European style' in terms of the way we produce and the way George directs in that we tend to follow Sarris's auteur theory of direction . . . I see my function as a producer in terms of providing George Romero with a brush, palette and canvas. And his creative control is absolute in terms of the film itself, that he's the scriptwriter, that he's the director and that he's the editor. It's totally the product of one man's vision – on a creative level.[4]

Rubinstein's comments iterate a fairly typical perception of independent cinema, where, as Thomas Schatz remarks, creative control is said to be 'exceedingly rare in major studio productions, while it is altogether common – if not taken for granted – in independent filmmaking. In this sense the indie realm is the province of the auteur.'[5] Although no prior scholarship exists on Laurel or its co-founder Rubinstein, Romero's status as an auteur has seen him attract more attention. His films have been praised for their aesthetic and ideological consistencies, especially when it comes to the bloody critiques of modern-day America found in his '*Dead*' films.

In a career that encompassed five decades, Romero directed six films featuring the walking dead, culminating with his final film, *Survival of the Dead*, in 2009. Scenes of ghouls devouring human flesh made *Night of the Living Dead* controversial upon its original release (industry trade paper *Variety* famously called it 'the pornography of violence'),[6] yet the film was quickly redrawn as a threshold moment in horror cinema, said to infuse cheaply made genre films with a political radicalism previously unheard of.[7] *Night*'s allegorical violence reflected simmering, potentially catastrophic tensions across sociocultural lines of race, family and class in late 1960s America, from a young girl butchering and devouring her parents to the bitter conclusion that sees the African American hero Ben (Duane Jones) shot dead by a white posse. The rural Pittsburgh location added immediacy (not to mention affordability) to its rhetoric, encouraging a '1970s generation of hand-to-mouth auteurs' such as Wes Craven, John Carpenter and Tobe Hooper to produce their own filmic blends of horror and engagement.[8]

Laurel's sequel, *Dawn of the Dead*, was equally impactful and placed its director at the heart of a serious-minded inquiry into horror cinema. In September 1979, Romero was a guest of honour at Toronto's Festival of Festivals where he was interviewed onstage by the organisers as part of a retrospective on the genre.[9] Alongside the accompanying *American Nightmare* booklet (compiled by festival organisers Robin Wood, Richard Lippe, Tony Williams and Andrew Britton), the retrospective significantly contributed to the study of horror, with Wood drawing upon Marxist and Freudian theory to conceptualise the genre as a subversive counterpoint to the dominant cultural hegemony. *Dawn of the Dead* neatly encapsulated this positioning, its vast shopping mall location (an 'important place' in the life and death of its zombie inhabitants, according to one of the film's protagonists) housing a full-blooded Technicolor satire of American consumerism. For Wood, the film's flesh-eating ghouls were nothing less than 'the logical end-result, the *reductio ad absurdum* and *ad nauseum*, of Capitalism'.[10]

In alignment with Schatz's comments on authorship, critics have equated Romero's freedom to transgress (politically and in the taboo displays of violence splattered across his best-known works) to his geographical distance 'far away from Hollywood'[11] – in other words, to his independence. Romero himself embellished his outsider status in the press, regaling interviewers with stories of Hollywood skirmishes and incredulous studio thinking,[12] and he shunned Hollywood for the greater part of his career. From the early 1970s to the 1980s, Laurel was a decisive factor in maintaining and reinforcing his independence, allowing Romero to operate from his Pittsburgh base supposedly free from mainstream interference. Notions of independence go hand-in-hand with the discourse surrounding Romero's director-auteur image, but what Romero in turn offers to a study of independent cinema has not been considered.

Analysis of the independent sector galvanised around films from the 1980s onward, where emergent young film directors such as Allison Anders, Joel and Ethan Coen, Jim Jarmusch, Spike Lee and Gus Van Sant were said to offer a 'fresh perspective, innovative spirit, and personal vision' unavailable in Hollywood.[13] Steven Soderbergh's *sex, lies, and videotape* (1989) is thought of as a climactic moment in this regard. According to Jennifer Holt, the film's substantial box office returns and inclusion at several high-profile award ceremonies (nominated for Best Original Screenplay at the 1990 Academy Awards and winning the prestigious Palme d'Or at the 42nd Cannes Film Festival) repositioned independent cinema as something that was 'profitable, viable and appealing to mainstream audiences'.[14] In the following decade, production-distribution companies including New Line Cinema, Miramax and later 'indiewood'[15] studio divisions such as Fox Searchlight and Paramount Vantage transformed the sector, in a manner that seemed to defy its status as an artistic-economic alternative to Hollywood, into a multi-million-dollar enterprise.

Though the independent cinema of the so-called 'Sundance-Miramax era' (1980s to 2010s) offered an attractive, if not altogether uncomplicated or entirely unbound alternative to Hollywood, the attention given to this strand tends to downplay historical developments. Leading independent cinema scholar Yannis Tzioumakis refers to events preceding the 1980s as a 'prehistory',[16] recognising the fact that this latter period is now an enclosed site of significance for numerous writers in the field. By the 1980s, however, independent cinema was far from the 'new phenomenon' described[17] and Tzioumakis (2017) and Greg Merritt (2000) have provided more comprehensive histories dating back to the dawn of cinema in the late nineteenth/early twentieth century. For his part, Romero's career advanced in parallel, if not exactly harmony, with movements that began in the late 1950s. To better understand his and his company's importance to a history of independent cinema (and why this importance has been contested), it is necessary to first trace the sector's growth as an industrial and philosophical alternative to Hollywood during this timeframe.

Romero's first steps into film production were, in fact, relatively conventional, using his summers between school to work entry-level positions on Hollywood A-pictures. This included 20th Century Fox's *Peyton Place* (Robson, 1957); Columbia's *Bell, Book and Candle* (Quine, 1958); and MGM's *It Happened to Jane* (Quine, 1959) and *North by Northwest* (Hitchcock, 1959). Coincidentally, 1959 also saw the completion of John Cassavetes's seminal indie film *Shadows*. For critic and future film director Peter Bogdanovich, *Shadows* was 'the first post-Golden-age-of-Hollywood independant [sic] film and it turned its back on all the glossy and bankrupt big movie rules and called for a new honesty, a final abandonment of the American studio formula'.[18] *Shadows* was self-financed and shot on location in New York City with a cast of non-professionals, and in the opinion of Tzioumakis asserted 'the very powerful and romantic ideology of the lone and uncompromised auteur . . . who goes to great lengths to see his distinct vision on the screen'.[19]

This promise of an uncompromising filmmaker with a 'distinct vision' was the stuff of heady discussion among cineastes and film magazines of the day. In the 1950s, cinema was increasingly advocated as a legitimate art form, a status that appeared to demand that a legitimate artist be placed at the centre of the conversation. Alexandre Astruc's 'la caméra-stylo' famously labelled filmmaking a means of personal artistic expression no different from painting or writing a novel, a sentiment later refined by *Cahiers du cinema* and François Truffaut as *la politique des auteurs*.[20] US critic Andrew Sarris's *Film Culture* article 'Notes on the Auteur Theory in 1962' further defined this status through three primary qualifiers: (1) the director must display technical competence; (2) the distinguishable personality of the director must be visible; and (3) the director must display interior meaning, which meant nothing less than the 'élan of the soul'.[21] For Sarris, the economic circumstances of production were irrelevant, permitting 'commercial' directors like Alfred Hitchcock to stand side-by-side with so-called 'pure' directors like Robert Bresson and Max Ophuls – with 'pure' indicating filmmakers deemed to make art for art's sake.[22] Not all commentators agreed with this estimation.

In 1961, *Film Culture* founders Jonas and Adolfas Mekas used the pages of their magazine to print 'The First Statement of the New American Cinema Group', a manifesto that distanced industry and the marketplace from the authentic creative process. The statement declared, 'we believe that cinema is indivisibly a personal expression. We therefore reject the interference of producers, distributors and investors until our work is ready to be projected on the screen.'[23] As the New American Cinema Group sought to establish an autocratic space for American Art Cinema, Mekas was never less than vocal about his expectations for this branch of non-Hollywood production. On seeing Cassavetes's *Shadows*, Mekas commended the film for catching 'the tones and rhythms of a new America',[24] awarding it *Film Culture*'s first Annual Independent Film Award. But to Mekas's dismay, Cassavetes continued to work on *Shadows* after its initial screenings, channelling additional funds into an extensive reshoot and re-edit to provide a clearer sense of narrative progression. Mekas despised this second version, deeming it a betrayal of the independent spirit, no more than 'a bad commercial film, with everything that I was praising completely destroyed'.[25]

Mekas was one of many prominent figures during this period to show concern over what American independent cinema should and should not be. On 8 January 1962, the Group launched the Film-Makers' Cooperative, a network that collated films for rental from a single distribution point. In spite of Mekas's misgivings about the second version of *Shadows*, he insisted that no film would be rejected by the Cooperative. This was in part a response to Amos and Marcia Vogel's Cinema 16 film society and their refusal to programme Stan Brakhage's *Anticipation of the Night* (1958). The Vogels' dedication to avant-garde and underground cinema was underpinned by their own sometimes restrictive valuations and they apparently found Brakhage's film to be 'an artistic failure'.[26] The Cooperative, on the other hand, initially sought to forge 'a middle ground where thematic seriousness and aesthetic integrity would meet popular accessibility'.[27] Andy Warhol's *Chelsea Girls* (1966) was an early success in this regard, mixing avant-garde technique, Warhol's saleable name and a salacious appeal to gross $300,000 in its first six months at New York's Regency Theatre. If *Chelsea Girls* suggested an independent cinema to come, the Cooperative steadily moved towards the same exclusive roster as

Cinema 16, influenced as much by a lack of support for the avant-garde at the New York Film Festival in 1963 as by their own limited financial resources.[28]

This doctrinal exclusivity was matched by an exclusivity of space, confining production largely to New York, or more accurately, Manhattan. David Curtis observes the importance of the region to the New American Cinema Group, identifying a 'loosely defined trade association of low-budget feature filmmakers, whose membership was based on personal association'.[29] Manhattan's Greenwich Village was central to this network and the large demographic of educated young people attending Columbia University and NYU helped sustain a localised avant-garde scene. Discourse during this period often treated 'New York' as an interchangeable word for 'independent',[30] downplaying the worth of other regional cooperatives and film societies in the United States (notably Bruce Ballie's Canyon Cinema in San Francisco). In the 1960s, it could be said that the face of independent cinema was one of provincialism. In spite of his own New York upbringing, Romero regarded this space as closed off. 'I never knew Manhattan; I was a Bronx kid . . . I fled before I even knew what New York was about', he later explained.[31]

What Romero did know about Manhattan was informed by a Bronx gang culture that regarded the borough, in his own words, as 'enemy territory'.[32] His only visits southward were made under the guardianship of a wealthy aunt and uncle determined to broaden his horizons through New York's theatre scene.[33] The young George Romero henceforth viewed Manhattan as urbane yet other, associated with prosperity, the arts and opposition. This world was far removed from his day-to-day upbringing as the only child of a first-generation Cuban father and a second-generation Lithuanian mother. Romero's parents emphasised the importance of education and job security, pushing him towards university at Pittsburgh's Carnegie Institute of Technology (also, as it happens, Warhol's alma mater; renamed Carnegie Mellon University in 1967), though he dropped out without earning a degree. Intriguingly, like his father, Romero trained to be a commercial artist and, as we shall see, this balance between business-related pragmatism and an artisanal life would be a source of tension and consolidation in his subsequent career.

In the 1970s, as Romero's production company Latent Image faltered and gave way to its Laurel subsidiary, American independent cinema elsewhere continued as a subject of discussion and development. This was propagated by inchoate funding bodies such as the National Endowment for the Arts (NEA), the Independent Feature Project (IFP), PBS's 'American Playhouse' series and private sector corporations including the Ford Foundation, the Jerome Foundation and the Film Fund. Within this infrastructure, home-grown independent feature films were voluminous enough to be labelled a 'movement'.[34] For all that, securing monies was still far from easy. Just as the Film-Makers' Cooperative found it could only support the avant-garde, the small pots of money available from the above institutions typically favoured first-time filmmakers, raising issues of longevity away from Hollywood.[35] Even the career of indie influencer John Cassavetes, an A-list actor who could funnel his star salary and connections back into indie productions like *A Woman Under the Influence* (1974) and *The Killing of a Chinese Bookie* (1976), offered no solutions for filmmakers emerging from without, rather than within, an established system.

In the early 1980s, critics were certainly alert to the problems of financing, penning articles that advised up-and-coming filmmakers on how to raise money and find distribution.[36] Gradually, these attempts to support the industry and, by and large, to say why these filmmakers deserved funding, gave way to an all-too-familiar need to define independent cinema based on its cultural worth. In 1981, Annette Insdorf's influential piece 'Ordinary People, European-Style' praised the 'social and moral' vision of films that included Barbara Kopple's *Harlan County U.S.A.* (1976), Robert M. Young's *Alambrista!* (1977), John Hanson and Rob Nilsson's *Northern Lights* (1978) and Victor Nuñez's *Gal Young 'Un* (1979), writing:

> These politically sensitive and geographically rooted directors resist Hollywood's priorities and potential absorption ... consistent with a European tradition that values a leisurely narrative over breakneck, television commercial-style pacing, reflection over action, and a depiction of political realities over sex and violence.[37]

Insdorf was essentially continuing where Mekas and the Vogels left off, determining to add specificity to an unwieldy sector that embodied everything from the avant-garde to pornography. In the late 1970s, as the NEA's regional States Arts Agencies helped move film production out of New York and across the country, regionality was suggested as a useful identifying factor, exemplified by the work of Nuñez in Florida and Hanson and Nilsson in North Dakota. Sundance Institute founder Robert Redford saw regional films as having their finger on 'the pulse of what is going on in this country'.[38] Even so, as the 1980s wore on, production increasingly gravitated back towards New York and LA, in no small part due to the larger networks of skilled professionals and media trade unions that naturally converged around pre-established industry centres. Critical interest followed thereafter.

More consistently than regional placement, 'quality' has been used as a benchmark, allowing critics to distinguish between so-called 'authentic' indies (films that are socially and politically motivated, formally disruptive and intellectually challenging) and those said to be more commercially minded.[39] Janet Staiger's assertion that independent features 'without an intellectual engagement might better be relegated to the traditional classical Hollywood cinema film practice'[40] is, however, problematic. Staiger fails to account for those independent practitioners who co-opt an 'aura of quality' as a marketing tool (or as a means of confounding the censors, as sexploitation producers such as Cambist Films did in the 1960s and 1970s).[41] More troublingly, this take also reinforces elitist notions of taste based on class, ethnicity and education. Michael Z. Newman says that such discernment is typical of the identity-forming of indie film consumers who, as per Pierre Bourdieu, court subcultural capital through a projection of their oppositional taste values.[42] The independent filmgoer denies the 'lower, coarse, vulgar, venal, servile' pleasure of low or mainstream culture to affirm a superiority based on their own refined sensibilities.[43]

Insdorf's 1981 article calls for a similar sense of distinction, distancing 'quality' independent films 'from filmmakers like George Romero, Tobe Hooper, John Carpenter, and David Cronenberg, who to one degree or another exist outside the industry orbit, but whose affection for Grand Guignol, violence, and sex has attracted commercial money'.[44] Though these filmmakers certainly saw the commercial potential of horror cinema, Insdorf's attempt to obtain specificity for American independent cinema by exclusion again overlooks a number of key factors, in this case: (1) that these filmmakers had interests in addition to the production of genre films; (2) that genre was far from the financial guarantor proposed; and (3) that the use of genre might not preclude artistry and/or a 'social and moral' vision.

Despite Robin Wood et al.'s efforts to reframe horror as a legitimate art form, the genre film has frequently been problematic for those tastemakers who worry over the 'erosion of a certain *idea* about art cinema'.[45] Jamie Sexton argues that horror offers a useful counterpoint to canonised independent cinema, the genre's exclusion as 'abject entity' serving to confirm the indie label as a homogenous generic construct through a reassertion of quality.[46]

In David Kehr's contemporary review of *Dawn of the Dead*, he detected an aggressive and 'antisocial stance' that as an independent film 'might be *too* independent – too fierce and original and threatening'.[47] For Kehr, independence and transgression appear to mean the same thing; Romero had simply taken this beyond the limits of acceptability (much to Kehr's overall delight, it should be added). *Dawn*'s affront to social mores flows from the film's graphic violence, which in the first fifteen minutes alone displays images of bodily assault, splattered gunshot wounds, decaying flesh, piled up corpses and gleeful close-ups of the undead devouring human flesh – the fifteen-minute mark was, incidentally, the point at which *New York Times* film critic Janet Maslin fled the press screening.[48] Linda Williams writes that such systems of excessive display have situated gross-out horror on the outskirts of a mainstream enquiry, with the genre only fractionally more credible than pornography as a site for study.[49] Harmony H. Wu adds that an embrace of what might be measured distasteful is actually one of horror's 'generic imperatives', consequently reiterating 'lowbrow' insinuations.[50]

The picture of American independent cinema painted above seems to leave little room for Romero's unique brand of cinema. Romero was geographically separated from dominant bicoastal industries, denied access to (the admittedly meagre) financial resources and the loose networks of film workers and artists that defined independent cinema from the late 1950s to the 1980s. Ideologically, Romero was drawn to the wrong kind of independent film, producing work deemed at once overtly commercial and aesthetically debased. His dismissal when it came to a homogenised American independent sector (determined by tastemakers whose definitions, it must be said, were far from universally agreed upon and often subject to in-fighting and internal debate) was, however, pivotal to his reputation elsewhere. This was nowhere more patent than in his status as a vanguard cult filmmaker, where notions of distaste, excess and distance from the mainstream are prerequisites for inclusion.

Abject Entities: Cult and Economics

What constitutes a cult film has long been a source of contention. Multi-platform studio properties such as *Star Trek* (1966-present) are famous for their dedicated cult followings, though cult is more typically associated with low-budget underground cinema. As with independent cinema, the 'sheer eclecticism'[51] of cult has seen theorists turn to the work of Bourdieu and cultural consumption as an organising principle. Mark Jancovich proposes that cult cinema aficionados seek to affirm their identity by rejecting mainstream entertainment and celebrating transgressive materials, perceiving viewers of mainstream product as the 'moronic victims of mass culture'.[52] If this sounds exactly like the indie film consumer, Jeffrey Sconce defines cult, or paracinema as he calls it, as a celebration of 'lowbrow' product, presenting 'a direct challenge to the values of aesthete film culture and a general affront to the "refined" sensibility of the parent taste culture'.[53] For Sconce, paracinema gathers up

> such seemingly disparate subgenres as 'badfilm', splatterpunk, 'mondo' films, sword and sandal epics, Elvis flicks, government hygiene films, Japanese monster movies, beach-party musicals, and just about every other historical manifestation of exploitation cinema from juvenile delinquency documentaries to soft-core pornography.[54]

David Chute writes that cult cinema's 'crucial social function is to overstep the limits of established taste',[55] an oppositional rallying cry that neatly summarises paracinema consumption.

By looking at cult through fan reception, Elena Gorfinkel argues that we have shifted 'from the "death of the author", to the (re)birth of the audience'.[56] Yet the director has not been entirely discarded and remains pivotal to fan cultures and academic writings. Ernest Mathijs and Xavier Mendik place a canon of auteurs at the heart of their own anthology on cult cinema, a list comprising of Dario Argento, David Cronenberg, Peter Jackson, Terry Gilliam, Alejandro Jodorowsky and George A. Romero. Of these directors, Gilliam is the only one not to turn his hand to horror, leading Mathijs and Mendik to observe the 'authority' of this genre when it comes to cult cinema. In terms of their own hand-picked selection, they confess that qualitatively, horror is the most prominent cult genre.[57]

Of course, not all horror movies are considered cult movies and fans will often dismiss a genre film if they find it to be 'too mainstream'.[58] Jancovich points out that an appreciation of the so-called 'cult auteur' can be a further source of distinction in fan communities, demonstrating capital through knowledge and expertise.[59] Notions of 'quality' are then not entirely thrown out for cult film fans. As we have seen, Romero's reputation as a cult auteur was restated through analysis of his *'Dead'* films, which 'provoked not just [a] visceral response but serious critical debate'.[60] Tony Williams has stressed auteurist propensities across all of the director's films, including lesser-known works such as *There's Always Vanilla* (1971), *Jack's Wife* (1972) and *Monkey Shines* (1988). Though admirable, Williams's intent appears to be to impart artistic seriousness via association, drawing parallels between these films and the work of Émile Zola and nineteenth-century literary naturalism.[61] Scholarship on cult cinema might argue that Romero fans do not need such associations with high culture to feel that his work is legitimised (quite the opposite in fact), and Romero has also implied that such equivalences, if they do exist, are entirely coincidental.[62] This points to a disconnect between certain text-centric readings and the filmmaker's approach to his own material.

Williams is, in fact, single-minded in his focus on textual analysis and ignores the industrial conditions that surround the production of Romero's films. This is not uncommon. In Kendall R. Phillips's work on horror filmmakers of the 1970s, he labels cinema 'one of the most expansive and collaborative of artistic endeavours',[63] yet ultimately abides to the classical auteur model when it comes to Romero's films. In these examples and elsewhere, important collaborators such as Rubinstein are consigned to the peripheries, and their impact on the filmic text goes with them.

In writings on cult cinema, industrial parameters are more commonly drawn upon as a counterpoint. Critics V. Vale and Andrea Juno's fans-eye-celebration of cult cinema *Incredibly Strange Films* (1986) asserts that lowbrow/low-budget cult films are 'transcendent expressions of a single person's individual vision and quirky originality', where the higher the budget, the longer the chain of 'lawyers, accountants, and corporate boards' that serve only to derail creativity.[64] As seductive as this may be, it again does not reflect, let alone scrutinise, the realities of filmmaking at any level. What is offered instead is a clichéd summation of working practices that subsumes industrial strictures into a broader agenda of fan identity-making. This perspective shrouds exactly how these cult films are made. What is the production process? To what extent does this process permit artistic transcendence? As we shall see, when Romero produced *Night of the Living Dead*, he and his collaborators were well aware of the commercial value of horror, but what Romero came to realise through his partnership with Rubinstein were the specific economic and industrial potentials of cult horror. An exploration of his firm's activities in this regard will make a fascinating addition to our current understanding of cult cinema.

As evident in the New American Cinema Group's First Statement, a diminishment of economic conditions was shared by American independent cinema's tastemakers. Greg Merritt's otherwise all-embracing overview of independent cinema also returns to the director-auteur as the sole creative force, and he ends his work by eagerly awaiting the moment 'the next great director – with a small budget and a big dream – calls "action!"'.[65] This statement is once again dislocated from the complex interplay of industrial personnel that facilitates calling 'action' in the first place. Chuck Kleinhans is more contemptuous of what he calls 'the authorship myth', upholding that 'independence is not just a state of mind; it is a set of potentials that can only be realized in a real-world situation with real economic institutions and constraints'.[66] Rubinstein himself boasted that Laurel operated in 'the European style' to support Romero as auteur, but what did authorship really mean to the company? Who were the stakeholders that had a say over output and how did their involvement complicate ideas of independent cinema as a sovereign space for the auteur?

The scholarship on independent and cult cinema identified above has attempted to overcome potentially 'slippery' definitions to coordinate these strands as specific analytical tools.[67] Yet in reality these arenas continue to intersect, and practitioners seem less willing to adhere to the same strict partitions as those proposed by the critics (as recently seen in indie forefather Jim Jarmusch's homage to Romero *The Dead Don't Die* [2019]). In regard to horror, the 2010s has seen the term 'indie horror' applied with a degree of frequency, used to describe either production contexts or as a familiar signifier of quality. Films such as Robert Eggers's *The Witch* (2015), Jordan Peele's *Get Out* (2017) and the work of Blumhouse Productions have helped sell this subgenre as a distinct brand. Geoff King (2005) and Jamie Sexton (2012) argue that the formal characteristics most associated with canonical independent cinema are identifiable in a number of earlier indie horror films, including George A. Romero's *Martin* (see Chapter 2). For King, the inclusion of genre-producing figures in an examination of independent cinema is therefore more 'open to debate'[68] than some of his peers have sanctioned.

With this in mind, Romero's commitment to auteurist independent cinema and gross-out violence would seem to place him at a nexus point between strands of research – 'somewhere between the art house and the mall', as Merritt once stated.[69] But as long as cult horror and independent cinema are so doggedly arranged around the text and reception, then debates will continue to surround this interconnexion. The value that one gives to the other, especially from the vantage point of workers in the field, is in danger of getting lost in the ideological shuffle. An industrial analysis of Laurel Entertainment's dual nature moves away from these value-laden polemics, harmonising cult horror and independent cinema through the pragmatic, everyday realities (and limitations) of non-Hollywood film production. Genre producers like Laurel Entertainment were part of a diverse American independent cinema landscape, and it is their very deviations that reveal a clearer picture of the opportunity structures, artistic incentives and creative concerns that shaped this sector across the United States.

As the title of this book implies, George Romero is a central character in this narrative, but it is the firm itself that takes the lead here. Indeed, the final chapter looks specifically at Laurel with its totemic figure *in absentia*, when in the late 1980s and 1990s he initiated stronger ties to Hollywood, while Rubinstein continued to navigate survival in the independent sector. This approach allows a clearer appreciation of 'George A. Romero's independent cinema' as both a creative and institutional force, one that, as per Philip Drake, problematises questions of authorship and independence.[70] Away from authorship, this book weighs genre's place within the firm's strategic agenda, particularly the extent to which a deliberate 'cultification' of horror cinema restricts and/or enable creative autonomy. What can this tell us about genre and cult's wider place within an economic history of cinema? How were concepts of authorship, genre and independence hierarchically arranged within the firm? To answer these questions, *George A. Romero's Independent Cinema* will step outside the established theoretical range to offer a more expansive methodological paradigm for understanding American film production practices.

Media Industries

Compound terms the 'entertainment industry' or 'media industries' imply the coming together of two distinct parts, a kind of marriage of convenience between creativity and economics. In reality, these two factors are not as separate as some may like and where one ends and the other begins can be hard to define. Even those films made far outside the studio walls, those Kickstarter movies or films funded with a parent's credit card, are significantly shaped by financing, since the budget will dictate aspects of the *mise en scène*, format, location, shot length, performance, special effects and so on. Tales of novel funding schemes, such as Spike Lee selling tube socks to finance *She's Gotta Have It* (1986), or Robert Rodriguez undergoing medical trials for *El Mariachi* (1992), also adhere to a wider economic agenda, with such stories quickly embellished as part of a film's marketing campaign. Indeed, to sell independent cinema as a purely artisanal pursuit, those collaborators who do the selling must remain hidden from the discourse.

The idea that art or 'fetish objects' are 'somehow sullied by the profit motif'[71] is gradually becoming outdated and scholars have begun to take a more holistic view when analysing media artefacts. A study of media industries has grown accordingly. As per Spicer, McKenna and Meir, social, economic, technical, legal, cultural and political contexts can deepen debates surrounding creativity, media historiography, national and transnational medias and authorship.[72] Holt and Perren iterate 'the need for a grounded, empirically based understanding of media industry practices, including the operations, business models, and day-to-day realities of the media industries, past and present'.[73] Herbert, Lotz and Punathambekar add that this discipline lets us look at cultural goods in '*historically and geographically contextualized ways*', recognising that the manner of production and release will profoundly impact the final product, imbuing it with additional artistic and industrial significance.[74]

Media industry studies assays a wide range of contributors, where the production of film art is more than simply the vision of a single auteur. In terms of production, participants might be producers, screenwriters, cinematographers, editors, production designers, composers and below-the-line workers such as teamsters, the technical staff and so on. At the financial level, this could be investors, shareholders, a board of directors, distributors, exhibitors or the marketplace itself. James Lyons has applied a 'value chain' model to film production, emphasising a 'process of assembly' that situates the director as a function (one of many) whose value diffuses or concentrates depending on the demands of specific stages of production.[75] The director-auteur remains pivotal to this process; they are simply relocated within a wider municipal.

Michele Hilmes proposes that by monitoring production in this larger context we can challenge some of the major critical theories that have shaped a study of film and media in the humanities, principally in terms of authorship, genre and the 'purely aesthetic textual exegesis inherited from literary studies'.[76] As we have seen, the auteur was of great use when presenting film as a serious topic of study and discussion in the 1950s, though media industry studies argues that this theory is no longer satisfactory in and of itself. Genre, meanwhile, was initially met with scepticism by the academy, dismissed as little more than a mass-produced commodity that stressed repetition and an alleged lack of innovation. Hilmes puts forward a more considered view, countering that the genre filmmaker's appropriation of past works is true of all creative artists, who frequently learn from, respond to, and reinvent that which came before.[77] Through an industrial lens, these disparate perspectives on genre can exist side-by-side, with genre serving as both a commodified product and as a conduit for artistry. A study of media industries exhibits complexity, rather than essentialisation.[78]

This field has already been of value to a study of horror and independent cinema. Kevin Heffernan (2004) has used an economic framework to evaluate changes in the genre, from the refinement of the early 1950s to the baroque stylisation of the 1960s (which culminated in the release of *Night of the Living Dead*). Editor Richard Nowell (2014) tracks an economic history of horror spanning from the Universal Monster movies of the 1930s to today's 'digital age'. Both works go some way to reframing the discussion around practitioners rather than spectators, allowing us to think about the text not in terms of what '"we collectively believe it to be" . . . but rather what they collectively believed it to be'.[79] Although cult cinema scholars Mathijs and Mendik also recognise that cult exists as 'part of an economic premise' as goods made for profit, they insist that 'something always goes wrong with cult films – there is always something unplanned intervening in one of the levels of production, promotion or reception'.[80] The industrial focus of my inquiry puts this claim to the test, asking how cult sits within the self-conscious economic undertakings of individual practitioners and a single production company.

Looking towards American independent cinema, Perren and Tzioumakis have led the way in instigating an industrial focus, with the former's analysis of Miramax (2012) the gold standard when it comes to a close case study of a single production company. Elsewhere, Perren has turned to films and filmmakers existing outside of the dominant discourse and her appraisal of Lions Gate surveys the firm's production and distribution of both in vogue 'quality independents' like *Buffalo '66* (Gallo, 1998) and films in tested genres, such as the horror film *Saw* (Wan, 2004).[81] Tzioumakis's edited collection *The Time of Our Lives* (2013), co-edited with Siân Lincoln, also discusses under-valued independents, in this case the lasting sociocultural and industrial impact of *Dirty Dancing* (Ardolino, 1987). Building upon these evaluations of marginal independents, I present a case study of a small-scale entertainment company whose economic and industrial autonomy was, for a large period, uniquely literal. Laurel takes us out into those regional spaces once deemed so vital to Robert Redford and the independent cinema 'movement', not in an ideological sense, but in a way that can help us appreciate the actual conditions of making films away from bicoastal centres.

To conduct this survey, this analysis will take place at the macro- and micro-industrial level. The macro-level casts a wide net, factoring in oligopoly, integration, the national/international economy, and so on. At the micro-industrial level, we turn to individuals, production companies and distinct territories.[82] A study of Laurel falls clearly into this latter category, but it is important to acknowledge the vast array of influences that impact the conduct of industry figures and institutions at both levels, from changes in national law to boardroom decision-making.[83] Horace Newcomb and Amanda Lotz argue that shifting between the macro- and micro-scale emphasises the dynamic interrelationship between six levels of activity: (1) national and international political economy and policy; (2) specific industrial contexts; (3) distinct organisations (studios, production companies, television networks); (4) individual productions; (5) individual agents; and (6) prosumers and produsage.[84] Moving with Laurel as they navigated these spaces will offer a comprehensive perspective on the company's actions.

Of these levels of activity, issues concerning national and international political economy have been an important consideration for media industry scholars. In its essence, political economy addresses the interrelationship between systems of governance and business/industrial entities, judging the impact of policy and the rule of law on the production, distribution and consumption of goods and services, and vice versa. In the 1940s, Frankfurt School theorists Theodor W. Adorno and Max Horkheimer made political economy fundamental to their inquest into the culture industries, expressing concern with American mass media entertainment and what they felt was its role in depoliticising the general population and eroding the country's democratic principles. Following on from this line of enquiry, a contemporary application of political economy remains bound to issues of moral philosophy and power relations, probing the ways that governments and media operators oppose or reinforce the dominant ideology. For Gamble, Kelly and Parkinson, political economy is 'concerned not just with how a particular social order works, but also how it might work and how it should work'.[85]

How a social order or business entity 'should work' is beyond the scope of this investigation into Laurel Entertainment. Political economy does play an important role here, principally when turning to the various governmental policies and changes in regulation that frequently prescribed Laurel's movements. Further, economist R. H. Inglis Palgrave emphasises that political economy is about more than the relationship between 'the government and governed' and is equally alert to the exchanges between individual practitioners.[86] The legal and personal relationships between Laurel co-founders Romero and Rubinstein will be crucial to this book, while ethical questions surrounding the firm's use of tax shelters, for example, will arise. Nevertheless, the moral implications of Laurel's activities will be left for others to condone or reproach as they see fit. Of greater interest is not what these figures should have done, but what they did do and why.

Following Lotz, these questions will be answered by applying a 'mixture of methodologies' encompassing sociohistorical, industrial and textual analysis.[87] Even further, this interdisciplinary approach incorporates business studies theory to supply a new, transportable model with which to examine film. The aim of business studies is to 'analyse, present, and explain' corporate behaviours without judgement.[88] It is designed to shed light on economics and management, offering practical, actionable guidelines for businesspersons and consumers that facilitate informed decision-making and on-site problem-solving.[89] Aspects of corporate governance come to the fore here. Sir Adrian Cadbury famously defined corporate governance as 'the system by which companies are directed and controlled'.[90] It is the method through which firms manage and internally coordinate the influence of stakeholders, either at the board level or in terms of management and employees. This ensures that all participants act in alignment for the overall betterment of the firm.[91] In this sense, corporate governance shares with political economy a focus on relationships, only here seen from the perspective of those involved. In Laurel's case, corporate governance was the strategy through which issues of creativity were administered as part of a robust business plan.

Laurel was a small business enterprise (SME) like any other, and business studies discloses parallels between corporate behaviour and internal systems of organisation across industries. Business theory on the founder-managed firm will tell us much about Laurel's maturation and corporate identity. Scholarship on risk and entrepreneurialism will highlight the indie film producer. Theories on the marketing concept and opportunity structures will offer new ways of looking at the independent sector as a whole. Factors relating to agency and media conglomeration will show the impact of business relationships at the macro- and micro-level. And business theory was not some esoteric concept for Laurel. Rubinstein was himself a business school graduate, obtaining a Bachelor of Science degree at the American University in Washington, DC and an MBA in business administration at Columbia University in 1971. What strands of analysis he sweated over in the classroom is not known, but we do know that he left education with a clear-minded and assured sense of how to run an SME. This analysis of his company will consequently draw upon this same discipline, using existing statistical findings from business studies (rooted in careful samplings and controls) as part of a comprehensive evaluation.

It is important to state that this is not an economic study and is not intended to tell businesses how to manage their operations. This book draws upon business studies as part of a comprehensive methodology, rather than as a research model in its own right. As a distinct discipline, media industry studies belongs to the humanities and the text remains a pivotal component. Addressing issues of economy, management, politics and policy brings us back to the construction of texts and images, offering additional insight into artistic decisions and meaning-making.[92] Hilmes posts the text as a 'preserved' artefact that remains ever present, the question that sparks the investigation.[93] With this in mind, each chapter of this book will examine a Laurel text through this industrial prism, revealing films such as *Martin*, *Knightriders* and the TV miniseries *The Stand* in an entirely new light. A study of media industries can consequently be of vital use to an enquiry into independent and cult/genre cinema, extending the scope, while remaining inclusive of the academic work that has gone before.

To create a holistic portrait of the firm and its output, data has been drawn from a number of places. Primary among this are the records taken from the US federal agency the Securities and Exchange Commission (SEC). From 1980 onwards, Laurel was a publicly owned company and was required to submit regular 'state-of-the-company' information to the SEC. This consisted of an array of reports, forms and exhibits. An Annual Report to Shareholders (AR) collated a letter from the Chief Executive Officer (in this case Richard Rubinstein) outlining financial data; results of operations; market segment information; a list of acquisitions; subsidiary interests; partnerships; plans for expansion; and future projects.[94] The SEC Form 10-K provided insight into the company's financial condition, including: production financing; details of assets (such as property and subsidiary companies); legal proceedings; profiles on executive officers; lists of capital resources and liquidity; staff remunerations (bonus payments and so on); and stock ownership.

SEC documents also contain a yearly Financial Statement and an Accountant's Report, permitting scrutiny of balance sheets; insurance payments; payments received (current and non-current); revenue from a film's release (Laurel's share of the box office rather than box office receipts); packaging and production costs; lease payments; and income tax payments. A Form 8-K attaches a number of exhibits, including: memorandums; employment agreements (Romero's and Rubinstein's are here in full); and end of contract plans. Excitingly, Laurel's 1984 Form 8-K contains Romero's contractual demands as an auteur, itemising the creative controls that were available to him (see Chapter 4). The information held within these records shows no less than the spine of the company's operations during its key years of activity. Post-1988, a flurry of merger and acquisitions (M&A) saw Laurel become a subsidiary to a number of larger firms, including Spelling Entertainment, Blockbuster Entertainment, Viacom, the CBS Corporation and ViacomCBS. As with Laurel, these publicly owned firms submitted annual documentation to the SEC and their reports illuminate the profound changes to infrastructure and output that occurred during the final stages of Laurel's life cycle.

In union with these corporate papers, the importance of ethnographical data cannot be discounted, as it offers vital insight into the behaviours and rationales of the firm and its agents. Interviews with Laurel personnel and associates are of benefit in additional ways, helping to interpret and contextualise empirical data and to fill in those gaps in knowledge where no prior data exists. As a consequence, I have drawn from a diverse sample of personnel, spanning various levels of corporate hierarchy and stages of pre-production, production and post-production from different periods of Laurel's life cycle. Interview subjects include *Night of the Living Dead* co-writer John A. Russo; composer, writer and director John Harrison; regional filmmaker Tony Buba; assistant cameraman and 'jack of all trades' Tom Dubensky; financial advisor Barney Guttman;

freelance producer, film accountant and completion guarantor representative David Ball; *Tales from the Darkside* (1983–1988) producer William Teitler; *Day of the Dead* (Romero, 1985) associate producer Ed Lammi; and Laurel vice president of production Mitchell Galin. Finally, and most importantly, George A. Romero was an essential contributor to this book and, in an interview conducted in April 2016, he provided insight into corporate structure and his personal expectations for the company he co-founded. All of these participants are speaking for the first time about their specific relationships to the company.

This ethnographic data is, of course, not without complications and we must be cautious of the self-representations media industry workers make. This is especially true when substantial time has elapsed since the events in question and subjects may be prone to shifting viewpoints, record-setting or lapses in memory. It is also worth saying that contributors here are only a representative sample and some leading personnel are notable by their absence. Previous researchers have observed the 'closed-door facade of the media industries',[95] with practitioners often mindful that any loquaciousness might compromise the value of their properties or their ability to do business. This may have been the case with Rubinstein. To date, he remains semi-active in the industry, most recently listed as an Executive Producer on Warner Bros. and Denis Villeneuve's *Dune* (2021). He is also the president and chief shareholder of the MKR Group, Inc., whose principal business is to 'monetize the value' of Laurel assets, from DVDs and T-shirts to action figures and Halloween costumes.[96] Given the continued ancillary value of these assets, it is unsurprising that Rubinstein's door has remained closed.

Compensating for this absence is a vast array of additional primary resources and empirical data. Trade publications, specialised periodicals, fanzines, the national and regional press and promotional materials add scope to this research. Through these materials, one can find extant interviews with leading personnel (Rubinstein's interaction with the press during Laurel's heyday was substantial); industry-focused advertising; box office reports; legal considerations; details on marketplace trends; release patterns; and information on funders and external partners. This information situates Laurel's efforts within a macro-industrial setting. Business studies theory will help correlate and make sense of this data in connection to recognised patterns of enterprise.

From this heterogenous perspective, the history of a firm can seem like a jigsaw puzzle, one with key pieces still missing. As such, a singular, uncontested 'real-world' truth may be unknowable. Yet as Hilmes advises, 'the concept of "industry" implies the coming together of a host of interests and efforts around the production of goods or services'.[97] The methodological approach of this work reflects the fact that the history of a firm is a collective history – one of contradictions, compromises and contested approaches to creative and economic matters. This is something that is as true for the American independent film sector as a whole as it was for this small entertainment company surviving on the margins of the industry.

George A. Romero's Independent Cinema is also only one case study. Although models of business may be applied across industries, we cannot assume that Laurel's working practices were universally employed by all independent production companies in the United States. Indeed, part of the value of this study is its emphasis on heterogenous conduct. But as economic geographer Bent Flyvbjerg reports, 'the advantage of the case study is that it can "close in" on real-life situations and test views directly in relation to phenomena as they unfold in practice'.[98] The interdisciplinary approach of this case study pushes closer to disclosing the everyday undertakings of the firm. It admits the social interactions, motivations, self-representations and problem-solving that made Laurel Entertainment the company that it was – and that made George A. Romero the 'Master of Horror' for which he will always be known.

Chapters

Chapter 1 presents a comprehensive examination of parent company the Latent Image, charting its growth from regional television advertising firm into an ambitious and entirely singular film production unit. Critical evaluation of Romero's work has so far overlooked the company's infrastructure and intent, ignoring the post-Fordist, egalitarian production culture that sat in determined opposition to traditional modes of filmmaking. Taking into account this corporate method for the first time strongly challenges an auteur-centric reading of Romero's early work, particularly *Night of the Living Dead*. Romero's first project as singular creative leader was the non-genre film *Jack's Wife*, a film that, though under-seen, I argue was a significant part of independent cinema's evolution in the early 1970s. Amid Latent Image's bold experimentation, the firm's unique industrial placement tended inevitable obstacles and the gradual reliance on exploitation product is assessed in the context of a restricted independent marketplace. At the same time, attention to the internal work relations and changing power dynamics uncovers the decision-making that led to the formation of Laurel. The integration of business theory on the marketing concept and leadership management enriches our comprehension of independent and exploitation cinema during this period.

Spanning from 1973 to 1979, Chapter 2 evaluates the business methods – instigated and led by Richard Rubinstein – that saw Laurel evolve from a subsidiary into an independent corporate entity. I investigate the company's polymorphic funding strategies in relation to production output and corporate agency, particularly Laurel's manipulation of state and federal laws and its moves into television and book publishing. I ask what Laurel's auteurist infrastructure meant during this period, contextualising this hierarchical remit within a broader business agenda. By observing the tactics used to maintain independence, this chapter explores risk and risk management to problematise classical notions of independence and authorship. Scrutiny of Laurel's efforts to manage risk leads to a discussion of corporate identity and branding, looking at the risk-reducing policies behind Romero's cult reputation as a 'horror auteur'. The effect of these elements will be made plain in a case study of Romero's vampire film *Martin*. The chapter concludes by appraising the international funding behind *Dawn of the Dead*, where the involvement of Italian horror filmmaker Dario Argento, an auteur whose cult reputation eclipsed Romero's in overseas territories, had further implications for the company's supposed auteurist mandate.

Chapter 3 surveys a period of professionalisation, dating from 1979 to 1982. Now a publicly traded company, Laurel faced growing responsibilities to shareholders and external partners. I review the influence this exerted on production content, infrastructure and Romero's on-set autonomy. Professionalisation has been under-explored in regard to independent filmmaking, appearing to contradict a rhetoric that situates this sector above corporate and regulatory interests. What these standardised systems of governance meant to Laurel as an independent film practitioner is measured against this apparent dichotomy. In part, Chapter 3 is a remedial to the idealisation of independent cinema, yet Laurel's professionalisation also sat at odds with its own corporate identity. As the firm sought permanence, the company brokered ties to the major studios for the first time, potentially contradicting Romero's anti-establishment persona. I assay the techniques employed to reassert (or reconfigure) an identity of dissent, both through engagement with the press and through Laurel's feature films. *Knightriders* provides an evocative case study, with the firm's changing structures of governance disclosing an entirely new reading of the film, one that conveys apprehensions about this period of maturity and Romero's feelings regarding a so-called 'spirit of independence'.

Assessing a period from 1981 to 1985, Chapter 4 foregrounds agency. This timeline takes us from the release of *Knightriders*, in many ways the zenith of Romero's creative ambitions, to his exit from the company on 19 June 1985, a withdrawal that formally ended the firm's auteurist mandate. I begin by framing Laurel within wider institutional circumstances, looking closely at agency in relation to marketplace trends and the implications on the company's projects-in-development. A case study of Laurel's unproduced collaboration with Marvel Comics, entitled *Copperhead*, asks how such material reflected the firm's wider objectives and unrealised plans for the future. The institutional delimitations placed on the company also came from its external affiliations and I compare Laurel's agency to that of its distributor-partner United Film Distribution Company (UFDC). Against this background, the material affairs that undermined Romero's creative authority and altered his intent for *Day of the Dead* are revealed. I conclude by reviewing 'agency theory' as a principle of economics, allowing a clearer understanding of the 'agency relationship' between Laurel's co-founders, not least in terms of the conflicting objectives that culminated in Romero's departure.

Chapter 5 looks at Laurel's regeneration in the wake of Romero's departure, giving special attention to the firm's merger with television producer Aaron Spelling Productions in 1989. An inquiry into media industry M&A traditionally falls upon top-level machinations and the moguls, conglomerates and major players who dictate the fate of the industry at large. Analysis of a subjacent player like Laurel offers a ground-level perspective, providing a rare case study of one of the many small business enterprises swept up (or swept away) by these waves of consolidation. The chapter looks at the impact of the Spelling merger on output and corporate identity, detailing Laurel's move into television and the production of 'event' programming such as the ABC miniseries *The Stand*. How *The Stand*'s onscreen content reflected this period of transition is then discussed. This is followed by an evaluation of the limits imposed by this merger, paying attention to the 1990s M&A wave and Viacom's purchase of Spelling in 1994, a transaction that resulted in Laurel's closure. From this unique vantage point, Chapter 5 demonstrates key distinctions between M&A waves, applied here to an analysis of the film industry for the first time.

Conclusion

In a 1979 interview with Chris Auty, Romero registered his determination to remain independent of Hollywood, professing amazement 'that anything survives the system at all'.[99] Yet Laurel's survival in the independent sector, a survival that traversed four decades of production, was perhaps even more remarkable. Rubinstein's suggestion that Laurel did little more than provide an auteur filmmaker with 'brush, palette and canvas' is in keeping with ideas of independent cinema's artistic and authorial providence. But Laurel was far more than that, and the division between creativity and business parameters was more complex and intertwined than either Romero or Rubinstein (for numerous conflicting and corresponding reasons) cared to admit. 'The Laurel story' – to borrow a phrase from one of Rubinstein's annual reports to shareholders[100] – enlarges the narrative of American independent cinema, shedding light on the diverse industrial practices, corporate partnerships, business methods, creative decision-making and opportunity structures that made survival away from Hollywood possible. Within this study, issues concerning auteur filmmaking and cult genre film are considered and expanded upon, revealing new ways of thinking about media entities and their real-world potentials across a heterogeneous landscape.

Notes

1. Unless otherwise stated, box office data is drawn from industry data and research site *The Numbers*, <https://www.the-numbers.com>
2. Holt and Perren, 2009, p. 5.
3. Yakir, 1979, p. 60.
4. Interviewed in *Document of the Dead*, 1985.
5. Schatz, 2009, p. 50.
6. Quoted in Hervey, 2020, p. 16.
7. See Gange, 1987, p. 38; Contreras, 2017.
8. Newman, 2006, p. 134.
9. The interview was published in *Cinema Spectrum* No.1 in 1980.
10. Wood, 1980, p. 31.
11. Spainhower, 1986, p. 183.
12. Goldstein, 1988; Dawson, 2008.
13. Levy, 1999, p. 3.
14. Holt, 2002, p. 303.
15. For more on 'indiewood', see King, 2009.
16. Tzioumakis, 2013a, p. 6.
17. 'The Independent Feature Movement', 1981.
18. Quoted in Kouvaros, 2004, p. 4.
19. Tzioumakis, 2017, p. 159.
20. The term was coined by critic André Bazin in a 1957 *Cahiers du cinema* article that actually voiced his misgivings.
21. Sarris, 1962–3, p. 7.
22. Ibid., pp. 5–7.
23. New American Cinema Group, 1961b, p. 131.
24. Quoted in MacAdams, 2001, p. 228.
25. Mekas and Hoberman, 2007, p. 241.
26. Tomkins, 1973.
27. James, 1989, p. 104.
28. See Decherney, 2005, p. 181; Sitney, 2000, pp. 71–2.
29. Curtis, 1992, p. 262.
30. For an example of this interchangeability, see New American Cinema Group, 1961a, p. 134.
31. Vallan, 2006.
32. Ibid.
33. Monell, 2008.
34. 'The Independent Feature Movement', 1981.
35. Grants such as those offered by the Jerome Foundation were only available to 'emerging artists' who had not previously received substantial sponsorship, from them or any other institution. See Cornwell, 1981, p. 80.
36. See Lamont, 1981.
37. Insdorf, 1981, p. 58.
38. Quoted in Edgerton, 1986, p. 44.

39. Geoff King has suggested that the term 'indie' be used as an entirely separate classifier, with 'independent' broadly referring to any film made outside of Hollywood's infrastructures, and 'indie' connotating a specific textual departure based on aesthetic and ideological concerns. See King, 2017. Despite King's best efforts, these terms remain, at time of writing, relatively interchangeable for most critics and academics. See Badley, Perkins and Schreiber, 2016; Murphy, 2019.
40. Staiger, 2013, p. 24.
41. Merritt, 2000, p. 276; See also Fallows, 2018.
42. Newman, 2009, p. 17.
43. Bourdieu, 2008, p. 391.
44. Insdorf, 1981, p. 58.
45. Hawkins, 2009, original emphasis.
46. Sexton, 2012, p. 81. Chuck Kleinhans writes that independent cinema's identity rests on its position as counterpoint, best understood in relation to the dominant system rather than as a totally autonomous entity. See Kleinhans, 1998, p. 308.
47. Kehr, 2011, p. 106, original emphasis.
48. Maslin, 1979.
49. Williams, 1991, p. 3.
50. Wu, 2003, p. 86.
51. Jancovich, 2002, p. 314.
52. Jancovich, 2000, p. 25.
53. Sconce, 1995, p. 376.
54. Ibid., p. 372.
55. Chute, 1983, p. 10. When trying to define cult and independent cinema through fan consumption, the boundaries between these fields can become blurry. John Fiske argues that cult films tend to appeal to disempowered groups of people, particularly in terms of class, race, gender and age. James Monaco strongly refutes such assertions, maintaining that the trash aesthetic of cult films like *Pink Flamingos* (Waters, 1972) and *El Topo* (Jodorowsky, 1970) indulge an educated, self-aware and emotionally distant viewing model. For Monaco, cult, like independent, cinema, appeals directly to the 'privileged children of the middle class'. See Fiske, 1992, p. 30; Monaco, 1984, p. 66.
56. Gorfinkel, 2008, p. 35.
57. Mathijs and Mendik, 2011, pp. 2–3.
58. Such films are frequently charged with tempering their scares to attract the widest audience possible. See Henry9785, 2019.
59. Jancovich, 2000, p. 28; see Chapter 2.
60. Vale and Juno, 1986, p. 182.
61. Williams, 2015, pp. 11–17.
62. Williams, 2001, p. 399.
63. Phillips, 2012, p. 7.
64. Vale and Juno, 1986, p. 5.
65. Merritt, 2000, p. 411.
66. Kleinhans, 1998, pp. 310, 326.
67. King, 2005, p. 9; see King, Molloy and Tzioumakis, 2013, p. 2.

68. King, 2013, p. 263.
69. Although this description was not used in direct reference to Romero, Merritt was describing similar practitioners who strove to blend 'thought-provoking' content with a broader accessibility. He cites L. Q. Jones's post-apocalyptic satire *A Boy and His Dog* (1975) as a primary example. See Merritt, 2000, pp. 268–9.
70. Drake, 2013, p. 143.
71. Spicer, McKenna and Meir, 2014, p. 1.
72. Ibid., p. 1.
73. Holt and Perren, 2009, p. 3.
74. Herbert, Lotz and Punathambekar, 2020, p. 7, original emphasis.
75. Lyons, 2014, pp. 200–2.
76. Hilmes, 2009, p. 25.
77. Ibid., p. 25.
78. Ibid., p. 21.
79. Nowell, 2014, p. 2.
80. Mathijs and Mendik, 2008, p. 7.
81. Perren, 2013, p. 109.
82. Schatz, 2009, pp. 46–51; Doyle, 2013, pp. 3–4.
83. Lotz and Newcomb, 2012, p. 78.
84. Ibid., pp. 72–8.
85. Gamble, Kelly and Parkinson, 2000, p. 2.
86. Quoted in Mosco, 2009, p. 23.
87. Lotz, 2009, p. 36.
88. Ghauri, Grønhaug and Strange, 2020, p. 17.
89. Ferrell, Hirt and Ferrell, 2017, pp. 4–6; Ghauri et al., 2020, p. 12.
90. Quoted in Abor and Adjasi, 2007, p. 113.
91. Mallin, 2019, pp. 10–12.
92. Holt and Perren, 2009, p. 2.
93. *An Interview with Professor Michele Hilmes*, 2014.
94. 'Glossary: Annual Report', n.d.
95. Mateer quoted in Freeman, 2016, p. 2.
96. See Capcom Co., Ltd v. The MKR Group, 2008.
97. Hilmes, 2009, p. 22.
98. Flyvbjerg, 2006, p. 235.
99. Auty, 1979, p. 28.
100. Laurel Entmt., 1987a, p. 3.

1. LATENT IMAGE(S): REVEALING INDUSTRIAL ALTERNATIVES, 1963–1973

When discussing his early impressions of the film industry, George Romero stated, 'I never imagined I'd be able to work professionally in film; I thought you had to be born royalty or something'.[1] If the Hollywood studios of his youth were not exactly sovereign, workforce structures were deeply hierarchical. Hollywood of the 1940s operated under a decentralised coordination of specialised labour inspired by the automotive industry.[2] Job roles were divided into production units and talent guilds (representing writers, directors and performers) and the IATSE labour union (representing technicians, artisans, craft persons and so on) reiterated compartmentalisation. The advent of television and the impact of the antitrust Paramount Consent Decrees in 1948, which sought to de-monopolise the industry by separating distribution and exhibition, created widespread uncertainty, and unions sought to protect experienced workers through a roster system that rewarded seniority. Accordingly, the number of new employees gaining a foothold in the industry declined and by 1957 only 6.4 per cent of workers were under the age of thirty, while 50 per cent were over fifty years old.[3] Jonas Mekas and the New American Cinema Group in Manhattan raged against unionisation, arguing that the restrictions put on non-union members had made Hollywood a 'closed shop'.[4]

As a teenager, Romero's brief entry-level work on studio A-pictures only reaffirmed his original impression of the industry, leaving him certain that he'd 'never be able to do anything but get coffee'.[5] More so, as a second unit assistant on MGM's *North by Northwest*, he despaired at seldom seeing director Alfred Hitchcock on set, instead finding a 'mechanical' system of separately operating divisions incongruous with his perception of an artist-driven medium.[6] His distaste for this infrastructure (an infrastructure overseen by absent kings) strongly influenced the formation of his own company the Latent Image four years later, and this chapter charts his firm's bold attempts to transgress institutional barriers in terms of production practices, corporate organisation and filmic content. Evaluating Laurel's prehistory through its parent company sheds new light on the prehistory of American independent cinema, where important developments in terms of product diversity and the national growth of the sector have been unexplored.

Television and Leadership

Television's post-war dispersion across the United States was rapid. By 1952, there were over 108 television stations in operation and by the mid-1960s over fifty million households with a television set.[7] Regional centres for television production were soon established and Pittsburgh's first station, WDTV, began operating on 11 January 1949. As a bicycle courier for Pittsburgh's WRS Motion Picture Laboratory, Romero witnessed first-hand 16mm news footage being processed, synchronised, mixed and edited, later remembering how he would sit in 'dusty old film labs ... with the editors, editing newsreels with real glue, smoking cigarettes all the while and gluing the footage together to try and get a coherent news story out of it'.[8] This tactile, hands-on environment (or at least Romero's perception of it as such) suggested filmmaking as something tangible and, in a working-class milieu, achievable – sitting fiercely at odds with his views on Hollywood at the time.

Romero made additional headway after purchasing a 16mm camera with $5,000 loaned from his uncle. With his friend Russell Streiner, he then set up a storefront office at 1829 E. Carson St in Pittsburgh's South Side, which essentially became a bohemian hangout for college grads and friends with an interest in filmmaking. Though their initial commissions were limited to weddings and baby photographs, work steadily increased and on 6 September 1962, the *Pittsburgh Post-Gazette* reported that 'camera crew director' George Romero was supervising a series of films on 'how to entertain youngsters in Pittsburgh' for WQED-TV.[9] Romero's crew included Streiner and Rudolph J. Ricci and the project was part of the Junior League of Pittsburgh's commitment to children's programming. This experience later paved the way for freelance work on WQED's ground-breaking children's television series *Mister Rogers' Neighborhood* (1968–2001), proving that old entertainment industry axiom that 'work begets work', at least as far as this fledging production company was concerned.

As the firm's reputation grew, in December 1963 Latent Image procured investment from local Roller Palace owner Vincent D. Survinski to ratify Latent Image as a regional advertising agency specialising in industrial and commercial product. Romero was the nominal president, Streiner became secretary-treasurer and Lawrence J. Anderson served as executive vice president. Each was a major shareholder in company stock. According to journalist Mike May, 1960s Pittsburgh was 'a nexus for advertising agencies', thanks largely to its thriving steel industry and status as the nation's third largest corporate headquarters.[10] For Banks, Lovatt, O'Connor and Raffo, this type of environment is crucial to the success of such SMEs, where cultural businesses thrive in the 'networks, clusters, embedded knowledge and informal infrastructures of the city'.[11]

Within this environment, Romero's knowledge of film production was another discernible advantage. Up until the late 1950s, in-product advertising was the industry norm, with a show's host typically promoting a product during a live broadcast – from *The Tonight Show*'s (1954-present) Steve Allen selling hair products from behind his desk to Howdy Doody singing about the benefits of Colgate Dental Cream. Yet by 1955, commentators were noticing a shift towards pre-recorded ads shot on film. Trade magazine *Billboard*, for example, listed as benefits the potential for 'open-end' syndication (where a filmed product could be resold across multiple networks) and the 'attention-getting eye appeal' of edited film footage.[12] By 1964, Latent Image had become a specialist in this field, able to take clients 'from the initial idea through to the finished product, in color, black-and-white, sound and what have you'.[13] Latent Image prided itself on the quality of its work, which it felt transcended 'the local look' (read 'amateurishness') of its competitors, and was soon winning awards for these pre-recorded, highly stylised advertisements, including an International Film and TV Festival Award for its one-minute Duke Beer spot.[14]

In April 1965, Southwest Pennsylvania credit corporation the Regional Industrial Development Company (RIDC) noted Latent Image's viability and advanced $40,000 for a studio and new equipment, now housed at 247 Fort Pitt Blvd in Downtown Pittsburgh. RIDC president Robert H. Ryan hoped the loan would stimulate the local growth of a fast-developing advertising industry and the investment allowed Latent Image to court higher-profile clientele.[15] This included H. J. Heinz, Calgon, US Steel and larger advertising firms such as Lando, Inc. looking to avoid the high cost of outsourcing to New York.[16] These commissions were reinvested into the company and by 1973 Latent Image boasted three 16mm cameras, a 35mm camera, a Super-8 camera, two Nagra-operated sound recorders, 1/4-inch record facilities and its own mixing and film editing bays.[17] When the firm moved into feature films and other forms of television production, these facilities enabled it to bypass heavy rental fees and union contractors.

Aside from providing fertile ground for industrial augmentation, advertising had a demonstrable impact on form. Jeremy G. Butler proposes that 'stylistic excesses and violations' are an intrinsic part of the sector's constitution, the bellicose aesthetic serving to disrupt the connection between viewers and the programme narrative to scream attention to the products on sale.[18] Commercials such as Latent Image's 1967 spot *The Calgon Story* (which parodied

Richard Fleischer's sci-fi film *The Fantastic Voyage* of the previous year) showcased rapid cuts, harsh edits, whip-pans and crash zooms, all slashed together with an absence of master shots. Romero's self-labelled 'cubist' editing style[19] would become an early trademark, most evident in *The Crazies* (Romero, 1973), which cuts entire sequences to the rapid tempo of a non-diegetic military drum. According to Stew Fyfe, *The Crazies* has an average shot length of around 2.8 seconds. In Hollywood during this period, the average shot length was between six and eight seconds.[20] This aggressive cutting style perfectly conveys *The Crazies*' overall theme of Vietnam War-era military invasiveness (onscreen, America's armed forces are turned against one of its own rural communities) and like Romero's best-known work asserts impact – impact as part of product differentiation and political engagement.

That this visual audacity emerged through specific industrial structures demonstrates a pragmatism in contrast to the ideology of the New York independents and avant-gardists. This said, like Mekas et al., Romero was looking for alternatives to Hollywood, particularly in terms of the segmented manufacturing process he identified during his brief internships. Latent Image therefore adopted a post-Fordist infrastructure that accentuated a 'new "flexibility" in labour practices and relations'.[21] For many, post-Fordism, or flexible specialisation, is, in its ideal (or perhaps that should be idealised) form, the solution to the rigid practices of mass or decentralised production. Keith Grint argues that flexible specialisation does away with the assembly line 'to increase the skill levels and flexibility of the workforce, to provide team work structures, and to seek out specialized niche markets for high quality, high value products and services'.[22] Christopherson and Storper argue that the vertical disintegration that followed the Paramount Decree actually saw Hollywood transition to flexible specialisation as well, albeit in a manner that called into question the association between flexibility and workplace stability, equality and fairness.[23]

At Latent Image, equality and flexibility were indispensable. Staff members operated without formalised job classifications, becoming part of a small, hands-on unit skilled in a number of production roles, including direction. Cultural studies theorists Chris Barker and Emma A. Jane advocate that the purpose of flexible specialisation is to eliminate rigid job demarcation lines and to 'create a more horizontal labour organization' where co-workers share responsibility for product quality.[24] Latent Image was to be a 'multi-trained, non-hierarchical workforce', reliant on a fluidity that maximised creative freedom and profit potential.[25] Romero's role as company leader was to facilitate knowledge sharing, passing on the technical expertise he had acquired from his informal apprenticeship at WRS. This coordination of skill levels evidences the company's democratic leadership style, a technique that empowered individuals at all stages and facilitated participatory decision-making.[26] Such democratic leadership is often associated with fresh ideas and creativity.[27]

In the context of industrial films and advertisements this method made sound business sense. As Latent Image cohort and shareholder John Russo recalls, the firm's burgeoning roster of clientele and overlapping assignments made having a skilled, independently minded workforce essential.[28] More surprisingly, as the company began to transition into feature films, this democratised infrastructure remained in place and Romero initially handed directorial control of *Night of the Living Dead* to collaborator Karl Hardman, and then to Russo.[29] Speaking in 1987, Romero stated that his intent was to create a 'communal sense of collaboration with creative contributions from all involved'.[30] Hardman remembers the production as 'a democratic group effort', with on-set decisions agreed to through compromise and discussion.[31] Richard Ricci adds that *Night* was 'not [done] the way it was normally done with a strong central authority'.[32]

This democratic atmosphere was in-keeping with then popular ideas of communalism, made famous in the mid-1960s by so-called 'hippy' communes such as Drop City, Tolstoy Farm and Ken Kesey and his Merry Pranksters. According to Timothy Miller, these communities were often 'devoted to radical politics, anarchism, sexual freedom, the sharing of labour, creation of arts and crafts, land development, ethnicity, and a dazzling array of visions of assorted seers and cranks'.[33] Though the firm's original E. Carson St office was a place for friends to hang out, play table hockey and clean up after the office monkey,[34] they were hardly cranks and worked hard to establish themselves as a viable and competitive local firm. But even after the move Downtown, the Latent Image colleagues shared at least some of these communalist values, most evident in the offscreen distribution of labour and the onscreen revolutionary politics of *Night of the Living Dead*.

In his auteurist analysis of Romero, Tony Williams situates *Night* and its follow-up *There's Always Vanilla* as the products of a singular vision. For Williams, *Night* anticipates the counterculture themes that would predominate in Romero's later work, notably the film's attack on government, the military and the media.[35] *Vanilla*, meanwhile, is said to contain 'several relevant autobiographical elements based upon the director's experience of filming television commercials'.[36] This may be true, but these films can be more fully understood by taking into account their collaborative production method, the result of an experimental corporate infrastructure that stressed flexibility of labour and shared decision-making. Thematically, issues tackled by *Night* can also be seen in later work by co-writer John Russo, particularly his 1982 independent horror film *Midnight* that explores the dysfunctional families, domestic abuse, racism and violence at the heart of rural America. Further, the 'autobiographical elements' Williams highlights in *Vanilla* belong to the group, not the individual. Streiner and Russo in fact appear onscreen as themselves, seen performing their 'day jobs' of directing and producing regional television commercials.

Given that Romero was a key creative member of this collective, it is not surprising that recurrent themes should appear in his later work. But in spite of his directorial credit, Romero was not the traditional creative authority and did not have final say over content. Romero was the most hands-on technically, typically handling the camera during production and almost entirely responsible for the physical task of editing, allowing easier comparisons to be made when looking at the 'cubist' montage style of *Night* and later Romero productions. This said, as far as Latent Image's first feature film is concerned, Streiner recalls that after the rough cut was assembled, the core creative team gathered to discuss all decisions relating to 'what should go and what should stay. In that regard it was committee edited'.[37] Latent Image's initial production method should not be overlooked in the headlong rush to valorise Romero as auteur, especially when what is revealed instead is a deviation from the rigidity of Hollywood practices and the presentation of radical alternatives to traditional production processes.

Pauline Kael's 1963 rebuttal of the auteur theory situates film as a collaborative medium, arguing that the role of the director is inextricable from the multitude of personnel that help shape production, from the producer to the front office. Her ire also fell on Mekas and his independent filmmakers, 'already convinced about their importance as the creative figures – the auteurs'.[38] By the late 1960s, *nouvelle vague* auteur Jean-Luc Godard was equally sceptical about notions of creative autocracy, initiating the Dziga Vertov Group to explore cinema's democratic potential. The Dziga Vertov Group, which was comprised of Godard, Jean-Pierre Gorin and numerous filmmakers and militants, determined to imbed their Marxist philosophy into the means of film production itself, thus distinguishing their methods from the dominant ideology of Hollywood and so-called Western 'imperialism'. The Group's feature film *Le Vent d'Est* (1970) makes plain this drive towards collectivism, where in a metatextual sequence early in the film we see the actors and crew form a general assembly to plan a scene. As the film's voice-over narration states, in the Dziga Vertov Group's ideal, 'the camera is at everyone's disposal'.

Back in Manhattan, Andy Warhol's turn to filmmaking also minimised authorial intervention, encouraging improvisation or spontaneity in his actors or, as with *Blow Job* and *Eat* (both 1963), using just one extended shot to diminish editorial choices. Unlike Godard, Warhol insisted that he was simply making an asset of limited finances, telling Joseph Gelmis that if you can make films 'look better bad, at least they have a *look* to them. But as soon as you try to make a better movie look good without money, you just can't do it'.[39] In spite of its own impoverishment, Latent Image rejected 'the local look' for a professional veneer that would be saleable on the open market. Flexible specialisation kept costs down, with principal crew members performing multiple tasks in front of and behind the camera. Figure 1.1 shows a complete budget for *Night of the Living Dead*, divided into four subsections that formally demarcate production roles.

AN IMAGE TEN PRODUCTION
The Image Ten, Inc.
247 Fort Pitt Blvd.
Pittsburgh, PA. 15222

1. Pre-Production:
    a. Casting
    b. Story
    c. Screenplay (scripting)
    d. Location Search
    e. Make-up Testing
    f. Talent Contracts
    g. Production Design
    h. Legal Fees
                                     TOTAL: $14,000.00

2. Actors Fees:
    a. Principals
    b. Extras
                                     TOTAL: $20,000.00

3. Production:
    a. Location Fees
    b. Sets
    c. Set Furnishings
    d. Equipment Rentals
    e. Crew
    f. Film Stock
    g. Music
    h. Editing
    i. Sound Effects
    j. Lab Work and Finishing
    k. Titles and Special Effects
                                     TOTAL: $60,000.00

4. Artwork and Advertising:
    a. Pre-sales Exploitation
    b. Miscellaneous Artwork and Ad Layouts
                                     TOTAL: $20,000.00

                           BUDGET TOTAL: $114,000.00

Prepared for Image Ten, Inc. by
Russell W. Streiner – Vice President
Vincent D. Survinski – Treasurer

Figure 1.1 *Night of the Living Dead* budget breakdown (Source: *Night of the Living Dead* budget breakdown, 2002).

In practice, these roles were loosely adhered to (no casting director, location manager or production designer are listed in the film's onscreen title sequence, while cinematography is collectively attributed to 'The Latent Image, Inc.'). Responsibilities were instead passed between colleagues as and when required in a collaborative workspace.

Latent Image was inspired by a practical method that had reaped dividends in the advertising sector. In the crossover to film production, the firm utilised a post-Fordist infrastructure to stretch resources as far as possible, saving monies across all areas of production to create a professional and competitive product. Romero and his Latent Image colleagues firmly believed in the artistic potential of democratised filmmaking, putting it to the test on their first feature film. As such, previous readings of *Night of the Living Dead* as the work of a singular auteur are, at the very least, a gross reduction, ignoring the innovative creative process behind its construction. In an understated, workaday manner, Latent Image pushed a creative radicalism that, as with the Dziga Vertov Group, defied traditional modes of production, even surpassing the auteur-focused Manhattan independents in this break away from institutional norms. By subduing the director-leader, Latent Image championed an egalitarian film art unheard of in bicoastal centres. This was at once far from Hollywood and the auteurist construct that its Laurel subsidiary would become.

Post-Fordism and Pragmatic Radicalism

The radicalism of Latent Image's corporate infrastructure was offset by a pragmatic evaluation of the marketplace. This 'pragmatic radicalism' was evident in *Night of the Living Dead*, the company choosing to make a film in a saleable genre that nevertheless went far beyond permissible boundaries of screen violence. Production was instigated by a limited partnership of ten individuals, comprising Latent Image employees and peers from the advertising sector, including Marilyn Eastman and Karl Hardman from Hardman Associates and attorney David Clipper. The collective was incorporated as Image Ten shortly after and legally separated from Latent Image to protect the senior firm from financial liabilities. Additional investors from the partner's commercial clientele brought the budget up to $114,000. These external backers reinforced an obligation to create a product that, at the very least, had the potential to return investments.

Latent Image's assessment that horror might provide a distinct marketplace advantage, one unavailable in other genres, was built on experience. Immediately prior to Latent Image's inception, Romero and Rudolph Ricci put together *Expostulations*, an anthology feature film concerning a day in the life of various Pittsburgh inhabitants and visitors (including a microscopic alien from outer space) that was filmed, but never completed. The team sent a playful promotional booklet out to local businesspeople across the region that emphasised the film's experimental nature, stating, 'Oh for crying out loud, it doesn't follow any standard story pattern ... it's ... it's ART!'[40] In the mid-1960s, Latent Image also sought funding for a 35mm colour feature film entitled *Whine of the Fawn*, a coming-of-age story set in England (though shot in Pittsburgh) during the Reformation era. Financing for this project also failed to materialise.

If raising production monies for such films was hard, then acquiring theatrical distribution would have been almost impossible. In the late 1960s, avenues for distribution were largely limited to the major studios, the avant-garde and exploitation cinema. Exploitation was initially known for its shameless mining of any and all popular trends and interests (ripped from either the headlines or the box office), but by 1968 was associated with transgressive displays of nudity, softcore sex and/or bloody violence. These films were mainly produced by independent companies outside the majors and exhibited in drive-ins and second-run or grindhouse theatres (such as those gathered on 42nd Street in Manhattan), adding a further sense of licentiousness to the cheap thrills onscreen. In the 1960s and 1970s exploitation trends included sexploitation, gang or biker films, Blaxploitation actioners, drug movies, kung fu and horror.

Part of exploitation cinema's growth came as a result of changing audience demographics. A Motion Picture Association of America (MPAA) survey in March 1968 indicated that 16-to-24-year-olds now made up 48 per cent of box office admissions.[41] Thomas Doherty records that exploitation companies had been catering to this audience from as early as 1955, narrowing focus to 'attract the one group with the requisite income, leisure, and gregariousness to sustain a theatrical business'.[42] As Doherty suggests, the studios were actually at the forefront of this shift – MGM's *Blackboard Jungle* (Brooks, 1955) displayed teen appeal with its rock 'n' roll soundtrack and themes of juvenile rebellion[43] – but the majors proved slow in abandoning a traditional (and monolithic) family audience. American International Pictures (AIP) co-founder Samuel Z. Arkoff held no such trepidation, boasting, '[w]e saw the rebellion coming, but we couldn't predict the extent of it, so we made a rule: no parents, no church or authorities in our films'.[44]

In economics, the production of goods to meet the consumer's needs is known as the marketing philosophy, or marketing concept. Here, the customer is placed at the centre of a firm's strategical organisation and profit planning, with corporate activities pointed towards finding the right product for the customer, rather than the right customer for the product.[45] Put simply, when following the marketing philosophy firms must ask themselves, 'what does the customer want and how can we give it to them?'. David Jobber and Fiona Ellis-Chadwick divide the marketing concept into three key elements: (1) *customer orientation*, which is based on satisfying the needs of the customer; (2) *integrated effort*, where the workforce aligns to take responsibility for customer satisfaction; and (3) *goal achievement*, which states that providing customer satisfaction is the best way to achieve organisational objectives. They summarise by saying that customer satisfaction is the backbone of all corporate efforts and one of the most effective ways of staying ahead of the competition.[46]

As firms look to better meet consumer needs, economists have explored the difference between market segmentation and market aggregation. In the former, the total heterogeneous market is divided up into several homogenous segments, while in the latter, it is the goal to attack the mass market and reach as many customers as possible.[47] Traditionally, Hollywood has fixated on an aggregated marketplace, and under the Motion Picture Production Code (PCA) – a one-size-fits-all censorship mandate founded by the MPAA in 1934 – product was designed to cater to a unified mass audience.[48] AIP espoused a more definitive single-segment concentration strategy, directing all of its resources towards a homogenous group of consumers. This was aided by a relaxation of the Production Code in the mid-1950s, permitting exploitation companies greater liberty to produce sensationalist, teen-focused material. Congruent exhibition spaces provided a convenient home for segmented product.

In 1965, *LIFE* magazine reported that AIP flourished in this environment, its 'first 150 releases – none of which cost as much as a million dollars to make and only its later efforts as much as half a million – have brought in a total of $225 million'.[49] Predictably, independent distributors such as Jack H. Harris Enterprises, Crown International Pictures and Allied Artists Pictures began to release similarly segmented exploitation films. With the market expanding, horror was a natural choice for Latent Image's move into features. Russell Streiner recalls that with no distribution agreement in place prior to production, 'we had to do the kind of picture that we were almost assured of being able to sell'.[50] The resulting film, *Night of the Living Dead*, revelled in scenes of bodily carnage, including decaying flesh, immolation, cannibalism and parricide. An aghast review in *Variety* on 15 October 1968 bewailed:

> Until the Supreme Court establishes clear-cut guidelines for the pornography of violence, '*Night of the Living Dead*' will serve quite nicely as an outer-limit definition by example. In a mere 90-minutes, this horror film (pun intended) casts serious aspersions on the integrity and social responsibility of its Pittsburgh-based makers, distrib Walter Reade, the film industry as a whole, and exhibs who book the pic, as well as raising doubts about the future of the regional cinema movement and about the moral health of filmgoers who cheerfully opt for this unrelieved orgy of sadism.[51]

As Image Ten eyed a consumable market, the film's nihilism actually alienated a number of distributors and, according to Romero, AIP turned the film down due to its fatalistic ending.[52] After Columbia Pictures also toyed with distributing the film, Image Ten turned to Continental Releasing, whose parent company Walter Reade was best known for importing high-profile international films such as the UK's *Saturday Night and Sunday Morning* (Reisz, 1960). In 1964, Walter Reade-Sterling, Inc. (renamed the Walter Reade Organization in 1966) reported annual losses of around $491,000, attributed by *Variety* to 'disastrous results from artie releases'.[53] Continental looked to offset this decline with a roster of more commercial features and *Night of the Living Dead* neatly fit the bill. The film was sold as an exploitation feature to the inner cities and drive-ins and the marketing campaign played up the violent content. Posters declared 'They keep coming back in a bloodthirsty lust for HUMAN FLESH!', while the theatrical trailer grouped together the film's goriest moments. And in a gimmick lifted directly from producer-director William Castle's *Macabre* (1958), Continental even issued a $50,000 life insurance policy to anyone who the film 'frightened to death'.[54] Such ballyhoo contributed to the global box office of around $30 million.

Perhaps more provocative than the violence was the apparent political radicalism that lay behind it. As seen in the introduction, much has been made of the film's address to contemporary sociopolitical concerns, principally its casting of African American actor Duane Jones in the lead and the thematic evocation of contemporary hot-button issues such as the war in Vietnam, brutal attacks on civil rights campaigners and the political assassinations that defined the decade. Romero himself has pointed to the revolutionary credo behind all of his *Dead* films, each depicting 'a new society replacing the old and devouring it – in this case, literally'.[55] Contrarily, critic Steve Beard is sardonic in regard to this radicalism, writing:

> [Romero] started out making commercials for US Steel, Alcoa, Heinz and Duke Beer, outfits similar to those whose mass-produced commodities he would later trash in *Dawn of the Dead*. His production company, Image Ten [sic], was set up in 1963 within earshot of Pittsburgh's declining steel mills, and occupied an ambivalent position in the economic fabric of the town. Parasitic upon the local branches of big Fordist companies for employment, it operated flexible post-Fordist labour practices and was staffed by a small 'family' of highly-skilled workers who treated the office as a home from home. It was within this makeshift environment that *Night of the Living Dead* was conceived, financed, filmed and edited. Schooled in selling corporations a flattering image of themselves, Romero took his revenge by defaming the reputation of the people they served.[56]

This so-called ambivalence between Pittsburgh as a Fordist corporate centre and Latent Image as a post-Fordist entity is intriguing, challenging the extent of the firm's ideological break from mainstream culture and modes of production.

As we have seen, independent cinema has been positioned as a progressive alternative to Hollywood, frequently placed in direct opposition to a dissolute mass culture. Indeed, the Frankfurt School's perception of American popular culture in the 1930s still echoes in an analysis of independent cinema today, where, 'controlled by giant corporations, the cultural industries were organized according to the strictures of mass production, churning out mass-produced products that . . . sold the values, lifestyles, and institutions of American capitalism'.[57] In its commercial work, Latent Image was literally selling 'the values, lifestyles and institutions of American capitalism', even as its feature films openly criticised these structures.

The company operated on the fringes of an established system, acceding to corporate commissions to generate space for politically aggressive cinematic work. Even as it concentrated on theatrical releases, Latent Image never abandoned its commercial work and, by 1972, the advertising department contributed $150,000 to its annual revenue.[58] This subsidised almost all of the firm's day-to-day SME primers such as payroll, utilities, rent, equipment costs, bills and other services. Latent Image's use of horror was equally utilitarian, appropriating a saleable framework on which to showcase its capacity for feature film production. *Night of the Living Dead*'s box office suggested to the RIDC the start of a 'Hollywood East' and in 1970 they invested $80,000 into Latent's next feature *There's Always Vanilla*.[59] When added to the financial speculation of local businesses, this totalled around $100,000. Latent Image's facilities, equipment and services were valued at roughly the same amount, bringing the total budget to $200,000.[60]

Latent Image's commitment to the commercial industry also disconnected its founders from a surrounding artisanal community. Benjamin Ogrodnik writes that by 1972 the NEA's Public Media Program was providing much-needed financial support for those 'filmmakers who refused to work within the commercial sector'.[61] This initiative was extremely attentive to regional development and in Pittsburgh was supported by the media arts centre the Film Section at Carnegie Museum of Art, founded in 1969. Under curator Sally Dixon, the Film Section served as a kind of networking hub/exhibition space/education centre for local artists, students and filmmakers. While the Film Section's Independent Film Makers (IFM) series curated screenings and personal appearances from directors such as Jonas Mekas and Stan Brakhage, neither Romero nor his Latent Image colleagues were invited to participate. After all, Latent Image's backing came not from the Endowment for the Arts, but from the RIDC, an institution supporting economic rather than artistic development. For Dixon and the Film Section, it appears that Romero did not fit the ideal image of an independent filmmaker. A familiar story.

Yet Latent Image began operating during a period that presented no clear pathways for regional film production. From 1963 onwards, the firm constructed new, entirely untested in-roads on its own terms, balancing artistic and infrastructural experimentation with a commercially minded output. For Beard this was hypocrisy; for the Film Section it was distasteful; for Latent Image it was pragmatic. Sherry B. Ortner writes, 'from very early in the history of the industry, there were challenges to the Hollywood hegemony, with various attempts to create alternative sites of movie-making outside of the big studios'.[62] Rather than a 'challenge', Latent Image's ideological opposition to cultural hegemony was more surreptitious. If the firm's compromises were far from the romantic polemics of the New American Cinema Group or John Cassavetes, Latent Image was a real-world alternative – independent cinema with an overhead.

With *There's Always Vanilla*, Latent Image took additional risks in terms of content, firmly pressing against the industrial barriers imposed on independent production to showcase artistic versatility and workforce adaptability. Taking the RIDC at its word, *Vanilla* abandoned the security of the horror genre to emulate youth-orientated Hollywood comedies such as *The Graduate* (Nichols, 1967) and *Goodbye, Columbus* (Peerce, 1969).[63] Like its Hollywood predecessors, *Vanilla* reveals a sense of disaffection behind its bold colour photography and pop music soundtrack, and for the film's free-spirited young lovers Chris (Ray Laine) and Lynn (Judith Ridley), their relationship is only a brief interlude, ultimately lacking the solace or sense of purpose that they were looking for.

In the late 1960s and early 1970s, youthful content was very much the order of the day. The $40-million domestic box office of thirty-three-year-old actor-director Dennis Hopper's *Easy Rider* (1969) had awakened Hollywood to this market's potency. The studios now sought to add greater teen appeal by placing age-appropriate talent in front of and behind the camera. Recently established film schools provided ripe picking ground, where graduate students emerged well-versed in popular theories of the day and with a conviction to put what they had learned into practice.[64] These precocious, self-styled auteurs included John Carpenter and George Lucas at USC; Francis Ford Coppola at UCLA; and Martin Scorsese at NYU. James Bernardoni adds that filmmakers outside of academia and Hollywood were equally, if sometimes indirectly, influenced by the auteur theory, 'since auteurist premises informed much of the critical community's commentary on their work'.[65] Kleinhans says that this was similarly true for the Manhattan avant-garde scene, where attention favoured those filmmakers who 'had access to the organs of publicity' and thus actively participated in their own extratextual construction as auteurs.[66] It seems reasonable to conclude that the auteur theory was in the air during this period, having a direct impact on films and filmmaking across sectors and sites of production. This was no less true within the offices of Latent Image, where an embrace of the auteur theory would redraw the firm's corporate mandate and approaches to leadership.

As the nominal director of *Night of the Living Dead*, Romero was at the forefront of critical interest in the film. Indeed, the lack of credit given to his collaborators became a source of resentment and Russell Streiner, John Russo and Karl Hardman would later sit down with *Cinefantastique* journalist Gary A. Surmacz to try to restate the collaborative nature of the film. Here, Russo namechecked a 1971 *Newsweek* article (that distilled production to being 'made in and around Pittsburgh by George Romero') as a specific annoyance.[67] How much this press attention influenced Romero's move towards auteurist filmmaking can only be speculated on, but during this period Latent Image's egalitarian infrastructure faltered. On *There's Always Vanilla*, Russo recalls the endless creative battles that began in pre-production and stretched beyond the film's completion.[68] Romero attributed this disharmony to their achievements on *Night*, where individual players, emboldened by success, were no longer willing to accede to their collaborators.[69] Not least of all Romero himself, who recalled being 'frustrated by the compromises, both creative and social, that were forced by our democratic process . . . I came out of it all wanting the controls, wanting to be the auteur'.[70]

Though effective on *Night of the Living Dead*, *There's Always Vanilla*'s lack of a strong central authority proved the partnership's undoing. Disagreements over content, coupled with ongoing commercial obligations, saw a planned six-week production schedule expand to over a year.[71] In his influential essay on leadership, Cecil A. Gibb recognises that 'the democratic leader has the complex problem of giving each individual satisfaction as an individual, protecting the group as a whole, and satisfying his own aspirations or benevolent intentions'.[72] Romero, it seems, was no longer able to balance such factors. More so, it was not clear who could now actually claim leadership, democratic or otherwise. Romero was the director of the company, but he had conceded creative leadership as part of the participatory corporate culture he initiated. Producers Streiner and Russo had vital agency and their shared command on set led Romero to verbally, if not formally, reject his directorial credit on *Vanilla*, dismissing it as a film that was not a legitimate representation of his work.[73]

Given the industry-wide push towards directorial authority, the failure of Latent Image's egalitarian infrastructure is perhaps unsurprising. After the frustrations of *Vanilla*, Latent Image pushed for a clearer hierarchy between departments and company leaders. Romero recruited Alvin C. Croft as a more formal executive vice president and general manager, a divisive move that led Russell Streiner to sell his stock and leave the company.[74] Alongside his brother Gary, John Russo and Rudolph Ricci, Streiner formed New American Films, Inc., a regional commercial production company in direct competition with Latent Image. Notwithstanding this marketplace rivalry, Romero was timorous about the separation, saying, 'I've always had a business partner and up until then it was Russ Streiner . . . and then all of the sudden I was out on my own'.[75]

His subsequent difficulty in guiding the company from a business perspective, a failure that essentially finished Latent Image as an active film production unit, reinforced his feelings that he needed a partner whose interests extended no further than the bottom line.

JACK'S WIFE AND THE 'PROTO-INDIE'

Romero's first major responsibility in his reorganised company was to court distribution for *There's Always Vanilla*. Latent Image had originally felt that the film's proximity to Hollywood youth films would easily return around $15 to $30 million at the box office,[76] but the lack of interest from distributors was now a concern. Even so, Romero was confident that he could sell the film, later citing the success of *David and Lisa* (Perry, 1962) as precedent, a $185,000 Pennsylvania-shot independent that earned around $2.3 million in rentals.[77] Like *Night of the Living Dead*, *David and Lisa* was released by Continental, but the distributor was unable to agree terms with Latent Image on its second film.[78] In the meantime, Latent Image attracted monies from a Pittsburgh-based brokerage firm committed to raising $750,000 for Romero's next three films.[79] Romero was undeterred by *Vanilla*'s inability to find distribution and planned the company's next feature film *Jack's Wife*, his first as authoritative leader, to be another character-led regional drama.

In *Jack's Wife*, Joan (Jan White) is a middle-class woman whose identity rests exclusively on her role as 'housewife-mother'. Her husband Jack (Bill Thunhurst) is consumed by work and her grown-up daughter Nikki (Joedda McClain) is increasingly independent, leaving Joan feeling old and isolated within their suburban home. Joan is envious of her daughter's youth and is attracted to Nikki's casual lover Gregg (Ray Laine), with whom she begins an affair of her own. She seeks further solace in therapy, medication, alcohol and is later intrigued by the gossip surrounding her neighbour Marion (Ginger Greenwald), who is said to practice witchcraft. As Joan's fascination with the occult intensifies (see Figure 1.2), she becomes progressively disturbed, culminating in the accidental murder of Jack when she mistakes him for a prowler that has been haunting her dreams. Now liberated, Joan has a clearer sense of her identity, boldly telling fellow guests at a house party, 'I'm a witch', though she is still introduced as 'Jack's wife'.

Despite the attention given to witchcraft in *Jack's Wife*, horror is not the film's central preoccupation. Instead, the narrative openly engages with second wave feminism and the ideas presented in Betty Friedan's bestseller *The Feminine Mystique* (1963), considering a disaffected American housewife offered 'no other road to fulfilment' beyond 'finding a husband and bearing children'.[80] The film draws us to themes of domestic entrapment, a struggle that has created a crisis point in Joan's psyche. Friedan called this 'the problem that has

Figure 1.2 Joan (Jan White) looks to escape her role as 'housewife-mother' in *Jack's Wife* (1972).

no name' and noted the large number of American women seeking psychiatric help in the 1960s.[81] Joan, too, pays regular visits to a therapist, although his glib, condescending manner ('the only person imprisoning Joanie, is Joan', he tells her) is infantilising and unsympathetic. Her husband's only expression of interest is rage (he assaults her when Nikki runs away from home) and Joan's life stretches out before her in a seemingly endless mass of household duties and dull social engagements.

By taking into account the film's interest in the women's liberation movement of the late 1960s and early 1970s, *Jack's Wife*'s use of witchcraft also comes into focus. The concurrent women's spirituality movement, or Goddess movement, gave way to so-called 'feminist witches' who rejected and opposed 'patriarchal structures of religious and social power' in support of women's rights.[82] Also making headlines in the late 1960s was the guerrilla theatre and action group WITCH (Women's International Terrorist Conspiracy from Hell), who on Halloween night 1968 took to Wall Street to put a hex on New York's financiers. The witch, a historical symbol of male oppression and female power, blended 'political and romantic rhetoric',[83] and interest in Wicca or pagan witchcraft as a serious religion and/or as a counterculture expression of defiance spread accordingly. Practitioners worshipped a pre-Christian matriarch and comprised a cross-section of everyday women (and sometimes men) like Joan, people far removed from the hell-bent supernatural Satanists of contemporary exploitation cinema such as *Mark of the Witch* (Moore, 1970) and *Daughters of Satan* (Morse, 1972).

Distancing itself from these exploitation presentations, *Jack's Wife* draws from the realities of 1970s America. The mystical elements of the film are ambiguous, and scenes in which Joan uses witchcraft are accompanied by a rational explanation, such as when she casts a spell to summon Gregg, only then to call him on the phone and invite him over – just to make sure. Joan believes in magic totally; for Gregg it is a 'cop-out'. The women's spirituality movement was also labelled an 'apolitical "cop-out" from feminist struggles' by some commentators, proposing escapism rather than practical challenges to patriarchal oppression.[84] Romero himself seems sceptical of this movement, or at least, of Joan's appropriation of it. Her obsession with spells and occult paraphernalia (all purchased on a MasterCard) at times seems little more than a bourgeois 1970s fad, in congruence with fondue sets and wife swapping. Finally, Joan's initiation to the coven implies another form of subjugation when high priestess Marion ties a leash-like cord around Joan's neck and pulls her down on all fours, an image that starkly parallels an earlier dream sequence in which Jack leads Joan around on a leash and then locks her in a dog pound.

Dreams play a central role in *Jack's Wife*, dominating the narrative and drawing heavily on overt symbolism and avant-garde filmmaking techniques to reveal Joan's repressed anxieties. The film begins in an autumnal forest. Jack walks ahead reading the *Wall Street Journal*, Joan is behind him, the camera at a distance. As they pass into the woods, Jack pushes away skeletal branches that whip back and slash Joan across her face. We see this in a close shot and from her subjective point of view. Their actions are silent. Strange electronic noises bubble on the non-diegetic soundtrack. From somewhere there is laughter. As they continue to walk, she serves him coffee and a boiled egg, which he devours ravenously. Joan sees herself on a swing, dressed in white. Later, she has a recurring nightmare about an intruder wearing the face of the pagan Green Man, whose association with death and rebirth mirrors Joan's own coming transformation. The Green Man's pursuit of Joan through a seemingly inescapable domestic space iterates her mounting desperation, where feelings of entrapment will culminate in a final, real-world act of violence.

Scaring his audience may have been secondary in Romero's mind, but the use of horror film paradigms allowed him, in his words, to 'walk the line' between marketability and personal expression.[85] In many ways, this articulated Jonas Mekas's original demands for the Film-Makers' Cooperative, inhabiting a 'middle-ground' of popular accessibility and aesthetic seriousness. *Jack's*

Wife was not alone in performing this balancing act and was preceded by what Janet Staiger calls 'the proto-indie', an assortment of similarly 'half-way' films made in 1950s and 1960s New York. In her review of these films, Staiger notes shared themes (usually a taboo or politicised subject matter); similar structure (deliberate pacing, narrative ambiguity); recurring characters (typically ordinary or offbeat); and a stylisation (location shooting, experimentation with form) that later came to the fore in more widely recognised expressions of independent cinema in the US.[86] Staiger's 'proto-indies' include Shirley Clarke's *The Connection* (1961), Jim McBride's *David Holzman's Diary* (1967) and Robert Downey's *Putney Swope* (1969). For Staiger, the 'affective point' of a number of these films was to voice 'a negative reaction to the contemporary bourgeois world',[87] a description that could be applied to *Jack's Wife*.

However, Staiger regards the 'proto-indie' as short-lived (lasting roughly from 1953 to 1970), soon replaced by a 'second wave' (late 1970s to 1989) that finally realised indie film's 'potential for profit making *and* for cultural prestige'.[88] This second period began with the indie 'movement' championed by Annette Insdorf and culminated with Soderbergh's box office giant *sex, lies, and videotape*. As with the avant-garde, Staiger's 'proto-indies' were 'very much a New York City thing', based on a concentration of talent, facilities, infrastructure, equipment and training.[89] It was only towards the end of the 1960s that independent film moved 'into other parts of the country, via the distribution channels of avant-garde, underground and midnight movies'.[90] The 'second wave', in fact, began with an emphasis on regionality, rooted 'in regional work characterized by stories about people nobody in a studio deems worthy of attention', according to former Sundance Film Festival director Geoffrey Gilmore.[91] As noted, this was evident in the work of Victor Nuñez in Florida, Eagle Pennell in Texas and Hanson and Nilsson's *Northern Lights* in North Dakota.

While Staiger's periodisation of American independent cinema is perhaps a little too neat (*David and Lisa* is just one example of a temporal and geographical deviation from her categorisation), it does help us consider the ways in which important trends have defined and redefined the sector at specific times. And if we categorise the period beginning in the late 1970s as a 'second wave', then the importance of films such as *Jack's Wife* and *There's Always Vanilla* is magnified. These films existed outside the concentration of interest and resources that permitted the New York 'proto indies' room to develop, while at the same time anticipated the direction independent cinema would take at the end of the decade (where the NEA and additional funding bodies supported regional production). In this sense, Latent Image's films serve to bridge the gap between Staiger's epochs, revealing an early manifestation of independent cinema as a national 'movement' that could produce artistically challenging work beyond the confines of the east coast.

Of course, given the lack of sympathetic partners during the early 1970s, sustaining non-genre regional film production was a Herculean task. Following the promised brokerage firm investment, Romero set aside $250,000 for *Jack's Wife* and secured a $100,000 bank loan to begin production. Mid-production, the brokerage firm declared bankruptcy, leaving Romero no way of paying back the loan.[92] Actress Jan White claims that to entice investors, Romero rewrote the screenplay to include explicit sex scenes that he never intended to shoot.[93] This subterfuge attracted exploitation distributor Jack H. Harris Enterprises who on seeing the final 130-minute cut pushed Romero to include the graphic material promised.[94] When he was unwilling/unable to do so, the film was taken from him, cut by 30 minutes and repackaged as the sexploitation film *Hungry Wives* in the Southern states of Texas, Ohio, Kentucky and Georgia. In the late 1970s, the film was rereleased as the horror film *Season of the Witch* to capitalise on the success of *Dawn of the Dead*, although it still struggled to find an audience. Irrespective of its pretentions, *Jack's Wife* ultimately failed to overcome the limitations of the marketplace. If Latent Image was going to survive, it would have to respond accordingly.

Auteurist Product, Exploitation Distribution

As Romero continued to look for a home for *There's Always Vanilla*, Russell Streiner's New American Films designed its first (and, as it transpired, only) feature film for the burgeoning sexploitation market, a market then thriving thanks to changes in the rating system and a voguish interest in adult film. Directed by John Russo, *The Legend of Cherry Jankowski* remained unreleased until 1976 when Constellation Films, a subsidiary of Sam Sherman's Independent-International Pictures, re-edited and re-titled it *The Booby Hatch* to add to its roster of soft-core sex comedies that included *The Naughty Stewardesses* (Adamson, 1974) and *Game Show Models* (Gottlieb, 1977). New American Films' calculated approach was understandable, especially given the successful use of market segmentation with *Night* and the limited number of independent distributors available.

Almost concurrently, John Cassavetes was struggling to find a distributor for his *A Woman Under the Influence* and despaired at the lack of supportive outlets, telling Ray Carney:

> [The distribution companies] take precautions against failure. They put unrelated violence in just because there is some kind of audience appetite for it. They'll put action scenes and production values in, things that don't have too much to do with the films that we make. I have to put a rape scene in or a nude scene, or I have to shoot somebody in the face for this film to be 'good'![95]

Cassavetes used his star cachet and personal wealth to release *A Woman Under the Influence* himself, experimenting with a self-distribution strategy that had been successful on films such as Tom Laughlin's *Billy Jack* (1971) and Mulberry Square Productions' G-rated *Benji* (Camp, 1974). New American also toyed with the idea of self-distributing *Cherry Jankowski*, beginning by four-walling it at the King's Court Theater in Pittsburgh before passing the nationwide release on to Constellation.[96]

Without reserves of capital, self-distribution was far beyond Latent Image's means and *There's Always Vanilla* was not released until 2 March 1972, almost two years after the completion of principal photography. Distributor Lee Hessel and his Cambist Films had made its name by releasing and producing sexploitation films, yet increased competition from 16mm hard-core pornography pushed Hessel to explore other avenues. The acquisition of *Vanilla* was Hessel's attempt to variegate, purchased as part of a package deal that included front-end financing on Romero's next film, *The Crazies*. Once outside of his familiar marketplace, however, Hessel seemed unsure of how to sell *Vanilla*, and like Jack H. Harris before him, eventually repackaged Latent Image's film as sexploitation. Now entitled *The Affair*, the new promotional material obscured the original text and the poster replaced Lynn and Chris with a black-and-white photograph of an undressed young couple (neither of whom appear in the film) passionately kissing on a brass bed.[97]

So limited were the theatrical releases of *There's Always Vanilla* and *Jack's Wife* that Robin Wood took to calling them Romero's 'unknown films'.[98] Critic Travis Crawford, albeit an admirer of these films, views Romero as 'idealistic and naïve' in thinking he could create an alternative industry in Pittsburgh outside of the horror genre,[99] even though, as we have seen, regional bodies such as the RIDC shared the director's optimism. In 1972, Alvin Croft determined that there were only two types of feature possible in the independent sector. The first was what he called an 'idea or theme' picture (that is, non-genre product such as *There's Always Vanilla*), which represented a 'gamble' because, as the firm had discovered, such films did not have obviously marketable components. Under Croft's risk-averse stratagem, Latent Image would direct its energies to the second type, exploitation, which he felt to be economically safe because of the apparent built-in fanbase that would see these films regardless of their overall quality.[100]

Croft's comments are telling, implying that for Latent Image to survive, Romero had to subjugate artistic imperatives for a fuller concession to marketplace trends, the antithesis of his motivation behind corporate restructuring in the first place. As president of the company (a company that now operated under a traditionally organised system of leadership), Romero had final say over this move to more saleable product, indicating his own resignation that the marketplace was limited. Insubstantial box office returns seemed to require a corporate rethink and the disastrous production of *Jack's Wife* left Romero with debts in excess of half a million dollars.[101] Romero later reflected that *There's Always Vanilla* and *Jack's Wife* demonstrated that 'the film industry is not going to accept serious little dramas from some upstart in Pittsburgh . . . those two films taught me what the odds were against that kind of small personal film'.[102]

In line with his reading of the marketplace, Romero redesigned Paul McCollough's original screenplay for *The Crazies* into a loose reworking of *Night of the Living Dead*, replacing undead ghouls with insane townsfolk and upping the violence. Romero told Dan Yakir that *The Crazies* was designed to go out 'into the drive-ins – it's a potboiler, a B-movie, an action melodrama, at least on the surface'.[103] The front-end deal with Cambist also ceded creative control, giving Hessel input into the screenplay and later permitting him to cut Romero's preferred version by 15 minutes.[104] Romero's self-conscious desire to make more personal films in the independent sector was not institutionally reciprocated, exposing limitations and demanding alternatives. A reliance on exploitation distributors undermined artistic freedom and his films repeatedly fell to the mercy of investors with their own ideas about the market. By 1973, Latent Image's industrial longevity seemed to necessitate a standardisation of product and corporate thinking.

Exploitation cinema is, of course, not totally anathematic to auteurism and filmmakers such as Russ Meyer have found the sector equitable to their personal obsessions. But the parameters are narrow. Like Romero, Roger Corman explored a diversified marketplace and in 1962 momentarily put aside drive-in features to self-finance *The Intruder*, a racially charged drama concerning political opportunism and integrationist tensions in the American South. According to Corman, *The Intruder*'s rave reviews and film festival awards did not prevent it from becoming the first film on which he lost money. From that point on, Corman says his films were designed to work on two levels, 'On the surface level would be an entertainment film, a genre film, an exciting film of a certain type, and on a deeper sub-textual level would be a film that would have some meaning to me'.[105] This 'two-level' approach was not dissimilar to Romero's own. Even on *The Crazies*, where Latent Image submitted to a fuller compliance to exploitation demands, the film still made space for sociopolitical commentary by indirectly placing Vietnam at the centre of the text. This included images of scared kids-as-soldiers invading a rural community and the self-immolation of a priest, the latter an uncomfortably close facsimile of real events in Saigon.

If genre offered a marketable hook for *The Crazies*, Romero also presented these elements as auteurist choices, defining horror (admittedly somewhat defensively) as a legitimate art form for which he had an especial interest.[106] In this context, Romero's auteurist proclivities seem closely integrated to an economic livelihood. At best, the filmmaker's relationship with genre was ambivalent. Publicly he lauded horror's artistic credibility; professionally he exploited its bankability. Nevertheless, he claims to have been limited by the reductive industrial parameters that forced him repeatedly into this sector. 'I'm trapped in a genre that I love', he later conceded,[107] highlighting a fascinating conundrum for both the company he founded and his future as an independent filmmaker.

For his part, Corman's own acceptance of marketplace restrictions was fuller than he originally intended. After forming New World Pictures in 1970, Corman shifted his attention from film direction to running an entire company, now responsible for a catalogue of feature films that were 'marketable within a highly-competitive industry'.[108] According to *Night Call Nurses* (1972) director Jonathan Kaplan, Corman imposed a strict working template on his filmmakers that 'laid out the requirements of the genre. Exploitation of male sexual fantasy, a comedic subplot, action and violence, and a slightly-to-the-left-of-centre subplot.'[109] This latter element, as Kaplan saw it, was little more than lip service to an engaged youth demographic, indicating an increased sagaciousness behind Corman's 'two-level' politicking.

This top-down approach to film production returns us once again to the marketing concept, where product is carefully orientated to meet customer demands. Market orientation, however, is not the only business philosophy recognised by marketing experts, and other strategic models have been appropriated based on differing corporate resources and desires. Table 1.1 provides a useful overview of four key business orientations (or philosophies as they are also known), divided into production, product, selling/sales and marketing.[110] The methods summarised in each category are not absolute or determinedly separate, bleeding into each other as different strategies are utilised at different times. With this in mind, the concept of business orientation, when applied in the context of independent and exploitation film practices for the first time, can help us understand the corporate thinking behind such production and distribution companies. More so, it underlines important differences between types of independent cinema, where, even within the exploitation sector, there was a divergence in activity, intent and marketplace valuations.

In the 1950s and 1960s, as the Hollywood studios came under fire for their sluggish adoption of modern market research techniques,[111] companies like AIP were *market orientated* from the start. AIP shrewdly allowed its target audience to dictate content, undertaking careful market research in schools, colleges and advertising agencies. Using this feedback, it would generate a title, a poster and a concept (in that order) before a writer was hired to pen the screenplay.[112] Although such methods did not necessarily produce inferior output, it is important to recognise that AIP's primary agenda was the manufacture of saleable goods. Corman took this philosophy with him to New World Pictures,

Table 1.1 Four types of business orientation (Sources: Blythe, 2014, p. 7; Kotler et al., 2020, pp. 11–13).

Orientation	Characteristics	Media Industry Examples
Production	Manufacturing focused. Emphasis on availability and low costs. Seeks to increase efficiency through cost-effective technologies and labour relations. Associated with mass production and distribution.	The Hollywood Studio System (1930s to late 1940s)
Product	Product focused. Favours quality and innovation. Inward-facing strategies can lead to market specificity (accused of being myopic).	New York independents; the Film-Makers' Cooperative
Selling/Sales	Selling focused. Relies on aggressive 'hard selling' techniques. Makes profit from quick turnover of product. Risk intensive due to potential loss of repeat business.	Cambist Films; Jack H. Harris Productions
Market	Customer focused. Responsive to customer demands and needs. Committed to delivering satisfaction. Demonstrates strong awareness of competition. Groups customers according to their needs.	AIP; New World Pictures

where common practice indicated that each production would only begin once executives had identified an exploitable subject matter based on its 'commercial potential'.[113] This project would then be passed down to a writer/director who would adapt the material within a defined template.

Exploitation producer-distributors including Jack H. Harris Enterprises and Cambist followed suit, carefully watching the marketplace to determine output. If releases failed to attract a sizeable audience, such companies revealed the *selling/sales orientation* at their core, using 'devious selling techniques'[114] to resell *There's Always Vanilla* and *Jack's Wife* as soft-core or sexploitation. Such repackaging was common in the exploitation sector. Independent-International's *Blazing Stewardesses* (Adamson, 1975), for example, was repeatedly repackaged and re-titled (as *Cat House Girls*, *The Jet Set* and *The Great Truck Robbery*) to take advantage of changing marketplace trends. In line with marketing experts, exploitation producer David E. Friedman argued that this technique was not viable for long-term survival, telling David Chute, 'the first rule is, you must never continually burn the sucker'.[115] Nonetheless, New World also used selling orientation when they felt it was called for. As Corman was fond of saying, 'there's no law that says every scene in a trailer has to be in the picture'[116], and (in)famously added the same stock footage of an exploding helicopter to any trailer he felt needed livening up.

In her examination of the relationship between business orientation and the arts, Simona Botti advocates that 'the Artist' must, at the level of creation, be scornful of market considerations, producing 'pure' artistic material that does not and should not contemplate marketing strategy and policies. Only once the work of art is completed can the marketplace be addressed.[117] This admittedly romantic *product-orientated* approach runs parallel with the ideology of the Manhattan avant-garde and the canonical independents that followed. Distinctions have been made between 'art for art's sake' and 'utilitarian or crafted objects' that are produced to the specification of external parties, be it a patron or a marketplace.[118] Elizabeth C. Hirschman takes a broader view, asserting that there are three potential audiences that a creative person must consider: (1) the public at large; (2) peers and industry professionals; and (3) the self. Hirschman insists that each audience can and will be considered during the creative process. Any prioritisation between the self and the mass 'is based upon the value orientation of the creative individual'.[119]

What then of the dominating value/business orientation of Romero and Latent Image? In print, Romero poured scorn over an industry that prioritised the marketplace over aesthetic concerns, telling journalist Edward L. Blank that 'the deal is the thing today. The product is usually secondary in the minds of the people creating the package.'[120] As a creative individual, Romero aspired to start from the bottom up, beginning with an evocative story or concept that granted room for his unique formal stylisation and sociopolitical subject matter. As president of a solvent production company, he could not be so single-minded, and each project contained vendible components that could later be teased out or exploited in the marketplace. His desire to 'walk the line' between auteurist self-expression and industrial continuance could be detected on screen, where even his feminist drama *Jack's Wife* alludes to commercially minded genre film tropes. As one critic observed, *Jack's Wife* is 'a strange, experimental film . . . torn between genre and art'.[121]

This push-pull between *product* and *market orientation* was something Latent Image never resolved. In 1973, under Alvin Croft's guidance and Romero's leadership, Latent Image sought to take fuller advantage of the exploitation market and with *The Crazies* sacrificed creative authority for the financial certainty the project seemed to imply. For all that, Lee Hessel's own optimism for the project was misguided and instead of targeting the drive-in markets and grindhouses, Cambist placed a large billboard in Times Square and on

23 March 1973 released the film simultaneously in three first-run New York theatres. *The Crazies* failed to recoup its budget and Romero was again left with a creatively compromised box office failure. As he told freelance journalist Richard Rubinstein shortly after the film's release, '[*The Crazies*] is still not a film I can say is totally mine . . . I'm still looking for that situation where I can do the film myself, which I still have yet to do.'[122] Fortuitously for Romero, his interviewer was a recent business graduate with his own ideas about independent film production.

Conclusion

While *Night of the Living Dead* used market segmentation to achieve commercial success, Latent Image's subsequent attempts to variegate output exposed a delimited independent sector, alluding to the economic assurance of cult/genre product. But if American distribution networks in the 1960s and early 1970s were largely restricted to the majors, the avant-garde and exploitation, a study of industry methods, specifically in reference to Latent Image's occupational environment and intent, betrays greater diversity. Latent Image's unique post-Fordist infrastructure initially favoured collaboration and democratic leadership, boasting an egalitarian organisational structure as radical as it was pragmatic and at odds with bicoastal practices (and, indeed, an auteurist reading of the company's early filmic output). Examination of the marketing concept further demonstrates a multitude of industrial approaches to the production of filmic texts, where output is determined by the value/business orientation of an eclectic array of filmmakers, producers, businesspeople and stakeholders. Latent Image exhibited a tension between product and market orientation, evident in proto-indie films such as *Jack's Wife*, positioning the firm somewhere between exploitation and an ideology later consistent with the canonical independents. This tension blurs the boundaries between sectors that have, for the most part, up until now been clearly defined.

Notes

1. Blackford, 2014, p. 50.
2. Gomery, 2004, p. 119.
3. Christopherson and Storper, 1989, p. 335.
4. New American Cinema Group, 1961a, p. 137.
5. Gange, 1987, p. 13.
6. Ibid., p. 13.
7. See Boddy, 1993, p. 51; Rielly, 2003, p. 39.
8. Romero, 2013.
9. 'Newest Fun for Kids', 1962.
10. May, 2010.

11. Banks, Lovatt, O'Connor and Raffo, 2000, p. 454.
12. Plotnik, 1955, p. 19.
13. Allan, 1964.
14. Ibid.; Fanning, 1967.
15. Allan, 1965.
16. Fanning, 1970.
17. Rubinstein, 1973, p. 23.
18. Butler, 2010, p. 117.
19. In the 1960s, a number of young television directors moved to feature film, including Robert Altman, Arthur Penn, Sam Peckinpah and Sidney Lumet. These filmmakers, each in their own way, were part of the changing face of Hollywood during this period.
20. Fyfe, 2008; Bordwell, 2002, p. 17.
21. Heffernan, 2000, p. 4.
22. Grint, 2005, p. 301.
23. Christopherson and Storper, 1989, pp. 345–6.
24. Barker and Jane, 2016, p. 168.
25. Russell, 1999, p. 108; Block, 1972, p. 23.
26. Gastil, 1994, p. 953.
27. See Goleman, 2000, p. 85; Bosiok, 2013, pp. 66–7.
28. Russo, 2012, pp. 26–7.
29. Ibid., p. 44.
30. Gange, 1987, p. 40.
31. Interviewed in *Reflections on the Living Dead*, 2005.
32. Interviewed in *Affair of the Heart*, 2017.
33. Miller, 1992, p. 75.
34. Russo, 2012, p. 14.
35. Williams, 2015, p. 34.
36. Ibid., p. 38.
37. Surmacz, 1975, p. 24.
38. Kael, 1963, p. 24.
39. Gelmis, 1970, p. 69.
40. Hart, 2020.
41. 'Pix Must "Broaden Market"', 1968.
42. Doherty, 2002, p. 2.
43. Ibid., pp. 57–60.
44. Quoted in Heffernan, 2015, p. 7.
45. Kotler, 1967, p. 11; Kotler et al., 2020, pp. 12–13.
46. Jobber and Ellis-Chadwick, 2019, p. 6.
47. Stanton et al., 1994, p. 82.
48. Given the use of genre, star and product differentiation, there is an argument that the studios engaged in a softer form of market segmentation, aiming diverse product at a variety of consumer segments. The implementation of the CARA ratings system in 1968 saw a stronger focus on segmentation.
49. Levy, 1965, p. 81.

50. Surmacz, 1975, p. 15.
51. Quoted in Hervey, 2020, p. 16.
52. Block, 1972, p. 22.
53. Quoted in Heffernan, 2002, p. 64.
54. Unlike *Night*, *Macabre* could at least connect this promotional device to the mechanisms of the plot, concerning a doctor's devious scheme to scare his father-in-law to death and get his hands on his life insurance money.
55. Biodrowski, 2007.
56. Beard, 1993, p. 31.
57. Kellner, 2002, p. 33.
58. Wylie, 1972.
59. Ehrich, 1970, p. 1; Crawford, 2017.
60. Russo, 2012, p. 102.
61. Ogrodnik, 2019, p. 148. Ogrodnik's article 'Forging an Alternative Cinema' (2019) provides a fuller insight into the Film Section.
62. Ortner, 2012, p. 1.
63. Yakir, 1979, pp. 64–5. *The Graduate* was actually financed by independent producer-distributor Embassy Pictures, though the film's $3 million budget allowed it to compete with studio releases of the time on an equal footing.
64. Schatz, 2004, p. 8.
65. Bernardoni, 1991, p. 8.
66. Kleinhans, 1975.
67. Zimmerman, 1971; Surmacz, 1975, p. 27.
68. Russo, 2012, p. 105.
69. Gange, 1987, pp. 55–6.
70. Ibid., p. 40.
71. Ibid., p. 44.
72. Gibb, 1969, p. 259.
73. See *Digging up the Dead*, 2005.
74. Russo, interview with the author, 30 June 2016.
75. Romero, interview with the author, 7 April 2016.
76. Ehrich, 1970, p. 1.
77. See *When Romero Met Del Toro*, 2017; 'Top Rental Features of 1963', 1964.
78. Russo, 2012, pp. 101–2.
79. Gange, 1987, p. 49.
80. Friedan, 1963, pp. 2, 14.
81. Ibid., pp. 1, 4.
82. Raphael, 1999, p. 22.
83. Rountree, 1999, p. 140.
84. Spretnak, 1982, p. xxii.
85. Scott, 1973, p. 13.
86. Staiger, 2017, pp. 210–12.
87. Ibid., p. 220.
88. Ibid., p. 213, original emphasis.
89. Ibid., p. 215.

90. Ibid., p. 215.
91. Quoted in Levy, 1999, p. 182.
92. Gange, 1987, p. 49.
93. See *The Secret Life of Jack's Wife*, 2005.
94. Scott, 1973, p. 12.
95. Carney, 1990, p. 356.
96. Russo, interview with the author, 30 June 2016.
97. For a detailed overview of Cambist Films and its relationship with Romero, see Fallows, 2018.
98. Lippe, Williams and Wood, 1980, p. 5.
99. Crawford, 2017.
100. Wylie, 1972.
101. Gange, 1987, p. 65.
102. Seligson, 2011, p. 77.
103. Yakir, 1979, p. 64.
104. Ibid., p. 64.
105. Dixon, 2011, p. 147.
106. Jones, 1982, p. 35.
107. Quoted in Fisher, 2017.
108. Corman, 2011, p. 91.
109. Hillier and Lipstadt, 1986, p. 44.
110. Blythe observes an emergent fifth business orientation called societal marketing, in which social, ethical and/or environmental needs are foregrounded, 2014, p. 7.
111. See Handel, 1953, pp. 304–5; Levitt, 1960, p. 45.
112. 'Guardian Interview', 2003.
113. Corman, 2011, p. 92.
114. Blythe, 2014, p. 7.
115. Chute, 1986, p. 61.
116. Abrams, 2015.
117. Botti, 2000, p.22.
118. Fillis, 2006, p. 32.
119. Hirschman, 1983, p. 47.
120. Blank, 1977.
121. Pirie, 2001.
122. Rubinstein, 1973, pp. 23, 24.

2. A NEW DAWN: CULT, RISK AND THE INDEPENDENT FILM PRODUCER, 1973–1979

On 23 April 1979, as *Dawn of the Dead* hit US cinemas, the *Village Voice* published a laudatory front-page article on George Romero predicting that his 'truly independent movie will pose the challenge of the decade to the way films are made, rated, and marketed in America . . . it's going to be the biggest cult blockbuster of all time'.[1] And *Voice* critic Tom Allen was not only impressed by the film and its writer-director-editor, he also marvelled at his production company's scope, noting that in six years Laurel had made two feature films, produced seventeen sports and entertainment documentaries for television, imported twenty-three foreign films for domestic distribution and placed thirty-eight books by authors including Anthony Burgess, J. B. Priestly and Dick Gregory with leading publishing houses. Despite the corporate potential this demonstrated, Allen determined that these machinations were all 'geared to one simple objective: To turn Romero loose'.[2] But if Laurel's public face was one of deference to an artist-leader, closer inspection of corporate activities suggests a more complex agenda. This chapter looks at Richard Rubinstein's entrepreneurial impact on Romero's work, exploring issues of risk and risk management to problematise classical notions of independence and authorship, while in the process reconceptualising ideas of the cult filmmaker.

Turbulent Environments: Capital and Risk Aversion

As Latent Image looked for a distributor for *There's Always Vanilla*, on 9 December 1970 attorney John F. Bradley applied for a certificate of incorporation for Laurel Productions of Pennsylvania on behalf of his client George Romero.[3] Laurel was to be a subsidiary of Latent Image and the certificate of incorporation established this new endeavour as an independent legal entity separate from its parent's shareholders and directors. Ultimately, no projects materialised under this banner and the timing of this application reaffirms the tempestuous atmosphere at Latent Image during this period. The collapse of the company's egalitarian infrastructure had a toxic effect, resulting in Romero's attempt to cultivate a pocket of autonomy away from the collective. The departure of the Streiners and John Russo et al., however, made Laurel Productions of Pennsylvania temporarily redundant, putting Romero back in the driver's seat and able to steer the parent company in whichever direction he pleased. But by 1973, following the back-to-back commercial failures of *Vanilla*, *Jack's Wife* and *The Crazies*, Latent Image ostensibly ceased operations as an active production house, a status affirmed in June when executive vice president Alvin Croft left for the Philadelphia-based advertising firm the Aitkin-Kynett Company.

Partnership with Rubinstein saw a revival of the Laurel brand. Gange writes that by using this already incorporated subsidiary, the partners were able to bypass the $500 fee associated with forming a new company,[4] but this explanation seems a little glib. What the Laurel entity actually offered was an opportunity to publicly distance the filmmakers from the string of Latent Image releases that had failed to return monies to investors. Even more significantly, as a subsidiary of Latent Image, Laurel had access to the facilities, personnel and holdings of its parent. And as a legally distinct unit, it did not share Latent Image's immediate debt or financial obligations. Latent Image would now serve as a studio space and house for equipment only, still situated at 247 Fort Pitt Blvd. Romero had described these facilities to Rubinstein in detail during his 1973 interview for *Filmmakers Newsletter*[5] and this wealth of physical capital seemed to intimate opportunity to the fledgling producer.

Rubinstein's interest in the creative industries dated back to his videotape production service the Ultimate Mirror, Ltd., formally registered with the New York Division of Corporations on 24 March 1972. The company was named after philosopher Marshall McLuhan's declaration that television was 'the ultimate mirror of society'[6] and Rubinstein, then only twenty-five-years-old, was looking for his own alternatives to mainstream small-screen production. At the time, television was controlled by the 'big three' networks of NBC, CBS and ABC and entrance by new contractors was deeply restricted. These networks may have sourced programming from independent production companies, but Mark Alvey reports that by 1963, as independents like Desilu and Filmways 'became top suppliers of prime-time product, and as producers teamed up with old-line majors or powerful agents, the term "independent" became more and more ambiguous, and sometimes meaningless in any "alternative" sense'.[7]

Rubinstein, in his own words, was interested in taking television 'out of the hands of the "establishment" and into the hands of the people'.[8] This intent to democratise television was aided by the release of lighter, more affordable technology, such as Sony's first handheld video camera the DV-2400 Video Rover Portapak, released in 1967. Armed with both the equipment and the intent, Ultimate Mirror began selling short video documentaries to high schools, colleges 'or anyone with an interest in art, sculpture or television'.[9] Projects included a conversation with George Nobel entitled *The Thing About Sculpture* (1971) and *Breathe Deep NYC No Charge* (1972). This latter video followed 'anarchitect' artist Gordon Matta-Clark as he handed out containers of pure oxygen from his 'Fresh Air Cart' to passers-by in New York's financial district. In this work with Nobel and Matta-Clark, Rubinstein seems far from the typical Columbia University business graduate, showcasing an attentiveness to the arts, and especially fringe artists, that would bear fruit in his relationship with Romero.

Indeed, the attractiveness of Latent Image's physical capital notwithstanding, Rubinstein was primarily investing in the company's founder; although where Latent Image began and Romero ended was not easy to establish. Gedajlovic, Lubatkin and Schulze's analysis of founder-managed firms describes the abiding link between corporate identity and creator-personality, viewing the nascent founder-managed firm as 'an incarnation of its founder'.[10] They continue to say that founder agency shapes corporate direction, driving decision-making through a refraction of individual experiences and informal influences, all of which are collated from the founder's upbringing, education, social interactions, cultural heritage and previous work in the field. This often results in an idiosyncratic output that reflects personal objectives rather than the larger corporate interests of the firm as a whole.[11]

If Latent Image/Laurel was George Romero in 1973, then it was far from a guaranteed investment. The economic success of Romero's filmic output was erratic at best and his determination to remain independent appeared led by an anti-corporate, anti-establishment agenda that rejected Hollywood out-of-hand. In 1972, Romero told journalist Alex Block that he was fearful of the compromises the 'studio system' would subject him to, ultimately preferring, if push came to shove, to abandon narrative feature film altogether rather than conform to industry standards of production.[12] Such thinking did not suggest a profit-maximising endeavour and had, as stated above, left Romero on the edge of bankruptcy.

Even without such caveats, the film industry is fraught with dangers for the would-be investor and as a recent business graduate Rubinstein was no doubt exposed to less irregular career pathways. Creative industries such as film, television and music have been described as 'turbulent market environments' where traditional bureaucratic, professional and craft leadership techniques offer no guarantee of financial success.[13] For Michael Pokorny and John Sedgwick, the film industry is particularly high-risk, and studio heads and financiers are repeatedly at a loss to predict, with any degree of accuracy or consistency, which of the year's releases will return or lose money at the box office.[14] In the creative industries, Mark Banks et al. extend this thinking about risk to include SMEs, where the economic fragility of start-up companies is especially 'embedded in risk', necessitating a need to be 'innovative, flexible, creative, ideas driven [and] constantly changing'.[15]

The connotations of risk on media production have been under-explored, largely confined to Mette Hjort's *Film and Risk* (2012) and Pokorny and Sedgwick's quantitative analysis of the economic risk associated with classical Hollywood and the blockbuster. Pokorny and Sedgwick determine that the major studios typically offset risk by producing a 'portfolio of films' of divergent content and scale, hoping that successful projects will compensate for the expected losses elsewhere.[16] Within this system, the issue of an individual film's profitability is less important than the overall profits of the collective portfolio. As Pokorny and Sedgwick attend, independent producers, on the other hand, do not have the financial resources to build a substantial portfolio of releases and are therefore more vulnerable to the box office failure of a single film.[17] If one accepts that this portfolio model is unfeasible for the majority of independents, an alternative analysis of risk management in this sector has not been put forward. Perhaps this is because the concept of risk aversion is too inconvenient a juxtaposition in the discourse on independent cinema – the sector, after all, is supposed to demonstrate 'bold moves' and creative risk-taking, not careful market analysis.

Without the capital of the majors, risk and risk management in independent cinema presents an entirely different set of problems for the entrepreneur or small enterprise. Risk was pre-eminent to Rubinstein's business management, and he applauded collaborator Salah M. Hassanein's 'enlightened sense of risk. He's *aggressive* about risk. He and I think very similarly', he told Gange.[18] This is a common outlook among self-styled entrepreneurs, and Sharon Gifford goes as far as to say that the entrepreneur can only function if their environment is uncertain, since entering into a marketplace with 'perfect information' and a guarantee of profit would not necessitate entrepreneurial behaviour to begin with.[19] Risk is therefore a vital characteristic of entrepreneurism.

At the same time, Banks et al. list a number of advantages for entrepreneurs when starting and running a small enterprise, including self-management, control over decision-making, localised industrial support structures and the 'relatively low financial risk' associated with start-up businesses, particularly in the cultural industries.[20] This was certainly the case with Laurel. When Rubinstein met Romero, the company was essentially ready-made, abundant in physical capital and with a knowledgeable workforce rich in experience. Economist Gary S. Becker has labelled worker knowledge an 'intangible resource', stressing the importance of schooling and on-the-job training to future real income and corporate profitability.[21] Becker calls this personal acquisition of skill, information, ability and experience 'human capital', which he breaks down into two types: (1) *general*, which proffers a broader, transferable knowledge base usually obtained independently at the worker's own expense; and (2) *specific*, where learning is facilitated on the job by the company and relates to tasks particular to that firm. For Becker, firms that provide specific on-the-job training often see a rise in workplace productivity.[22]

Even though Romero's egalitarianism was a thing of the past, Laurel's infrastructure remained relatively loose, offering informal apprenticeships to almost anyone interested in regional film production. In turn, these trainees would freelance on Laurel productions in a variety of roles and at a reduced wage.[23] With an abundance of freelance workers, the number of employees on Latent Image's annual payroll was reduced. Rubinstein was not officially associated with Laurel's parent company, but nevertheless was given licence to manage staffing levels, convincing Romero that there was not enough business to justify a large salaried workforce. 'I was rather ruthless in slashing the staff and overhead back to a manageable level . . . I became the hatchet man, to some extent', he later said.[24] Indeed, Laurel's growth was about more than just the so-called human capital of its freelance workforce, it was dependent on the personal human capital of its new co-leader Richard Rubinstein and his self-acquired business expertise.

Contrary to his boastings about risk, Rubinstein's rise from videotape documentarian to co-head of a full-service regional production company necessitated little in the way of personal risk or financial investment. Banks et al. posit that the entrepreneur's 'real investment comes from the subjective (personal) knowledge which they are prepared to commit to the project',[25] in other words, their human capital, immediately demonstrated here by Rubinstein's management of company overheads. Before Laurel, Rubinstein invested time developing his capabilities through education and personal and professional experience. During his two years as a Wall Street brokerage consultant, Rubinstein handled clients investing in feature film production, while his father, an investment banker, had experience in film investment through then lucrative tax shelter schemes.[26] Ultimate Mirror provided insight into small-scale media production, and Rubinstein determined to use his amassed knowledge to bypass the production barriers imposed by television's oligarchs. Romero may still have seen himself as a feature film director, but Laurel spent its formative years producing small-screen content only. To reinforce Rubinstein's agency, the company's provincial moniker was renamed Laurel Tape & Film, Inc., formalised on 25 February 1975.[27]

Shelters, Sport Stars and Ancillary Markets

In April 1975, Rubinstein evidenced his acute understanding of the television industry in an article written for *Filmmakers Newsletter*. Entitled 'The Selling of O. J. Simpson: Independent Production for Television', the article focused on ten sports documentaries made by Laurel Tape & Film and sold to ABC. In his appraisal, Rubinstein considers the relationship between audience aggregation, demographics, network affiliate stations and potential profits. This reading was complimented by a knowledge of both show pitching and potential gaps in the marketplace. Rubinstein claims that Laurel prospered due to a dramatic increase in the number of sports programmes in the early 1970s. To enter a marketplace dominated by the major networks, he determined product differentiation to be key, achieved through Romero's highly stylised filmmaking and Laurel's access to a number of leading sports stars of the day, including American footballers O. J. Simpson of the Buffalo Bills and Franco Harris of the Pittsburgh Steelers.[28] Harris was the subject of the first produced episode 'Good Luck on Sunday', though the Simpson episode 'Juice on the Loose' served as the series pilot.

In this *Filmmakers Newsletter* article, there are a number of details that Rubinstein leaves out. For instance, the decision to base these specials around ten athletes is intriguing, since Rubinstein writes that he and Romero shared a general disinterest in sports.[29] Even more curious was the decision to produce ten episodes on speculation, instead of just one pilot episode, which was then the industry norm. Rubinstein gives no explanation as to why this decision was made, stating only that the company went ahead after receiving monies from clients of a securities broker 'seeking high risk/high income potential investments with protection on the downside by a tax-related investment structure'.[30] Further, he omits how Laurel obtained access to these 'superstars' of the sports world. By way of explanation, Rubinstein writes that these documentaries were attractive because they gave the subjects agency, 'their chance to say what they wanted' unfiltered by the interpretations of mainstream sports journalists.[31] A 2016 episode of the NFL Network's *The Timeline* (2015–2018) entitled 'Night of the Living Steelers' also turned its attention to Laurel's documentaries without shedding substantial light on their production backgrounds.

Laurel's sports series (ultimately titled *The Winners*) was in fact based on an informed offset of risk and Rubinstein's expertise/human capital. In late December 1974, Laurel reported they had received financing for the show from Babb Investments, a subsidiary of the regional insurance broker Babb, Inc. who offered professional investment counselling with an expertise in tax shelters. Principally, a tax shelter offers individuals in high-income brackets the opportunity to generate losses on high-risk investments that offset tax on all of their collective income, promising deductions and credit far in excess of their investment.[32]

As Calvin Johnson puts it, 'a tax shelter is an investment that is worth more after-tax than before-tax'.[33] Tax shelters are usually managed through a limited partnership, which limits investor liability (they cannot lose more than they put in) and allows income and losses, and the taxation there within, to flow directly through to the investors. These schemes were all the rage in 1970s media production, and David Cook records that tax shelters financed 20 per cent of all films produced between 1973 and 1976, adding that in 1975 over half of the films in production or released by majors Columbia, Warner, Paramount and United Artists (not to mention independents including Allied Artists and American International Pictures) were at least part financed by tax shelter monies.[34]

Rubinstein learned of the relationship between tax shelters and film production from his father's investments and saw Pittsburgh as ideally suited to applying this stratagem. For him, this was a city that understood tax shelters because of the large percentage of high-income executives and businesspeople working and/or living in the region.[35] Alongside the advice given by Babb Investors, Laurel was aided in tax shelter financing by the Pittsburgh-based law firm Berkman, Ruslander, Pohl, Lieber and Engel, whose clients included a number of regional sports personalities. In point of fact, the firm's managing partner Marvin S. Lieber provided legal representation to both Romero and Franco Harris and just happened to be an expert in taxation.

In 1982, as the IRS looked to retrospectively disallow a number of these tax shelter write-offs, names of the scheme's high-income beneficiaries became public knowledge. The local press situated Laurel Tape & Film at the centre of these tax court cases and discovered its investors to be a 'disparate group of celebrities and old-line Establishment types'.[36] This included a department store executive, a former US attorney, baseball star Willie Stargell, Franco Harris and his Steelers teammates L. C. Greenwood and Rocky Bleier. All of these aforenamed sports stars appeared in front-of-camera on *The Winners*; the opportunity to set the record straight perhaps not as important as the promise of large, tax avoidance savings. 'Good Luck on Sunday' was credited to the limited partnership Television Documentary Associates, and in April 1974 Harris and partners of Berkman et al. commissioned Laurel to produce two more sports documentaries through the limited partnership Television Documentary Associates II. Two months later, Television Documentary Associates III was formed to instigate additional content. This was followed by a number of limited partnerships serving the same function: A. J. Associates, J. R. Associates and Front Four Associates.[37]

The loopholes exploited by these limited partnerships were closed by the Tax Reform Act of 1976. The IRS utilised an 'at risk' solution as a deterrent, meaning investors could now only claim deductions on their own monies, rather than against promissory notes or non-recourse loans, as they had done with Laurel. In the case of investment into 'motion pictures and similar productions', the 'at risk' solution was backdated to 30 June 1975.[38] In 1976, Ed Blank reported on the resultant anxiety in the independent film sector, with regional producer Maurice W. Gable forecasting nothing less than the end of independent film production in the United States. 'This is an incredibly high-risk business, and it's going to be much tougher to persuade persons to invest', said Gable. In this same article, an unnamed 'Latent Image' spokesperson added that the Tax Reform Act would affect financing 'less in feature films than in the production of such things as our one-hour sports documentaries'.[39]

Laurel's use of tax shelters, however, went much further than that and Rubinstein's knowledge of this scheme was enhanced by his strong relationships with a number of disparate business colleagues and associates, not least his mentor Irvin Shapiro, for whom he had worked as an administrative assistant at Films Around the World. Shapiro's company gained prominence as a leading distributor of foreign language films, including classic titles *Battleship Potemkin* (Eisenstein, 1925) and *À bout de souffle* (Godard, 1960) and acted as sales agent for a number of domestic production companies. In this latter capacity, Films Around the World mediated the distribution of US films on the international market, a service it had rendered on *The Crazies* in 1973. Rubinstein valued Shapiro's advice and it was on his say-so that he began his association with Romero.[40] Former Laurel employee Tom Dubensky asserts that it was Shapiro who instructed Laurel to transfer their tax shelter expertise into the acquisition of foreign films, advice that Rubinstein readily followed.[41]

Laurel consequently purchased the US rights to several European co-productions, including *Ten Little Indians* (Collinson, 1974), *Le Secret* (Enrico, 1974) and *Where There's Smoke* (Cayatte, 1973). As with the television product, films were sold to limited partnerships (established and overseen as tax shelters by Laurel itself) and then sold again to more experienced distributors. On the sale of the Italian *giallo* film[42] *Spasmo* (Lenzi, 1974), distributor-buyer Libra Films re-hired Laurel to shoot graphic inserts for the US release. The *giallo* subgenre was made famous by Mario Bava (in films such as *Blood and Black Lace* [1964]) and Dario Argento (*The Bird with the Crystal Plumage* [1970]) and violence in these films was often explicit, sexualised and operatic. Lenzi, however, designed his film as a conscious break from such paradigms. Under Romero's direction, additional footage was shot in Laurel's first-floor studio space, these new scenes depicting a killer in a leather fetish mask committing brutal acts of murder. This masked killer, admittedly a part of *giallo* iconography, served to disguise the fact that here he was played by a Laurel crew member and not one of the original Italian cast.[43]

Such alterations, though common in foreign film acquisitions, rest uneasily alongside Romero's auteurist proclamations. His initial incentive behind Laurel was to obtain control of material and to safeguard productions against interference (either internal or external). To sustain this space, Romero appeared willing to sacrifice the authorial voice of other filmmakers. Lenzi was incensed when he heard about these changes, disdainful of this process of re-cutting international releases without directorial approval. He regarded Romero's actions as 'reprehensible. He should have refused, or at least he should have notified me. I would never do such a thing . . . I have my ethical code as a director.'[44] From 1973–6, as Romero's filmic expertise was rechannelled to facilitate tax shelter deals, Laurel's auteurist remit was subsumed. Romero later conceded that working on *Spasmo* was his 'most embarrassing moment',[45] yet could at least console himself that these schemes kept him working as a media producer. This said, Rubinstein's business expertise continued to dictate corporate movements and in 1976, and despite the looming Tax Reform Act, he expanded the partnership's shelter schemes even further.

Rubinstein's next shelter partnership led Laurel into book publishing and through the brokerage firm Resource Investments, Inc. instigated at least two more limited partnerships, including J. W. Associates and Scorpio '76. A detailed description of these partnerships can be found in the 18 May 1983 Tax Court hearing *Fox* v. *Commissioner*, which sought to determine the extent to which seventeen investors (referred to as petitioners) could deduct their distributive share of the firm's losses through 1976 and 1977. When petitioners filed a redetermination of tax liability, the court questioned 'whether the purported acquisition of book publishing rights by these partnerships was a sham, serving no business purpose and lacking any economic substance'.[46]

These limited partnerships were typically overseen by a general partner, usually a person or persons with a specialised knowledge of the industry and tasked with managing day-to-day operations. On 28 June 1976, Romero was made general partner of J. W. Associates, though he had no experience in book publishing whatsoever. As revealed in *Fox* v. *Commissioner*, 'Romero did little more than acquiesce in all decisions' and sign whatever paperwork Resource put in front of him.[47] The focus of J. W. Associates' front-facing activities was the publication of John Wilcock's *An Occult Guide to South America* (1976). Rubinstein's Ultimate Mirror, though long since inoperative as a media content producer, was revived to serve as sales agent, receiving a 10 per cent fee for connecting the limited partnership to New York publisher Stein & Day. In turn, Stein & Day charged an excessive 35 per cent distribution fee, higher than usual due to the book's 'limited market potential'.[48]

In a letter to Resource dated 10 May 1976, Laurel voiced concerns over the impending Tax Reform Act, aware that J. W. Associates was under audit by the IRS. To demonstrate a legitimate 'for-profit' motive, Romero signed a two-sentence letter to Stein & Day wondering if a discount might 'spur some sales', while on 7 December Irvin Shapiro inquired about the film rights to Wilcock's book.[49] Rubinstein was ultimately undeterred by the IRS audit and on 30 June that same year established Scorpio '76 to purchase six books from Stein & Day, including Dick Gregory's autobiography sequel *Up from Nigger*; Jean Stubbs's crime novel *The Golden Crucible*; pharmacology study *Forbidden Cures* by Steven Fredman, M.D. and Robert E. Burger; and *The Virile Man: 60 Minutes to Greater Potency* by Sheldon L. Fellman, M.D. and Paul G. Neimark. All were released in 1976. Many of these books had underwhelmed in advance sales, leading the Inland Revenue Commissioner to conclude that 'these were not bona fide attempts at profitable book publishing'.[50]

It is important to clarify that *Fox* v. *Commissioner* was about a redetermination of tax liability, not about prosecuting those involved for tax evasion. The kind of tax avoidance exploited here has been strongly criticised, since it gives wealthy individuals a means to circumvent their 'fair share' of tax contribution to public services such as education, physical infrastructure, healthcare and defence.[51] Mark Rowney calls such tax avoidance 'the grey area between compliance and evasion',[52] but these measures are not illegal. Pittsburgh-based filmmaker Tony Buba says that tax shelters actually support regional development, encouraging 'investment in something that would be considered high risk in order to promote job growth. A lot of filmmakers and film techs got their start because of the shelter.' There is a clear ambiguity surrounding the use of tax shelters, yet Buba insists that it was this system that allowed Laurel to thrive, and in turn to instigate a regional base of trained professionals who would continue to work within the industry. 'There's a whole crew base [in Pittsburgh] because of Laurel', says Buba.[53]

Romero later recalled his frustration at Rubinstein's funding strategies, accusing his partner of 'always looking for sleazy little deals. I kept saying "Man, let's make another movie!"'[54] This depiction of Rubinstein as the scheming producer, stereotypically at odds with an artist only concerned with making art, is typical of the wider perception of non-creative talent in the cultural industries. Nonetheless, it was Rubinstein's so-called 'human capital' that lead the way, using his business and marketplace knowledge to establish a solvent production company based on degrees of risk and risk aversion. These tax shelter schemes cannily offset risk, producing content where economic failure was not merely an irrelevance, but something actively solicited by high-income investors. And as demonstrated in the *Village Voice*, Laurel's tax shelter moves into television, distribution and book publishing could later be re-spun, presenting an expansive, multifaceted entity with broad-ranging capabilities.[55] Yet within this context, questions arise as to what exactly Romero's auteur status meant; was it the ultimate objective, as Allen suggested, or simply an additional means to offset risk?

George A. Romero's *Martin* and Cult Film Branding

Between 1969 and 1972, the seven major studios reported record losses in excess of $500 million, an economic downturn that, among other things, pushed the studios towards a proactive distribution of more affordable foreign imports.[56] Academy Award Winners such as Italy's *Investigation of a Citizen Above Suspicion* (Petri, 1970) at Columbia Pictures demonstrated the viability of overseas acquisitions, and by 1981 UA Classics had become the first studio division solely dedicated to the release of domestically produced art films and foreign titles. US independent distributors looked to offset this incursion into their territory in a number of ways, promising overseas producers a higher profit against their smaller overheads[57] and adding more attention-getting content to the roster. Ben Barenholtz's Libra Films, for example, acquired provocative titles such as *Sebastiane* (Humfress and Jarman, 1976), *Maîtresse* (Schroeder, 1975) and Laurel tax shelter imports *Where There's Smoke*, *Le Secret* and *Spasmo*.

Aside from distribution, Barenholtz also ran the Elgin Theatre in Manhattan and in 1970 instigated the midnight movie craze with the exhibition of Alejandro Jodorowsky's psychedelic western *El Topo*. Late-night screenings of *Pink Flamingos* and *The Rocky Horror Picture Show* (Sharman, 1975) followed, cementing the midnight movie's reputation as a confrontational, anti-establishment alternative to mainstream sensibilities. Even as this trend spread nationally, the Elgin remained central and J. Hoberman suggests that 'by experimenting for several years, Barenholtz developed a sense of what could play well at midnight – what would develop a cult or become a fashionable must-see and what wouldn't'.[58] Barenholtz himself countered that 'you can't make a cult film intentionally, it doesn't work. It's the audience that creates the cult, it's not the filmmakers.'[59] As noted in the introduction, this is in keeping with a critical analysis of cult cinema where, as Matt Hills says, cult is 'linked to subcultural audience discernment, recognition and valorisation rather than marketing-led or industry/PR-related constructions'.[60] Closer analysis of Laurel's branding in relation to its film *Martin* will, however, demonstrate that a self-conscious, market-led utilisation of cult is entirely possible.

Though Romero had been absent from film production for almost three years, his cult appeal remained high. In its review of *Martin*, *Variety* labelled him 'a Pittsburgh-based auteur' whose 'insistence on bloody and dramatic closeups' would be eaten up by an identified fanbase.[61] The *Pittsburgh Post-Gazette*, meanwhile, observed 'a popular cult director among movie buffs because of the enduring appeal of his first feature film'.[62] This appeal expanded when *Night of the Living Dead* hit the midnight circuit in Washington, DC, leading *Newsweek*'s Paul D. Zimmerman to label it a 'bona fide cult movie for a burgeoning band of blood-lusting cinema buffs'.[63] Jancovich situates the midnight movie as something of a ground zero for cult, a phenomenon that brought together an eclectic assortment of films 'defined by a sense of distinction from "mainstream, commercial cinema"' and positioned as entirely separate from the economic considerations that drove the industry elsewhere.[64]

Director John Waters, on the other hand, sees the midnight movie as an implicitly commercial endeavour, where 'the very fact that [a film] was playing at midnight was almost a brand name, it was a genre'.[65] Contradicting Barenholtz's above comments, Waters argues that his *Pink Flamingos* was designed as cult, purposefully delivering to audiences shocking content (a singing asshole, cannibalism, vomit, chicken copulation and his star eating dog faeces) to differentiate product and attract attention.[66] If cult status had to be acquired authentically, Waters suggests that product could also be self-consciously pointed in that direction. The notion of the midnight or cult movie as a genre, or in relation to genre, is therefore an important one in terms of a media industry investigation. While genre is often discussed in terms of semantics or syntax, industry and economic experts draw attention to genre's box office appeal, where large returns have been generated from relatively small investments and practitioners have been able to build content and orchestrate strategies for release around codified systems of production, marketing and audience recognition.[67] As discussed in Chapter 1, such calculated, risk-reducing strategies are not limited to Hollywood and were apparent in the production of Latent Image/Image Ten's *Night of the Living Dead*.

Through Latent Image's early commercial failures, Romero came to understand the difficulty of selling films without a clear marketable hook. As such, Laurel's first feature film, *Martin*, readily adopted horror film tropes. Originally entitled *Blood* and developed for exploitation distributor Joseph Brenner Associates – whose releases included *Virgin Witch* (Austin, 1972) and the *giallo* import *Torso* (Martino, 1973) – the film instead raised its $85,000 budget through regional investment. *Martin*'s financial service provider Barney C. Guttman states that the film was not directly funded by tax shelters and, contrary to the incentives behind tax shelter schemes, the backers all made a healthy profit on their investments. According to Guttman, 'this wasn't serious money, it was more "let's have some fun with an investment"', and the backers contributed around $10,000 each into the production.[68]

While a genre framework seemed less economically risky (though not entirely without risk, as the box office failure of *The Crazies* had shown), Romero's use of horror was far from straightforward. This is most evident in *Martin*'s ambiguous narrative, where the titular protagonist (John Amplas) can be viewed as either an eighty-four-year-old vampire or a teenage boy driven to think he's a vampire by years of systemic family abuse. The film begins with Martin's arrival in Braddock, PA, a working-class industrial town ravaged by the collapse of the US steel industry. His vampiric curse is regarded as a 'family shame' borne across generations, now falling to the charge of his elderly cousin Tata Cuda (Lincoln Maazel). Cuda reluctantly invites Martin into the home he shares with his adult granddaughter Christina (Christine Forrest), warning him, 'you may come and go, but you will not take people from the city. If I hear of it, a single time, I will destroy you without salvation'. Instead, Martin preys upon women in the suburbs, but a consensual relationship with a lonely housewife (Elyane Nadeau) causes him to question his identity. When she commits suicide, Cuda immediately suspects Martin of her death and drives a wooden stake through his heart.

Martin has an instant, almost aggressive sense of realism, the film's washed-out colour aesthetic acting almost in defiance of the supernatural elements elsewhere. Cinematographer Michael Gornick's 16mm camera moves through dilapidated streets and the seedy red-light district of the city, while interior action is confined to drab domestic spaces – Cuda's kitchen, Martin's attic bedroom, the suburban homes of his prey. Martin haunts these locales, silent, watching, listening, often positioned to the side of the frame or at a distance from the people around him. But Braddock is more than a backdrop for Martin's nocturnal activities and its decline is imbedded within the narrative. Christina's boyfriend Arthur (Tom Savini) is a mechanic who laments the lack of work, eventually leaving in search of greener pastures. The only industry we see are cars being crushed in a nearby scrapyard, another overt symbol of broken Fordian prosperity. Poverty is rampant and in the final act Martin stalks the town's homeless people in search of a victim he assumes no one will miss. Braddock here is a place without a future, 'a town for old persons' as Cuda puts it, a tomb befitting a modern-day vampire.

This clash of *vérité* regional filmmaking and Gothicism is one of the many juxtapositions that *Martin* explores. Braddock's destitution is placed against the affluence of the surrounding middle class; Martin's boyish nature embodies both innocence and monstrousness (best exemplified as he shyly buys an ice cream sandwich while stalking his next victim); age is placed against youth; fantasy against reality. In this sense, the film speaks to a fractured American psyche. Martin's alleged vampirism is debated at length by the characters onscreen and Cuda and Christina come to represent each side of the film's dual positioning. Cuda fanatically adheres to the ancient books that document the curse, while Christina is less bound to familiar traditions:

> CHRISTINA: He's unbalanced. He's mad and you and those books have driven him to it.
> CUDA: He is *nosferatu*. He was born to Elena Borassa and Rudy Mathias in the old country in 1892. He is young for *nosferatu*. There have been nine such accursed in the family. There are three still alive. Martin is one.

Geoff King categorises *Martin* as a 'genre-complicating film', recognising the oft-seen 'indie' film compulsion to at once embrace and deviate from what came before.[69] Horror film conventions are important to *Martin*, but aside from the numerous Hitchcockian suspense sequences, particularly Martin's breathless cat-and-mouse invasion of a suburban home, the film is more of a dialectic address to genre tropes than a total adherence. Under the alias 'the Count', Martin calls a late-night radio talk show to debunk traditional vampire lore, avowing that real vampires are unaffected by garlic and sunlight, and entirely without the hypnotic powers of seduction associated with Bram Stoker's *Dracula* (1897). This play with genre is established in the opening sequence, as Martin boards an overnight train and stalks a female passenger. Picking the lock to her door (a hypodermic needle clutched between his teeth in place of fangs), Martin imagines her (or remembers a similar victim) waiting readily within, dressed in a loose nightgown and with her arms outstretched. These black-and-white memories/fantasies jar against her emergence from the toilet in a green face pack. And nor is she willing, instead desperately fighting back as Martin sedates her, rapes her and slashes her vein with a razorblade to drink her blood. 'There isn't any magic, it's just a sickness', Martin later tells us.

When *Martin* was obtained for domestic distribution by Libra Films, the promotional material played up more conventional horror film iconography. Posters featured either glaring vampire fangs dripping blood or skeletal hands reaching down for a crucifix. The theatrical trailer also centred on *Martin*'s use of archetypal motifs, such as the garlic that hangs in Cuda's house or close-ups of the rosary beads he desperately clings to. A scene from the film in which Martin dons a cape and fangs to make fun of Cuda's superstitions is also cut into the trailer, but in the context of this montage loses its sense of ironic commentary. Furthermore, the black-and-white sequences of a remembered or imagined past appear in the trailer in full colour, downplaying the film's ambiguity to suggest a mystical narrative progression that follows Martin from the nineteenth century to the present day.

Romero described *Martin* as his most personal, human story[70] and he allowed himself to empathise with Martin's sense of alienation. The fusion of horror and auteur filmmaking returns us to issues of cult and subcultural reception, where fan communities are said to rely on cultural status for affirmation within peer groups. Jancovich points to the 'intrageneric conflicts' that can emerge between fans of a certain genre, where status can be earned within the subculture through a recognition and valorisation of so-called 'cult auteurs'.[71] These consumers can then position their taste values as authoritative, hierarchically above fans whose passions are for apparently lightweight mainstream genre product. Fandom surrounding the 'cult auteur' allows subcultural capital through the display of knowledge, differentiation and connoisseurship.[72]

Rubinstein was aware of Romero's potential in this context from the very beginning, telling the director when they first met,

> I can see two separate markets for [*The Crazies*]: the neighborhood drive-ins as an exploitation film, and a second audience of people who know your work from [*Night of the Living Dead*] and are hip to what you're saying about the army and bureaucracy.[73]

Romero may have utilised horror as a marketable hook, but what Rubinstein recognised was that the cult status of *Night of the Living Dead*, alongside the widespread media ignorance in regard to the film's egalitarian production process, had made Romero himself an even more valuable hook. Romero was a seditious auteur rich in subcultural appeal; all Laurel had to do was tap into that. Latent Image's commercial failures had made Romero a risk for investors, and the Laurel moniker initially offered a degree of distance between founder and company. Now that connection was reaffirmed, turning Romero's potentially hazardous anti-establishment, anti-corporate posturing into an economically advantageous brand.

Rick Altman writes of the importance of branding to Hollywood studios, comparing marketing strategies to the advertising of household products in a supermarket, where brand names promise 'fantasy, quality, style and individuality'.[74] As the majors underscore 'restricted qualities' (star, budget, director and so on), Altman stresses that genre can be strategically employed as a selling point for producers of divergent financial means, even if they must still 'compete on equal grounds with all other producers of genre films'.[75] Away from Hollywood, Laurel indicates how branding can be applied in the independent sector. Just as the horror film market offered a reduction of risk, careful branding of Romero's image meant Laurel did not have to 'compete on equal grounds' with other genre practitioners. Stealing a move from star-director Alfred Hitchcock, on *Martin* Romero's name appeared on posters as part of the title, promising 'a new nightmare from the director of *Night of the Living Dead*'. The trailer meanwhile teased 'another kind of terror', situating auteurist differentiation (that is, 'restricted qualities') alongside the seemingly diametric quality of genre familiarity to sell the film.

Placing the director's name in front of (or as a part of) the title would become a common strategy among genre filmmakers seeking marketplace distinction, utilised on John Carpenter's *Halloween* (1978), Wes Craven's *A Nightmare on Elm Street* (1984) and again on Romero's *Dawn of the Dead*. Theorists Timothy Corrigan and Meaghan Morris have written convincingly about the auteur's brand-name potential, a potential that is actively cultivated in extratextual modes of packaging and promotion and that ultimately directs our understanding of the filmic text as a whole.[76] In the late 1970s, Laurel hired public relations firm PMK to increase Romero's profile, and he began to appear on talk shows and in magazine articles with a degree of frequency. These interactions emphasised his vanguard status (on PBS's *The Dick Cavett Show* in 1980, Romero was the only filmmaker in a panel of genre novelists comprising Stephen King, Ira Levin and Peter Straub) and allowed him to differentiate his films from low-budget (and, for Romero, lowbrow) 'slashers' such as *Friday the 13th* (Cunningham, 1980).[77] For Laurel, cult distinction was therefore not something ascribed in fan reception; it was consciously embedded within the text and reinforced through Romero's managed auteur persona.

The self-conscious application of cult, authorial distinction and its role within the firm can be summarised in the business wheel shown below (Figure 2.1), representing a cyclical intersection of objectives and outcomes. On a film like *Martin*, the Laurel partners agreed that to reduce risk, genre presented a sound framework in which to package auteurist product. In turn, this focus on more offbeat, personal work offered an unusual, 'genre-complicating' film that differentiated *Martin* from other products on the market, attracting a 'discerning' cult film audience in the process. Romero's cult auteur status could then be co-opted and recycled as a form of branding, framing filmmaker intent and identification for a specified market segment and once again reducing the high-risk associated with independent film production. Auteurist demands sit firmly within this business wheel, an integral part, if far from the ultimate outcome.

Figure 2.1   Laurel business wheel.

Within an equal partnership built around Romero (or the Romero brand), Rubinstein's entrepreneurial drive shaped what Ulrich Witt calls the 'cognitive commonalities' within the firm, harmonising seemingly disparate business and creative demands to execute a collective agenda. In discussing the entrepreneurial leader, Witt goes on to explain that

> a multi-person firm is an organization with an internal division of labor which serves the purpose of accomplishing jointly the conception which the entrepreneur is unable to realize by her/himself. This purpose is attained if all firm members decide, within their respective area of discretion, in a co-ordinated way, and if their decisions are consistent with the entrepreneur's business conception. To achieve this, the entrepreneur's conception must be transmitted to, and adopted by, the firm members.[78]

Rubinstein's brilliance was to create a company that satisfied the demands of both partners, where providing a platform for Romero's creative agency (albeit within fixed parameters) was in harmony with a sound business plan. If Rubinstein regarded Romero as a 'creative profit center',[79] Romero was equally gratified by the partnership. As he told journalist Cynthia Heimel in 1980, Laurel demonstrated a way 'to stay true to your aesthetic and still resolve your business problems', offering as close to total creative freedom as the industry allowed.[80] The 'cognitive commonalities' nurtured by Rubinstein meant that this creative freedom could in turn be fed back into the distinct, and highly competitive corporate identity deemed vital to success in this high-risk industry.

Martin premiered out of competition at the 30th Cannes Film Festival in May 1977, immediately attracting distribution in France, Spain and Australia, while negotiations in the UK and Germany were ongoing. Romero explained to George Anderson that this quickly put the film 'in the black', marking the first time since *Night of the Living Dead* that one of his films had returned money to investors.[81] *Martin* was also the midnight hit that Barenholtz intended, playing for forty-three consecutive weekend nights from August 1978 to May 1979 at the Waverley Theatre in New York. Branding had built a platform for the film's success and, in sequence, became another building block in the construction of that brand. *Martin* re-established Romero's name as a commercial, yet sociopolitical independent horror filmmaker. His next film, however, would cement his reputation as one of the genre's leading lights, giving Laurel additional means for corporate expansion.

Author, *Autori*: Overseas Investment and the X-rating

As the decade drew on, Romero's cult appeal expanded beyond domestic shores, creating space for Laurel's planned sequel to *Night of the Living Dead*. Romero's debut film had impressed at the international box office, generating

$18 million in overseas returns. According to R. H. W. Dillard, *Night* was the highest grossing film in Europe in the year of its release. Though these claims have not been corroborated, *Night* co-writer John Russo has also boasted of the film's European success, writing that it played for more than a year and a half in cinemas in Madrid and Rome.[82] In an attempt to capitalise on *Night*'s popularity, the walking dead became a popular fixture in 1970s Euro horror and among the film's successors/imitators were the Spanish-Portuguese co-production *Tombs of the Blind Dead* (Ossorio, 1972) and the Italian-Spanish *The Living Dead at the Manchester Morgue* (Grau, 1974).

Irvin Shapiro recognised the overseas potential of a *Night of the Living Dead* sequel and in his role as Laurel's foreign distribution agent sent a partially completed screenplay to Italian producer Alfredo Cuomo, who in turn brought in writer-director Dario Argento to raise monies. Like Romero, Argento was an important horror auteur who regarded industrial independence, in his own words, as 'one of the most important things in artistic life'.[83] When unable to attract financing for his first feature film *The Bird with the Crystal Plumage*, Argento and his producer father Salvatore established the production company Seda Spettacoli to make it themselves. The film's success established Seda Spettacoli as an industry player, and throughout the 1970s Argento productions such as *Deep Red* (1975) and *Suspiria* (1977) were regularly among Italy's top-grossing films. In 1973, Dario's brother Claudio joined the family business and served as a producer on *Dawn of the Dead*.

Romero and Argento appeared creatively simpatico and Argento even regarded *Night of the Living Dead* as one of his favourite horror movies.[84] More than fannish enthusiasm, investment into the renamed Laurel Group[85] made financial sense. Between 1974 and 1979, the Italian film industry suffered a massive decline in cinema attendances, largely due to competition from television. In 1976, the monopoly of the state-sponsored broadcasting company RAI (radio audizioni italiane) was deemed unconstitutional, and new television stations were now permitted to enter the marketplace. With audiences staying home with more frequency, and US films and imported television shows dominating small-screen programming schedules,[86] the number of domestically made feature films in production fell by almost 50 per cent. Argento was alert to these developments and viewed investment into overseas production as 'a good way of keeping the wolf from Seda Spettacoli's door'.[87]

In this climate, Dario and Claudio Argento in partnership with Alfredo Cuomo agreed to finance half of *Dawn of the Dead*'s budget in return for international distribution rights in all non-English language territories, with the exception of Latin America. The UK was a contested territory and split between parties. Economists often point to the large degree of risk involved in international trade, where importers-exporters are exposed to risk on everything from foreign exchange and intellectual property rights to credit and political risks. Friederike Niepmann and Tim Schmidt-Eisenlohr state that risk is especially high when dealing with partners who are far away or in countries whose legal differences make the contract hard to enforce, though such risk can be offset through 'specialized trade finance products offered by financial intermediaries'.[88] The Italian investment arrived as a letter of credit (LC), a form of payment organised through intermediary banks that guarantees payment to the seller. Once again, Rubinstein's apparent audacity, bypassing American financers entirely, was balanced by calculated risk management. With half the funds secured, Laurel drew an additional \$325,000 from a consortium of friends, family and investors. Romero and Rubinstein themselves personally invested \$25,000 each.[89]

Investment into *Dawn of the Dead* gave Seda Spettacoli considerable creative input. In pre-production, every page of Romero's screenplay (finished and overseen in Rome) had to be read, approved and initialled by the Italian consortium. Dario Argento even received a script consultant credit on the finished film. More dramatically, in post-production Argento insisted on editing his own version for release in European territories. Here, the film was re-titled *Zombi* or *Zombies* (or, in the divided United Kingdom release, *Zombies: Dawn of the Dead*). More than simply cutting or trimming scenes, Argento essentially edited Romero's footage from the ground up, using alternative takes, moving or removing some shots and extending others. In the first seven minutes alone, which mostly takes place in a chaotic regional news station as the world outside collapses, critic Tim Lucas records 'at least 10 subtle variations of montage, including a different presentation of the title onscreen, different music, a reduction of cutaways to the scientist being interviewed on TV, and additional dialogue'.[90] As just one example, Argento's edit has lead character Fran (Gaylen Ross) refer to the undead as 'the enemy', while Romero cuts this dialogue, leaving them without any definite appellative.

In Lucas's opinion, Argento's changes were designed to remove the film's satirical focus on a bankrupt, 'materialistic society'.[91] This is an overstatement, and Romero's bombastic approach to political commentary makes it hard to nullify totally the ideological concerns (*Dawn of the Dead* is, after all, a film about mindless consumers as zombies greedily wandering around an American shopping mall). Even so, in the European edit, sociopolitical intent is downplayed. In Romero's cut, after the protagonists find refuge in the mall, the space becomes a bourgeois prison of their own making. They live in a storage unit converted into a luxurious apartment with all mod cons and, as the narrative progresses, the sense of boredom becomes palpable. In one scene towards the conclusion we watch as they drink expensive whisky, play cards with real (albeit now worthless) money and squabble about whether the TV should remain on or off: 'what have we done to ourselves?' asks Fran. This scene was cut entirely from the European edit, indicative of Argento's decision to extract moments of quietude or pointed annotation. Claudio Argento maintains that Romero's version was simply 'too long'[92] and their edit is around eight minutes shorter than the US release.

One of Argento's most noticeable changes was to emphasise the music by Goblin (billed here as 'The Goblins, in association with Dario Argento'). Romero utilised some of these tracks himself, placed within an eclectic soundtrack of library music, muzak and pop. The inclusion of Goblin, however, created an authorial problem for Romero. By 1978, Goblin's synth-pop scores for *Deep Red* and *Suspiria* had made the group synonymous with Argento. Romero therefore minimised their place on the American soundtrack because of this close association.[93] This was, after all, to give the film its full US title, *George A. Romero's Dawn of the Dead* – a factor as important to Romero's artist-ego as it was to the film's domestic branding.

The LC from the Italian consortium had additional repercussions on Romero's authorial voice. *Dawn of the Dead* camera assistant Tom Dubensky recalls that Argento insisted the film be shot using Technicolor stock, taking advantage of a pre-arranged deal between Seda Spettacoli and the film processing laboratory that dated back to *Suspiria*.[94] Caetlin Benson-Allott believes that at this point all the Technicolor dye-transfer laboratories in the US had closed down, meaning that processing would have been done in Rome, giving the Italians even more control over the product.[95] This is, however, incorrect, and Dubensky and cinematographer Michael Gornick remember completing all processing and colour-timing at Technicolor's east coast labs in New York – all under Gornick's supervision. The Italians did work on their own cut at Technicolor Italiana, perhaps resulting in Benson-Allott's misunderstanding.[96] Romero was also able to work this contractual obligation to satisfy his own artistry, using the Technicolor process to flatten the image and emphasise the pop art reds, blues and yellows in emulation of the four-colour EC comic books *The Vault of Horror* and *Tales from the Crypt* he had adored growing up.

In terms of day-to-day production, the Italian consortium remained hands-off. Though they bound Laurel to a delivery date, they were entirely flexible when it came to the filming schedule. As with *Martin*, the regional shooting location allowed Laurel to circumvent union regulations and *Dawn* was shot over a leisurely four-month period, from November 1977 to February 1978. This accommodated a mandatory three-week break over Christmas, during which time Romero decided to emphasise the film's comedic elements. When shooting recommenced, Romero dropped the downbeat conclusion (in which the last of the survivors commit suicide) to one of escape and went so far as to improvise a custard pie fight, situating the zombies as the literally deadpan recipients of this slapstick standard.

The European edit of *Dawn* complicates issues of creative authority and Romero displayed concern when the Goblin score threatened to displace his status as the primary creative figure. This said, on the whole Romero seemed unconcerned as long as the Italian consortium did not interrupt his hands-on creative process. Romero has stressed the importance of improvisational freedoms to his ideas of authorial independence,[97] and for him authorship was largely expressed in the on-set process – it was the art of creating, the invention, the discovery and, providing that the final decisions were ultimately his to make, the collaboration.

That *Dawn of the Dead* was ultimately the work of multiple filmmakers was extremely rare in American cinema, independent or otherwise. Director of *The Neon Demon* (2016) and Argento superfan Nicolas Winding Refn called *Dawn* 'the only example of one movie having two parents'.[98] In many ways, *Dawn*'s production was a unique culmination to the egalitarianism Romero had begun on *Night of the Living Dead*, only here creativity was compartmentalised, divided into equal parts and sent out into separate territories. As a consequence, Romero's autonomy on set was maintained, even as his creative control in other areas of production and release was rescinded or denied.

Also divided was the very concept of the auteur, split between the classical notion championed by Sarris et al. and the idea of authorship as something commercial. Romero was not naïve about the economic potential of this collaboration, telling *Variety* in 1978 that he and Argento were each better placed to cater material to their designated markets.[99] As the *Independent Film Journal* observed on 21 March of that same year, 'with Argento's reputation abroad, and Romero's cult status in the States, the paring would seem a commercial certainty'.[100] James Naremore proposes that 'in certain American contexts, [auteurism] became useful as a kind of marketing strategy',[101] but he need not have cast his net so narrowly. Notwithstanding *Night of the Living Dead*'s international success, and Romero's subsequent cult capital in this marketplace, Argento was himself a regular box office draw on his home turf. His name reinforced *Dawn of the Dead/Zombi*'s Italian heritage for domestic audiences and the Italian promotional material astutely ran under the banner 'DARIO ARGENTO presents a film written and directed by GEORGE ROMERO', allowing both auteur brands to work side-by-side, with Argento's taking precedent.

On 18 October, *Dawn of the Dead*'s Italian distributor Titanus ran a two-page advertisement in *Variety* proclaiming that 'the zombies are eating up [Italian] box office records!', reporting an impressive $1.2 million in its first thirty-six days of release. The second page reprinted a memo from Titanus head Goffredo Lombardo addressed to Dario Argento, reading, 'Opening release of *Zombie* is sensational. Congratulations and thanks both to you and George Romero. Titanus is proud to be distributing this box office giant'.[102] This boast of massive, rapidly acquired ticket sales in a North American trade paper had a dual purpose: to bolster the international reputation of all parties involved, and to help Laurel attract a US distributor.

The biggest obstacle in acquiring domestic distribution had been the film's violent content, certain to receive an X-rating from the MPAA. Romero upheld that the violence was crucial to the film's aesthetic power, 'it speaks to our fragility, it shocks you and makes you wake up', he later said.[103] Unfortunately for Laurel, the X-rating, as *Night of the Living Dead* distributor Walter Reade told *Variety* in 1969, 'for all practical purposes was basically connected with dirty pictures for a large number of the film going US public'.[104] Although many distributors were quick to exploit this association (the poster for 1972's *Fritz the Cat*, directed by Ralph Bakshi, proudly proclaimed, 'We're not rated X for nothin', baby!'), restrictions in terms of audience and exhibition made the X-rating, outside of pornography, relatively uncommon. In a 1972 *New York Times* article, Stephen Farber and Estelle Changas reported that approximately 50 per cent of US theatres refused to play X-rated films, while a number of major national newspapers and regional television stations would not advertise such product. For many, the X was a 'brand of shame', or worse, 'box office poison'.[105]

Rubinstein claims that Laurel only received three serious offers for a North American release. The first came from Warner Bros., who put forward $1 million for an R-rated cut. Filmways Pictures wanted *Dawn* on the same terms, but Warner's offer essentially priced them out.[106] The third offer came from Egyptian mogul Salah M. Hassanein and his United Film Distribution Company (UFDC). Hassanein was then executive vice president of United Artists Theatre Circuit (UATC), the exhibition arm of United Artists Communications, Inc. (UA). By 1977, UATC was one of the largest cinema chains in the United States (see Table 2.1) and UFDC was established to provide an additional stream of content. Overseen by Salah and his son Richard Hassanein, UFDC output was infrequent, yet diverse, and releases included the West German soft-core porno

Table 2.1 Leading US cinema chains in 1977 (Source: Beaupre, 1977).

Cinema Chain	Number of US Domestic Screens (Approx.)
General Cinemas	500
United Artists Theatre Circuit (UATC)	500
Mann Theatres	250
Commonwealth	200
ABC Theatres	185
Cinemette	150

The Sinful Bed (Gregan, 1973), the Mexican Jaws facsimile *Tintorera: Killer Shark* (Cardona Jr, 1977) and the US feature-length sketch-comedy *The Kentucky Fried Movie* (Landis, 1977).

UFDC was alone in committing to an uncut version of *Dawn*, reflected in its reduced offer of $500,000, which Laurel accepted. Rather than concede to an X-rating and its association with pornography, Laurel and UFDC planned to release the film unrated. In place of the X, promotional material ran the following warning: 'There is no explicit sex in this picture. However there are scenes of violence which may be considered shocking. No one under 17 will be admitted'. Throughout the film's first and second run, the Laurel partners continued to do the rounds on the national press circuit, taking any opportunity to iterate the film's lack of sexual content, while not forgetting to enthuse that the film did contain 'blood aplenty'.[107] As Rubinstein explained in July 1979 (and not for the first or last time) 'no major company will release a film with an X rating. The flaw in the rating system is that X carries the connotation of sex. There is no sex in "*Dawn of the Dead*". Not even a kiss.'[108]

In *Variety* on 20 June, United Artists called for a new adult grading distinct from the X, citing the artistic merit of their Pasolini acquisitions *The Canterbury Tales* (1972) and *Arabian Nights* (1974) and UFDC's *Dawn of the Dead*.[109] Such public rallying against the X-rating continued in the marketing of independent films well into the 1990s, becoming a key release strategy for Miramax. As Perren details, when a Miramax film such as Peter Greenaway's *The Cook, the Thief, His Wife & Her Lover* (1989) was given an X-rating, the company parlayed the surrounding controversy into additional 'inexpensive' press. On the one hand, Miramax decried the X-rating and expressed outrage at the censorship of such a prestige picture. On the other hand, they used the publicity to draw attention 'to the film's racy content' and attract audiences beyond the arthouse.[110]

Like Miramax, Laurel's disavowal of the X and its associated 'racy content' was eagerly transferred into considerable media attention. By defending the film's more extreme content, Rubinstein was reinforcing the Romero brand, using the director's association with violent horror and *Dawn*'s rejection of the ratings system to promise uncensored, licentious thrills; at the same time authenticating the director's anarchic, counterculture persona. If *Dawn of the Dead* were, as Tom Allen predicted, the 'biggest cult blockbuster of all time', it was a status carefully nurtured by Rubinstein's shrewd judgement of the marketplace.

Getting an unrated *Dawn of the Dead* onto American cinema screens had been a calculated risk for Laurel. From the film's debut at the Cannes Film Festival in May 1978 to its national release, *Dawn* spent nearly a year looking for a US distributor who would protect Romero's directorial vision (domestically at least). But in the background, Laurel had legitimate offers for distribution from Warner and Filmways to fall back upon, and Rubinstein did contemplate removing some of the film's more graphic material if an R-rated release became their only option.[111]

Risk was then further offset by partnership with the Hassaneins and UFDC. *Dawn*'s lack of a rating threatened restrictions on exhibition and advertising, two factors that drove Warner Bros. and Filmways to demand an R-rating. UFDC, on the other hand, was a subsidiary of a leading North American cinema chain and had no problem with the film's exhibition. On 20 April, Richard Hassanein opened *Dawn of the Dead* in 200 cinemas across twenty-five cities, with plans for a saturation release of 500 cinemas depending on the film's initial success.[112] *Dawn* immediately exceeded expectations and within three weeks flaunted strong box office returns of just under $1.5 million, making it the fifth highest grossing film in the week ending 2 May 1979.[113] This bright start convinced other exhibitors to run the film and Rubinstein says that in the end only UATC's major competitor General Cinemas refused to play it.[114] By the final count, *Dawn of the Dead* had a collective worldwide box office of over $55 million.

In June 1979, Rubinstein claimed 'the key to our success is the creative control we've had in the past. I believe that's simply good business.'[115] As he makes explicit, Romero's 'creative control' was part of a good business plan, one facet of a corporation strongly driven by entrepreneurial acumen and risk management. Although in the 1970s risk management had not yet become an integrated part of business infrastructure (then mostly associated with insurance buying or financial derivatives), it nevertheless remained a prerequisite when engaging with any marketplace, particularly a 'high-risk' industry such as independent film production. Gifford connects risk to Becker's concept of human capital, suggesting that entrepreneurial activity is not necessarily guided by an individual's greater propensity for risk, but more so by the accumulated knowledge that allows them to better assess the marketplace and its potentials.[116] It's about expertise more than risk for risk's sake. In the case of Laurel, such human capital investment saw Rubinstein take a near-dormant regional production house and transform it into a key player in the independent film sector.

Conclusion

Creative risk-taking is seen as an essential component of independent film production, even if notions of economic risk management in this sector have been under-explored. How typical Laurel's behaviour was during this period remains to be seen, and this chapter calls for additional scholarship in this area. This said, risk did play a crucial part in Laurel's establishment, dictating method and influencing output. Attraction to risk has been seen as a determining factor in the behaviour of the entrepreneur, yet as Laurel's activities from 1973 to 1979 demonstrate, risk-taking was calculated, offset by investment into human capital, knowledge of the marketplace and strategic partnerships with investors at home and abroad. The demands of the independent 'cult auteur' sat in accord with such industry navigation, and films such as George A. Romero's *Martin* were situated within a business plan that emphasised product differentiation and brand appeal. Inside this infrastructure, Romero's creative output was also flexible, exhibited by two very different versions of *Dawn of the Dead*. Far from a simple objective to 'turn Romero loose', Laurel was more diverse, guided by entrepreneurism and risk management, rather than total artistic abandonment.

NOTES

1. Allen, 1979, p. 1.
2. Ibid., p. 45. So taken was Allen with Laurel that in 1984 he joined the company, serving as script consultant on *Tales from the Darkside* until his sad passing in 1988.
3. Bradley, 1973.
4. Gange, 1987, p. 64.
5. Rubinstein, 1973, p. 23.
6. Quoted in 'Richard P. Rubinstein: Breathe Deep NYC No Charge', 2006. McLuhan's writing was very much in the air during this period and his notion of 'cool media' also permeated in Haskell Wexler's *Medium Cool* in 1969.
7. Alvey, 1996, p. 146.
8. 'Richard P. Rubinstein: Breathe Deep NYC No Charge', 2006.
9. 'VT Program Guide', 1973, p. 49.
10. Gedajlovic, Lubatkin and Schulze, 2004, p. 902.
11. Ibid., p. 902.
12. Block, 1972, p. 24.
13. Peterson and Berger, 1971, p. 97.
14. Pokorny and Sedgwick, 2012, p. 181.
15. Banks et al., 2000, p. 453.
16. Pokorny and Sedgwick, 1998, p. 209.
17. Pokorny and Sedgwick, 2012, p. 188.
18. Gange, 1987, p. 62, original emphasis.
19. Gifford, 2011, p. 303.
20. Banks et al., 2000, pp. 458–9.
21. Becker, 1962, p. 9. Understandably, Becker's term has not been without controversy, deemed by some to reduce people to cold, calculated machines. In 2004, a panel of German linguists voted *Humankapital* the most offensive word of the year, see 'Six Big Ideas: Gary Becker's Concept of Human Capital', 2017.
22. Becker, 1962, pp. 12–13, 17.
23. See Buba, interview with the author, 16 June 2016; Dubensky, interview with the author, 16 June 2016.
24. Gange, 1987, p. 65.
25. Banks et al., 2000, p. 458.

26. Gange, 1987, p. 63.
27. Eger, 1975.
28. Rubinstein, 1975, p. 28.
29. Ibid., p. 30.
30. Ibid., p. 28.
31. Ibid., p. 30.
32. See Little and Drasner, 1976, pp. 67–8; Williams Jr, 2003.
33. Quoted in Braithwaite, 2005, p. 17.
34. Cook, 2000, p. 338.
35. Gange, 1987, p. 65.
36. Kiely, 1982, p. 1.
37. Ibid., pp. 1, A18.
38. United States, Joint Committee on Internal Revenue Taxation, 1975, p. 15.
39. Blank, 1976. This is one of the few occasions where Latent Image was credited as a source of information after the formation of Laurel Tape & Film. Whether this was a typo, a miscommunication, or a distancing move made to protect the subsidiary's image is unknown.
40. Gange, 1987, p. 64.
41. Dubensky, interview with the author, 16 June 2016.
42. The *giallo* subgenre takes its name from Italy's notoriously lurid yellow-jacketed crime paperbacks.
43. Dubensky, interview with the author, 16 June 2016; Romero, interview with the author, 7 April 2016.
44. Lenzi interviewed in Revokcom, 2010.
45. Romero, interview with the author, 7 April 2016. In Romero's defence, this was something that also happened to him when distributor La Superstar International drastically recut *Martin* for its Italian release in 1979. The film was re-titled *Vampyr* and given a new score by Goblin in an attempt to capitalise on the success of *Dawn of the Dead*, released in Italy in 1978.
46. *Fox v. Commissioner*, 1983, p. 974.
47. Ibid., p. 979.
48. Ibid., p. 982.
49. Ibid., p. 990.
50. Ibid., p. 1018.
51. Payne and Raiborn, 2018, p. 474.
52. Rowney, 2015.
53. Buba, interview with the author, 16 June 2016.
54. Romero, interview with the author, 7 April 2016.
55. If Tom Allen's summation is correct, and Laurel published around thirty-eight books, then the firm's tax shelter schemes were far more wide-reaching than the endeavours listed here.
56. See Belton, 1994, p. 302; Allen, 2003, p. 78.
57. Segrave, 2004, p. 197.
58. Hoberman and Rosenbaum, 1991, p. 314.
59. Interviewed in *Midnight Movies: From the Margin to the Mainstream*, 2005.

60. Hills, 2013, p. 22. Hills is speaking specifically to cult film stardom, though his analysis remains transferable to issues surrounding cult as a whole.
61. Poll, 1979.
62. Anderson, 1977.
63. Zimmerman, 1971.
64. Jancovich, 2002, p. 317.
65. Interviewed in *Midnight Movies: From the Margin to the Mainstream*, 2005.
66. Waters, 2005, p. 12.
67. See Holt and Perren, 2009, p. 10; Gomery, 2013, p. 49.
68. Guttman, interview with the author, 13 January 2017.
69. King, 2005, pp. 167, 191.
70. Yakir, 1979, p. 63.
71. Jancovich, 2000, p. 28.
72. Ibid., pp. 26–8.
73. Rubinstein, 1973, p. 23.
74. Altman, 1999, p. 115.
75. Ibid., p. 115.
76. Corrigan, 1990, p. 45; Morris, 1989, p. 123.
77. Hanners and Kloman, 1982, p. 77.
78. Witt, 1998, p. 167.
79. Harmetz, 1982, p. H15.
80. Heimel, 1980, p. 48.
81. Anderson, 1977.
82. Dillard, 1987, p. 15; Russo, 2012, p. 110.
83. Argento, 1996.
84. Shipka, 2011, p. 125.
85. This name change coincided with the firm's shift back to theatrical feature films, but it is also worth noting that the Laurel Group was, in fact, an entirely different corporate entity to Laurel Tape & Film, emerging as a wholly owned subsidiary of Rubinstein's Ultimate Mirror in 1977. Why the partners felt it necessary to create a new business entity is unknown.
86. Brunetta, 2009, p. 247.
87. Rigoletto, 2014, p. 7; Argento quoted in Shipka, 2011, p. 125.
88. Niepmann and Schmidt-Eisenlohr, 2014, p. 1.
89. Rubinstein and Martin, 2004.
90. Lucas, 1997, p. 42.
91. Ibid., p. 42.
92. Shipka, 2011, p. 125.
93. Lippe et al., 1980, p. 7.
94. Dubensky, interview with the author, 16 June 2016.
95. Benson-Allott, 2013, p. 221.
96. Dubensky, interview with the author, 16 June 2016; Axl and Jscott, 2013.
97. Romero, interview with the author, 7 April 2016.
98. Bennyx, 2016.
99. Werba, 1978.

100. 'Romero and Argento Aim Ghoul Tale for Exposure at Cannes Marketplace', 1978, p. 12.
101. Naremore, 2004, p. 11.
102. Titanus, 1978.
103. Porton, 2002, p. 5.
104. Quoted in Wyatt, 2000, p. 243.
105. Farber and Changas, 1972, p. D15.
106. Rubinstein and Martin, 2004.
107. Thomas, 1979.
108. Ibid.
109. 'UA Argues X, Stigma of Porno', 1979.
110. Perren, 2012, p. 44.
111. See *Document of the Dead*, 1985.
112. 'Italo *Dawn of the Dead* Goes to United Film', 1979; Anderson, 1979.
113. '50 Top-Grossing Films: Week Ending May 2', 1979.
114. Perry, 1979.
115. 'Romero-Rubinstein "*Knights*"', 1979, p. 26.
116. Gifford, 2011, p. 304.

3. 'CAMELOT IS A STATE OF MIND': PROFESSIONAL PRODUCT, INDEPENDENT SPIRIT, 1979–1982

The financial success of *Dawn of the Dead* at the global box office evidenced a skilful cultivation of the George A. Romero brand. His tendency towards auteurist production had been an impediment to Latent Image's solvency, yet in the hands of entrepreneur Richard Rubinstein became an integral part of the Laurel Group's differentiated, and now exceedingly profitable, corporate identity. Laurel was mutually beneficial to its two founders, a space where independent filmmaking could be a means of personal expression and economic sufficiency, each propelling the other and stimulating growth. From Rubinstein's point of view, growth meant legitimacy, a self-made business with the means to meet competitors on a professional level. For Romero, it meant a larger canvas, not just in terms of scale and budget, but also in terms of scope. This bore fruit in the company's next feature film, *Knightriders*, a $3-million production that abandoned genre entirely in favour of an apparent autobiographical narrative. When the firm incorporated as Laurel Entertainment, Inc. at the end of the 1970s, Romero's creative agency seemed, if only for a moment, to be limitless.

Encompassing a period from 1979 to 1982, this chapter details the transformation that took Laurel from privately owned to publicly listed firm, a metamorphosis that dictated a more formal business infrastructure with a greater accountability to a range of stakeholders. I consider how this threatened to contradict Romero's anti-establishment persona, inspecting the company's efforts to harmonise diametric entreaties for 'anarchic' creativity and professional responsibility. A study of Laurel's professionalisation gives us a unique platform from which to explore seldom discussed issues of non-Hollywood corporate governance and independent filmmaker (self)image-making.

Sale of Stock and Professionalisation

Laurel Entertainment, Inc. was established on 14 December 1979 in legal distinction from previous holdings bearing the Laurel name. In November, the domestic box office of *Dawn of the Dead* had risen to around $16.1 million, giving Romero and Rubinstein the capital needed to float their company on the public stock exchange. On 24 April 1980, underwriters Rosenkrantz, Ehrenkrantz, Lyon & Ross, Inc. listed one million shares of Laurel's common stock for sale at $3.25 per share, with $2.95 going directly to Laurel. These were sold on a 'best efforts' basis and Laurel and its investment bank set the minimum sale of shares at 650,000.[1] Stock was then advertised in publications such as *Barron's National Business and Financial Weekly* and the *Wall Street Journal* that same week. By 19 June 1980, Laurel was reporting the sale of 675,000 shares of common stock, allowing the company to begin trading on the NASDAQ American stock exchange. This sale of common stock realised proceeds of $1,852,280.[2]

Taking a firm public begins with what is known as an initial public offering (IPO). Here, shares of stock are listed on a stock exchange and sold to the general public as a means of generating additional capital. Once a firm begins operating as a public company, it is required to file regular public reports to a governmental body such as the SEC.[3] Floating a company on the public stock exchange is an expensive procedure and direct costs include legal fees, audit fees, filing fees, printing costs and, finally, payment of a percentage of the profits to the underwriters.[4] The total cost of Laurel's own public offering (which also included stock insurance) was approximately $341,470, an amount deducted from their total IPO.[5] Given this expense, questions arise as to why the partners felt public trading was necessary, particularly since the monies earned from *Dawn of the Dead* could theoretically be funnelled back into production of another feature film, allowing the company to maintain a clearer sense of autonomy.

Economists identify corporate growth as a fundamental part of a firm's organic life cycle. An IPO represents a crucial threshold in this development, moving from private, grassroots entity into a larger, more professional enterprise. Aside from the release of additional capital, issues of risk reduction also play a part. Gedajlovic et al. have observed numerous problems facing the privately owned 'founder-managed firm', noting that small-scale businesses often struggle to achieve marketplace legitimacy and find it difficult to initiate cooperative ties with skilled colleagues and external distributors.[6] Further, Gedajlovic et al. argue that the private firm's lack of transparency can also be a deterrent to potential investors, given that it restricts their ability to monitor how their investment is being utilised.[7] Going public reduces risk by tempering these facets. For Yung-Chih Lien and Shaomin Li, the process of professionalisation that follows an IPO adds further currency, facilitating the recruitment of resources, while enhancing 'the firm's productivity and competitiveness'.[8]

It is hard to answer definitively why firms go public, especially given the low rate of success for post-IPO companies.[9] Success is dependent on a number of variables, based on size, managerial ownership retention, venture capitalist following, the reputation of the investment bank and risk. Jain and Kini argue that 'entrepreneurs need to grow their businesses to a certain efficient scale before attempting to go public, thereby increasing the chance of survival. It also follows that the transition to these states will be dependent on risk'.[10] As we have seen in Chapter 2, Rubinstein was both drawn to risk and skilled in managing its effects. Speaking to the *New York Times* in 1982, he boasted of his intent to reduce risk by building Laurel into an accomplished business with a five-year plan.[11] The success of *Dawn of the Dead* presented a window of opportunity to begin this elaboration, the firm now at an 'efficient scale' to formalise growth through an IPO.

Laurel preceded this IPO with a flurry of activity and throughout 1979 the company frequently appeared in the trade papers. On 9 May, *Variety* announced that Laurel's next film *Knights* (later re-titled *Knightriders*) would be part-financed by United Artists' international division through foreign pre-sales.[12] Little over a month later, on 27 June, *Variety* ran a larger report on the company, recording, 'with *"Dawn"* maintaining its b.o. levels, and still facing heavy summer playoff, the Laurel Group partners may be close to that position of power that they once envied [in the majors]'.[13] Alongside *Knights*, the Laurel founders detailed two additional feature films, including a sequel to *Dawn of the Dead* and a 'sci-fi spoof' entitled *Shoo-Be-Doo-Be-Moon*, the latter written by Rudolph Ricci.[14] This marketplace activity included a re-release of *Martin* (repackaged to appeal to arthouse audiences) and the sale of the non-theatrical distribution rights to *Dawn* and *The Crazies* to Cinema 5, Ltd's 16mm division.[15]

In Laurel's 1980 *Sale of Common Stock Prospectus*, the company listed a number of additional projects at various stages of development, each identified for aspiring investors within a specific genre. These nine projects included *Knightriders* (dubbed an 'action-fantasy'), *Shoo-Be-Doo-Be-Moon* ('comedy'), *Day of the Dead* (a 'horror-action' sequel to *Dawn*), *Creepshow* (an 'anthology horror film') and *Cat People* ('horror'). Also included on this list was *The Stand* (a 'thriller-fantasy' adapted from Stephen King's best-selling novel of 1980), Italian co-production *Necronomicon* ('thriller-fantasy'), *Gunperson* ('action-western/parody') and *Out of This Furnace*, a 'dramatic' adaptation of Thomas Bell's 1941 novel concerning immigrant communities in Pennsylvania.

Creepshow and *The Stand* showcased a burgeoning relationship with Stephen King and the prospectus logged that King would pen the screenplays to both.[16]

This flurry of activity extended into ancillary markets. A *Dawn of the Dead* soundtrack album was released by leading film music producer Varèse Sarabande Records in 1979; an officially licensed board game made by Simulations Publications, Inc. came out in 1978; and novelisations of *Dawn of the Dead* and *Martin* co-written by Romero and Susanna Sparrow were published in 1977 and 1978 respectively. During this time, George Lucas famously affirmed the potential of these supplementary markets when he deferred a salary on *Star Wars* (1977) in favour of licensing and merchandising rights. By the end of 1978, toy manufacturer Kenner had sold more than 40 million officially licensed *Star Wars* action figures for a gross sale of more than $100 million.[17] It follows that ancillary markets and tie-in merchandising became more important than ever before to Hollywood release strategies.[18] And if this could be effective in Hollywood, Laurel proved that the same synergetic augmentation could be applied in the independent sector.

Ancillary markets would later become a vital revenue for canonical independent filmmakers such as Spike Lee and Kevin Smith. Through his production company View Askew, Smith opened the retail store Jay and Silent Bob's Secret Stash in 1997, offering a wide selection of tie-in products. Of all people, auteur theorist Andrew Sarris wrote that Smith's 'flair for merchandising and recycling the fruits of his labor is one of the reasons I'm betting on him to break out of the low-budget ghetto and into the movie mainstream'.[19] With his 40 Acres and a Mule production company, Spike Lee cultivated strong ties with sportswear manufacturer Nike, directing several of the corporation's television commercials in the late 1980s. He also appeared onscreen as his *She's Gotta Have It* character Mars Blackmon. Lee used this association with Nike to launch his own retail clothing store Spike's Joint in August 1990, stacking the shelves with tank tops, T-shirts, baseball caps, trainers, beanies and an array of merchandise all branded with logos from Lee's films. That some of this apparel was adorned with the Malcolm X quote 'by any means necessary' somehow neatly encapsulates the canonical independent sector as bold, provocative, political and co-opted.

Aside from additional revenue, in 1979 Laurel's move into ancillary markets, alongside the development of several new projects and the exploitation of its back catalogue, can be seen in the broader context of its IPO. These activities were widely reported on, and as former SEC attorney Robert G. Heim has written, 'a new company must have an exciting "story" to tell investors', a narrative of business activities that will entice the general public to invest their money into the company's future.[20] Posturing in the trade and regional press was part of a shrewd business strategy. *Dawn of the Dead* demonstrated Laurel's skill at crafting saleable product and the company's expansion across multiple platforms suggested additional sources of remuneration. Pursuant to its 1981 Form 10-K, taking Laurel public gave the company stability and proceeds from the sale of common stock were 'sufficient to meet the Company's cash requirements at least through June, 1982'. Management believed that this capitalisation would 'meet cash requirements at least through June, 1983'.[21]

An IPO is a period of great transition for a firm, signifying a move from one phase of development to the next. As such, passing this threshold necessitates significant changes to structures of corporate governance, pertaining specifically to the internal organisation of the firm in terms of a system of practices, decision-making and control.[22] Changes to corporate governance post-IPO are the culmination of the legal demands of becoming a publicly run enterprise and those necessitated by the desire to expand. Filatotchev, Toms and Wright record:

> the entrepreneurial firm has a narrow resource base. It is, as a rule, owned and controlled by a tightly knit group of founder-managers and/or family investors, and the level of managerial accountability to external shareholders is low. As the firm grows, it requires access to external resources and expertise that may fuel and support this growth, and it opens up its governance system to external investors ... At this stage, the balance between resources and accountability starts to shift towards greater transparency and increasing monitoring and control by external providers of resources ... [an IPO] represents a dramatic shift from an entrepreneurial firm to a 'professional' firm with a fully developed governance system.[23]

As a legal requirement of the IPO, all publicly owned firms must install a board of directors to oversee and authorise decision-making. This is part of a public firm's movement towards increased monitoring, transparency and accountability. This said, Rubinstein and Romero were not about to relinquish control so readily. In the election of Laurel's board, voting was done on a non-cumulative basis, meaning that each shareholder got to cast one vote per share owned. In such instances, it follows that the majority shareholder gets the most votes, and as such is entirely responsible for electing the board of directors. Romero and Rubinstein owned equal shares of 525,000 (approximately 57.5 per cent combined), giving them majority ownership.[24] The voting-in of the board took place at Laurel's first annual shareholders meeting in 1980 and, in the final count, Romero was elected chairman; Rubinstein was president, treasurer and director (as well as president and director of numerous Laurel subsidiaries); Michael Gornick was appointed vice president of operations and staff director of photography; and David E. Vogel became vice president of finance. The board was completed by Alvin Rogal, Lester Rosenkrantz (serving as a designee of the underwriters) and Rubinstein's father Frank.[25]

This organisational structure appears to have been fairly typical. Jonas Gabrielsson concludes that small companies usually initiate a skeletal board of between three and seven members, comprising of the owner-manager(s), the owner-manager's family members and outside directors with a personal-professional relationship to the owner-manager, such as a family attorney, a banker or a close friend. This type of board is sometimes referred to as a 'paper board' or a 'rubber-stamp board' and as Gabrielsson explains, 'the paper board is constructed just to meet legal requirements [while] the rubber-stamp board meets only to formally approve what the owner-manager has already decided to do'.[26] Though boards in SMEs have been described as 'passive entities',[27] they can nevertheless exhibit agency by proffering expertise and by giving advice to the owner-manager(s) as and when required. In this capacity, the board of directors sits in an 'advice providing role' and only convenes when called upon.[28]

Once Laurel's board was in place, its first official responsibility was to hire staff members to manage the day-to-day activities of the firm, beginning by appointing Rubinstein as president and treasurer and Romero as corporate secretary. Romero's role here is surprising. A corporate secretary is an administrative role largely responsible for ensuring that the company stays in compliance with regulatory requirements and statutory laws. Duties cover record-keeping, minute-taking, orientating new staff, providing regulatory advice to colleagues, facilitating training and executing the strategic agenda of the board – hardly the kind of duties one would associate with a 'maverick indie director'. More so, as the firm's 'two key employees', Rubinstein and Romero entered into a three-year employment agreement with their company and were paid salaries of $60,000 in the first year, increasing by $10,000 in each subsequent year of employment. Laurel also afforded substantial life and disability insurance policies of at least $250,000 for each partner.[29] By 1984, these employment agreements included annual vacation time of six weeks and, for Romero, an annual expense allowance of $5,000 for which no accounting was required.[30]

Laurel's additional salaried employees included Michael Gornick and David E. Vogel. Since 1973, Gornick had been a key collaborator, working as post-production supervisor for Latent Image and later becoming Romero's director of photography on *Martin* and *Dawn of the Dead*. Like many Laurel collaborators, Gornick was a 'Jack of all trades' and he also directed *The Winners* episodes 'I'm Back: The Rocky Bleier Story' and 'Thank God I'm a Country Boy: Terry Bradshaw', both in 1975. Vogel joined the firm in 1979, by his own account simply turning up at Laurel's Fort Pitt Blvd. offices and expressing a desire to 'work six months for free doing whatever they needed him to – sorting mail, answering phones, anything'.[31]

Though Vogel's above experiences may sound apocryphal, Laurel crew member Tom Dubensky also remembers the firm's laissez-faire recruitment policy, which required nothing more than a display of willing and knowledge of Laurel's business address.[32] Over the next decade, Laurel's accessibility allowed the firm to build strong relationships with a number of filmmakers and production services working in the region. This included the Image Works, whose founders John Harrison, Pasquale Buba and Dusty Nelson became important collaborators from the early 1970s onward. Like Gornick, Harrison is a creative polymath (serving at various times as composer, assistant director, writer and director), while Buba (brother of Tony) was a skilled editor who later worked on Hollywood productions such as *Heat* (Mann, 1995). Laurel's system of governance was far from the egalitarian infrastructure of the Latent Image days, but what remained, at least as far as its crew was concerned, was still relatively loose. Jeff Menne argues that the sense of freedom offered by small companies can emancipate 'film talent in all spheres of operation', liberating them from the rigidity of the 'studio-factory',[33] and sidestepping the narrow avenues for entrance and progression associated with Hollywood. At Laurel, its employees were given a unique opportunity to either experiment in a number of roles, or to specialise and express their talents in one particular field.

This being said, such practices were once again part of Rubinstein's canny offset of risk. As noted in Chapter 2, Laurel's utilisation of eager young talent kept wages down, while costs could also be minimised by hiring this talent film-to-film, rather than on a permanent basis. Each production was delegated to a separate subsidiary company, meaning that these single-purpose entities were legally accountable to just one film or television show and the parent was protected from liabilities and financial failure. By 1981, Laurel subsidiaries included Laurel-Knights, Inc., initiated to produce *Knightriders*, Laurel-Show, Inc. to produce *Creepshow* and Laurel-Moon, Inc. for *Shoo-Be-Doo-Be-Moon*.[34] During a production year, staffing could rise to up to seventy personnel, yet responsibility to these employees was limited to a Laurel subsidiary and a fixed-term contract that expired with that production. Gornick and Vogel were the only permanent members of staff during these formative stages of Laurel's IPO.

Despite his above comments, David Vogel was far more than just another of Laurel's waifs and strays. Like Rubinstein, he was a Columbia business school graduate and, as Laurel made clear to shareholders, had previously served as a management consultant at Booz, Allen and Hamilton, one of the largest consultancy firms in the US.[35] Vogel was hired as the company's first professional manager, that is, a high-level employee trained in management rather than in the company's particular product or market. The business expertise of the professional manager presents a number of advantages to the firm, bringing a degree of objectivity to decision-making and leading corporate activities for the good of the shareholders, not the personal incentives of the owner-founder.[36]

Vogel's presence allowed Rubinstein opportunity to focus on the numerous film and television packages Laurel was juggling at that point. Vogel's role soon expanded beyond vice president of finance to include aspects of film production and, by 1984, to the corporate secretary tasks previously governed by Romero. In terms of production, Vogel replaced Rubinstein as the on-set producer (aka the line producer), positioning him as the key point of contact between the business leaders above (in this case Rubinstein and the board of directors) and the creative team on the floor. This granted Vogel authority over the day-to-day organisational demands of filming and his responsibilities would have included overseeing budget and scheduling, hiring key personnel, managing below-the-line employees and mediating between the director and the cast and crew when necessary. Vogel appeared to welcome such responsibilities, displaying an ambition that by 1993 placed him as president of the Walt Disney Motion Picture Group. In the meantime, as far as Romero was concerned, Vogel was another corporate voice to whom he would have to justify some of his actions.

Vogel's supervisory role can be seen as another step in Laurel's move towards a formalised infrastructure based on mainstream industrial standards. *Knightriders'* $3 million budget was the largest handled by Laurel up to that point, and the increased scale brought about an increased scrutiny from outside parties. Employment of professional talent on *Knightriders* meant dealing with Hollywood unions such as the Screen Actors Guild (SAG) for the first time, something Romero had previously avoided to facilitate a looser, more improvisational shooting schedule. Janet Wasko recognises Hollywood as a 'highly unionized' industry and Laurel now had to contend with strong, potentially prohibitive regulations concerning minimum salary (known as scale), working conditions, hours worked, residual payments, and so on.[37] *Day of the Dead* producer Ed Lammi says that this system of employing SAG actors was still in place on subsequent Laurel productions. In the case of *Knightriders*, although all the onscreen talent would have been union, the below-the-line employees would not be. In fact, some of the above-the-line crew members, including the director and producer, were also non-union, allowing a degree of latitude in regard to scheduling.[38]

Even so, unionisation did create additional difficulties elsewhere. Ironically, *Knightriders'* principal photography took place during a SAG strike beginning 21 July 1980 and shooting was only allowed to continue because Laurel had not received the sixty days' notice required to halt operations. Christine Forrest (another Laurel polymath whose roles included actress, casting director and assistant director) recalls that a number of SAG members felt uncomfortable working during this industrial action, creating an on-set disharmony incongruous with the family dynamic typically claimed in the press by Laurel crew members.[39]

Away from union concerns, Laurel now had other external partners to consider. In another first for the company, *Knightriders* went into production with a domestic distribution deal already in place, with UFDC stepping in to provide half of the $3.5 million budget. This became the first of a three-picture deal and, according to UFDC president Richard Hassanein, it covered the domestic release of *Knightriders*, a second film of Laurel's choosing and a sequel to the highly profitable *Dawn of the Dead*.[40] Under these terms, filming for this sequel could begin no later than 18 January 1985. Romero would receive $100,000 for three screenplays, with an additional $100,000 in director's fees. Richard Rubinstein earned $100,000 in producing fees. These payments would increase by $50,000 to $150,000 each if the films received a net profit. This investment granted UFDC final approval over each screenplay and approval as to whether Romero would direct and Rubinstein produce. No project would be given a green light unless a representative of UFDC signed off on all three of these aspects.[41]

UFDC was clearly attracted to the sequel rights to *Dawn of the Dead*, but Laurel's professionalisation was another facet when courting such potential investment partnerships. The firm's IPO and its responsibilities to shareholders implied trustworthiness, presenting a serious-minded, fully capable business partner that a distributor such as UFDC could bet on. Management and PR expert Cara Reed observes that a central facet of professionalisation is a firm's 'legitimization claims', where primary value is drawn not from changes to internal infrastructure and management, but rather from the branding potential and how this displays the firm to the industry at large.[42] Magali Sarfatti Larson adds,

> most professions produce intangible goods: their product, in other words, is only formally alienable and is inextricably bound to the person and personality of the producer. It follows, therefore, that *the producers themselves have to be produced* if their products or commodities are to be given a distinctive form.[43]

Changes in Laurel's corporate governance presented an industrially legitimate entity with a capacity to do business at the highest level. Kevin James Vella and T. C. Melewar acknowledge that 'through a *strong, distinct, inimitable*, and *immediately recognizable identity*, firms attain their strategic objectives and gain sustainable competitive advantage over rivals'.[44] Marketing and economic data analysis points to a clear link between a firm's corporate identity and its performance in the marketplace, where a strong brand image feeds into and moderates the company's reputation as a whole.[45] A good reputation can simultaneously increase a firm's market share and reduce risk. Firms that are in the market of producing 'intangible' goods need somehow to 'tangibilise' such products in the marketplace.[46] A firm's reputation/image can act in this capacity, serving as a representation of quality that is difficult to quantify in other areas of business operations.[47] Laurel's professionalisation enhanced its reputation industrially, becoming a strategic tool through which to attract internal shareholders and external investors.

If corporate identity can be defined as 'the set of meanings by which a company allows itself to be known and through which it allows people to describe, remember, and relate to it' as Vella and Melewar argue,[48] then Laurel's own identity was in danger of developing a schism. Attempts to brand the company, and by definition the personality of the producer, as a conservative, formally run entity sat in stark contrast with Romero's persona as an anti-establishment radical; a persona readily cultivated by the Laurel partners throughout the company's infancy. More so, as Laurel began this professionalisation, discourse on American independent cinema began to rest upon the sanctification of the amateur. Laurel's professionalisation placed Romero's authentic cult status (a status with its own financial restitutions) in jeopardy, and vice versa. Balancing Laurel Entertainment as something both corporate and anarchic, however incompatible these identities might seem, would require skilful negotiation by its founders.

Corporate Partnerships and Identity Management

Dawn of the Dead's success saw an increased interest in Romero and his work. Reporters took his 'maverick' status at face value, celebrating a 'staunchly independent' filmmaker who refused to 'sell out' to corporate Hollywood.[49] In keeping with his cult image, in interviews Romero continued to vocalise a mistrust of Hollywood, dismissing it as a quagmire of deal-making and cynical market analysis. For him, the 'economic mechanism' of the studios had 'nothing to do with movies' and Romero alleged that real success in Hollywood could only be achieved through a total abandonment of one's morality.[50] His status as Laurel's chairman of the board and corporate secretary, where he was beholden to shareholders, professional managers and enjoyed a healthy annual salary with numerous benefits, was not discussed during this period of enhanced engagement with the media.

I do not wish to insinuate that Romero's distaste for Hollywood was anything other than a genuine reflection of his feelings. Nonetheless, it is important to understand the usefulness of such rhetoric, factual or otherwise, to Laurel Entertainment at that moment in its development. Extratextual engagement not only boosted Laurel's IPO (elaborating on an enticing story to tell potential investors), but also granted a platform from which to restate Romero's brand identity. Laurel's relationship with public relations firm PMK is further evidence of this self-conscious approach to identity management. Aside from Romero, PMK possessed an enviable roster of then A-list clients, including Woody Allen, Robert Redford and Chevy Chase. Such PR firms function to help influence or control, as much as is possible, the brand image of an individual or company, liaising with journalists, the press, television producers and so on to present a clear, consistent and positive impression of their client to as wide an audience as possible. Control in the case of Romero meant separating his valued cult image from the realities of his corporate activities.

This separation was crucial. As Joe Tompkins writes, Romero's brand situated him as a 'vanguard director whose supposedly distinctive counter-cultural approach revolutionized horror by issuing a radical challenge to society . . . Romero's reputation promises audiences an authentic cult experience'.[51] Romero proudly emphasised authenticity through his regional distancing, frequently painting this space as something prescriptively amateur; his films made by an informal 'troupe' of friends whose primary motivation was a shared love of the movies.[52]

A coalescence of amateurism and authenticity is common in writings on the independent sector, where critics stress the 'grassroots' context of filmmaking – placing inexperience and youthful passion centre stage. As mentioned in the introduction, in the late 1970s and early 1980s, this focus on first-time independent filmmakers was often based on a desire to assist growth in the sector. *American Film*'s special report and Austin Lamont's article 'Independents Day' (both 1981) paid close attention to the challenges facing the first-time director, mapping out the industrial terrain and pointing towards the state, private and overseas funding bodies that could offer support. In this regard, Lamont singled out up-and-coming independent filmmakers Robert M. Young, Victor Nuñez, John Hanson and Rob Nilsson, observing 'a conviction that makes them tenacious in reaching their goals. Filmmaking is not their job, it is their need. They do it because they have to'.[53] Numerous independent filmmakers have also positioned their own work in this manner. Jim Jarmusch calls himself 'an amateur filmmaker, not a professional, in the sense that "amateur" means love of something, for the form'.[54] John Cassavetes, meanwhile, famously referred to himself as a '"professional" actor and an "amateur" director'.[55]

Media educator David Buckingham views this as typical of the arts as a whole; the amateur's self-determined status, which sits apart from economic and commercial considerations, said to unlock a creative freedom unavailable to the professional.[56] At its most straightforward, a professional-amateur dichotomy is easily defined by payment or non-payment, leading James M. Moran to label the perpetual slippage of the term 'amateur' from 'descriptive economic category . . . into prescriptive aesthetic and ideological judgement' a misuse.[57] In the case of Laurel, this slippage was beneficial to the firm and its marketplace agenda, masking potential distasteful corporate realities to restate the 'authenticity' of Romero's cult director image. Theorists must therefore be careful not to take such prescriptive notions of the amateur at face value.

As Romero reasserted his amateur/authenticity by decrying the cynical 'economic mechanisms' of Hollywood, behind the scenes Laurel benefited from closer ties to the majors, particularly Warner Bros. Under the stewardship of executive John Calley, Warner had developed a reputation as an auteur-friendly studio, forging significant relationships with the likes of Stanley Kubrick and Clint Eastwood at home, and John Boorman, Federico Fellini and Luchino Visconti overseas. Romero was also on the studios' radar in the 1970s and the inability to agree to terms on an R-rated *Dawn of the Dead* did not dissuade Warner from continuing to pursue his services, even as control of Warner's operations passed from Calley to Robert A. Daly and chief operating officer Terry Semel in the early 1980s. Warner's interest in Romero finally resulted in the studio's distribution of *Creepshow* in 1982.

Aside from its attraction to auteurs, Warner's courtship of Romero and Laurel was part of a growing trend in Hollywood, as the major studios sought to cultivate ties with so-called 'prestigious' independent production companies.[58] Warner had actually been at the forefront of this interest when they agreed to finance Francis Ford Coppola's American Zoetrope production company in the previous decade, though they quickly reneged on this multi-picture deal after seeing Zoetrope's first film *THX 1138* (1971), an avant-garde sci-fi experiment directed by twenty-seven-year-old upstart George Lucas.[59] The premature termination of this deal notwithstanding, Warner continued this stratagem with a degree of success in the 1980s, evidenced by subsequent partnerships with Orion Pictures and the Ladd Company. If Laurel was not entirely 'prestigious', the company could at least be seen as a reliable partner that was well-versed in the production of commercial genre product.

During this period, Warner was also interested in the work of horror novelist Stephen King and approached Laurel to adapt his second book, *Salem's Lot* (1975), for the big screen. By the late 1970s, King was boasting six best-selling novels released over a six-year period, well on his way to becoming the household name/superstar novelist that he is today. His first novel, *Carrie*, published by Doubleday in 1974, was adapted for the screen in 1976 by United Artists and director Brian DePalma, generating around $14.5 million in US rentals. As with Warner's *The Exorcist* (Friedkin, 1973), *Carrie*'s box office success and Academy Award nominations (Sissy Spacek for Best Actress and Piper Laurie for Best Supporting Actress) evidenced the commercial security and growing critical acceptance of the horror genre. Warner was already awake to King's potential in this context and, three months prior to *Carrie* hitting theatres, John Calley personally sent the unreleased manuscript for King's *The Shining* to director Stanley Kubrick. Kubrick's adaptation was released in 1980.

The *Salem's Lot* adaptation was ultimately passed to writer-producer Paul Monash at Warner Bros. Television (WBTV), airing as a two-part miniseries on CBS in November 1979 and directed by *The Texas Chain Saw Massacre*'s (1974) Tobe Hooper. In its stead, on 23 January 1980, Warner and Laurel entered into an agreement to develop *Cat People*, a film based on an original screenplay by Michael Laughlin and Bill Condon[60] and not a remake of Jacques Tourneur's 1942 film of the same name. That Romero's *Cat People* failed to materialise did not dissuade Warner from entering a bidding war with Universal and Paramount for the domestic rights to *Creepshow*.[61] *Creepshow* was originally financed by UFDC as part of its three-picture deal with Laurel, yet the Hassaneins, not unwisely, took advantage of studio interest in the hope of a more expansive, and therefore more profitable, nationwide release. Under Warner's charge, *Creepshow* was held back to accommodate a revised ad campaign, and Romero used this time to trim the film by seven minutes and to convert it to a Dolby Stereo soundtrack. Warner was confident enough in the film to give it a saturation release and *Creepshow* hit 1,042 theatres in the United States and Canada on 10 November 1982.

This prolonged courtship with Warner did little to temper Romero's disdain for the majors, instead becoming another vessel through which to exhibit his anti-establishment credentials. Discussing *Salem's Lot*, Romero derided the corporate thinking that led Warner to suggest the project in the first place. As he told it, Warner executives came to him after seeing *Martin* at the Utah/US Film Festival in 1978, and 'in typical studio fashion they reasoned that *Martin* was about a vampire in a small town, Steve [King] had just written *Salem's Lot*, which was vampires in a small town, so they thought we should meet!'[62] Similarly, in 1981, Romero explained that *Cat People* had been abandoned after going

> through the typical studio process of a couple of script drafts and blah-blah-blah . . . and it became one of those development deals that never happened. So it's not that I resist studios in the right situation. I don't *need* a studio.[63]

Again, there is no reason to suggest that Romero's distaste for the studios was inauthentic,[64] but his independent status was no longer as straightforward as he intimated.

Romero bragged that his independence allowed impunity from Hollywood decision-making, yet Warner's investment into Laurel strongly stimulated corporate growth. The 'pay or play' deal on *Cat People* agreed that Laurel would receive a development fee to continue revisions of the script, penned by a screenwriter whom they found acceptable, and payable whether the film went into production or not. If the film had gone into production, Laurel would have been contracted to receive a total of $300,000 plus 15 per cent of the net profits.[65] The decision not to go ahead meant Laurel only received around $20,000. Though this amount might seem minimal, when taken alongside income earned on short-term interest-bearing securities, this was the company's only source of revenue for the fiscal year ending 31 March 1981.[66]

Good relations with Warner Bros. paid off more substantially on *Creepshow*. Aside from the enhancements made to the film's release (in terms of the scale of distribution, the revised ad campaign, the space made for additional post-production work and the inclusion of a Dolby Stereo soundtrack), Laurel received $541,577 in a deal that included the sale of cable, cassette and TV rights down the line.[67] Deferred until the fiscal year ending 31 March 1983, these earnings allowed Laurel to report its first year of positive net income since its IPO. This increase in revenue was entirely attributed 'to the completion and delivery of the feature film "*Creepshow*" during the first quarter of fiscal 1983. "*Creepshow*" was responsible for all of the revenue recognized by the Company during fiscal 1983.'[68]

On 7 July 1982, *Variety* reported that *Creepshow* had amassed additional revenues of $1,062,500 and corresponding liabilities of $383,330, thus propelling Laurel out of the development stage.[69] A firm is classified as a development stage company when principal business operations have either not yet begun (with the firm still focused on planning and/or research) or if revenues from its early operations have been insignificant. Such entities are subject to greater scrutiny and disclosure regulations. Moving out of the development stage is therefore a major step forward in a company's life cycle. As Rubinstein wrote in his annual report to shareholders in 1982, '[h]aving withstood the long inventory cycle associated with the making of "*Creepshow*", we enter our third year as a public corporation, no longer as a development stage enterprise but as a productive business entity'.[70] Laurel's deal with Warner legitimised the company, establishing its reputation as a professional independent production partner able to do business at the highest level.

Equally important to Laurel was Warner's suggestion to collaborate with Stephen King. Romero derided this proposal as an example of 'typical' Hollywood thinking, but King soon became a major partner in Laurel's enterprise, penning the screenplay for *Creepshow* and selling the company the film rights to *The Stand*. Rights to the latter were renewed until October 1983 and King himself worked on several drafts of the screenplay. King's involvement was further indication of the company's credibility and this partnership was encouraged by talent agents Adams, Ray and Rosenberg, Inc. who, on 25 April 1981, entered into a two-year agreement with Laurel for domestic representation.[71] The agency specialised in 'talent packaging', an industry-standard process in which key personnel (typically above-the-line talent such as star, director, producer and writer) are assembled and sold to a studio or independent financer hoping to profit from this collated marquee value. Apropos of this packaging, *Creepshow* posters and trailers relayed the dual credits of its 'masters of terror and the macabre', belaying a growing corporate influence on Romero's output.

That Romero publicly downplayed the importance of these transactions is not surprising. As already discussed, Romero's branding affirmed shared values with a subcultural audience, something John Caldwell views as equally typical: '"creatives" can spike the value of their own personal brands by mocking or dismissing the prestige institutional brands that launched their careers. In this way, creator brands frequently pose as institutional anti-brands.'[72] Although mainstream institutions played no part in launching Romero's career, Caldwell's reading does reflect the filmmaker's disavowal of Warner and the studio system. In 1980, Laurel's professionalisation made this identity management more complicated. Having used Romero's 'anti-brand' as a way of authenticating cult/counterculture output, Laurel also needed to present a positive, formalised brand image that would be proportionately attractive to external business partners and investors.

To manage these divergent identities, Rubinstein's visibility in the press increased. Here, a disparity between co-founders was strongly enforced, playing on stereotypical notions that segregate the creative and the commercial. On 7 November 1982, Aljean Harmetz's *New York Times* profile piece on Laurel entitled 'From the Cecil B. DeMilles of Pittsburgh' depicted the partnership as a kind of marriage of convenience, a union between distinct individuals that 'don't even like the same films'.[73] Rubinstein, we are told, is a business school graduate with a five-year plan, while according to a quote from Michael Gornick, 'George's chief characteristic is anarchy'.[74] Harmetz further observed this incongruence in their separate working spaces in Pittsburgh and New York; the former apparently facilitating Romero's creative autonomy, the latter a strategic corporate headquarters from which Rubinstein could conduct business. Even so, Rubinstein makes it clear that their skillsets complement each other, stating, 'as a practical matter, I give up my authority in the creative area 100 percent except as regards to budget and George gives up his authority in the business area 100 percent'.[75] Yet Romero's position as corporate secretary, as just one example, contradicts such neat compartmentalisation.

As well as the trades and the national and regional newspapers, the producer engaged with a wide array of publications, including specialist magazines with a fannish eye on genre. In an interview with science fiction magazine *Starburst* in 1982, Rubinstein echoed his familiar summation of the partnership, drawing clear lines of distinction between his business responsibilities and Romero's role as creative leader. As he told interviewer Tony Crawley, 'I see my job as providing George with the brush, palette, paint and canvas . . . I'm there on the set. I represent the clock ticking away'; the responsible hand behind Romero's artistic impulses.[76]

On the surface, talk about contract negotiations, stock options and development funds in fan magazines such as *Starburst*[77] may seem counterproductive, a potentially unappealing context in which to discuss one of the genre's most lauded cult auteurs. But Rubinstein's business perspective again served a wider purpose. Broadly speaking, it offered a consistency of their image across medias, affirming Laurel's corporate identity as a professionally run enterprise that championed artistic risk-taking. Additionally, Rubinstein used fan magazines to showcase his own shared values with Romero and, not least, Romero aficionados. In a second interview with *Starburst*, he joked that 'New York is the business office. Pittsburg [sic] is the production office. Hollywood is penance.'[78] Geoff King identifies such self-professed shared values as common among independent film executives, who stress that their skill in business is lent through a passion for the medium and creative enterprises, not as something solely defined by commercial considerations.[79] In public, the partners repeatedly separated the industrial and creative sides of their infrastructure, at the same time remaining in unison (and ideological superiority) in regard to the authenticity of their independent status.

As we have seen, the production of media goods is determined by a number of economic and creative factors, and it is frequently hard to unpick where one ends and the other begins. Yet Laurel's careful management of its corporate identity demonstrates how useful a clear separation of these factors could be in regard to branding. Rubinstein's media visibility allowed Laurel to present itself as a responsible corporate entity without sacrificing Romero's saleable image as an anti-establishment cult filmmaker. In reality, these 'autonomous bits of turf'[80] were not so clear cut. In the press, Romero's business responsibilities were downplayed, while the company's relationship with Warner Bros. was refracted to either affirm Romero's 'anti-brand' or to emphasise corporate legitimacy, as and when required. Extratextual engagement by both partners created a holistic corporate identity based on divergent yet mutually beneficial skills. Selling this identity of 'professional independence' was central to Laurel's concerns following its IPO. Done with forthrightness in their engagement with the media, it was also mediated more subtly through artistic work of this period, notably 1981's *Knightriders*.

KNIGHTRIDERS AND CORPORATE IDENTITY

Laurel's professionalisation was pivotal to the firm's post-IPO identity. Yet even scholars with an interest in Romero's industrial manoeuvrings tend to overlook the importance of this development. In his insightful analysis of the American horror auteur, Craig Bernardini recognises the self-fashioning that played a large part in Romero's success, marking an appealing display of dissidence and ordinariness, simply a small businessman with something important to say about his country. This blue-collar identity is central to Bernardini's assessment, in which he writes:

> [Romero's] legend and legacy are due as much to the success of Laurel, the company he founded with Richard Rubinstein in 1973, as to his films. The financial vicissitudes of being an independent in an age of conglomerates – digging up investors, deferring payments, and all the

other seat-of-your-pants solutions independents find to get films made – certainly account for the themes that have obsessed Romero throughout his career: his quixotic exuberance for tilting at the windmills of corporate power (a trope best represented by Billy in *Knightriders*).[81]

This colourful overview of the firm may have been true in the days of Laurel Tape & Film and the Laurel Group, but by 1980 Laurel Entertainment was much changed. Following its IPO, the company was now a publicly run enterprise with $2 million in the bank. It had additional responsibilities to shareholders and was also bound to partnerships with distributors such as UFDC and Warner Bros.

Romero's identity as a 'seat-of your-pants' independent 'in an age of conglomerates' continued to serve as a context for his persona and work long after it was actually the case. As with Bernardini's above summation, this was seen most prominently in the reception of *Knightriders*, a film repeatedly framed as Romero's reflection upon his own independent status.[82] But by analysing *Knightriders*' supposed autobiographical narrative in the context of the firm's corporate evolution for the first time, we will gain a clearer understanding of the film and its thematic intent. *Knightriders* follows an unconventional Renaissance fair and its attempts to maintain a communal way of life entirely apart from mainstream America; the troupe serving as an obvious surrogate for the film crew on the other side of the camera. According to *Fangoria*'s Bob Martin (in an interpretation consistent with reviews elsewhere), the troupe's leader, the self-professed King Billy, or Sir William the Knight (Ed Harris), 'could be viewed as Romero, the king of the independents ... determined to see things his own way, regardless of the hardships'.[83] At the time, Romero hesitantly admitted to identifying with Billy, but later proclaimed with more conviction that *Knightriders* is 'emotional and a bit autobiographical. It's me saying, "I won't compromise."'[84]

An understanding of Laurel's professionalisation, however, reveals this autobiographical reading to be far from straightforward. With the firm's corporate activities in mind, *Knightriders* becomes less about a dogmatic refusal to compromise (symbolising the bold endeavours of a determined indie artist vs. the system) and more pointedly about the very nature of compromise in real-world terms. In this context, the film can be seen as either a justification for Laurel's corporate growth or as Romero's attempt to work through and discuss these changes artistically. From either perspective, *Knightriders* seeks to reinforce, or perhaps recontextualise, Romero's authenticity as a counterculture figure.

To re-orientate the film in this regard, it will be advantageous to first summarise the narrative: *Knightriders* follows a travelling 'living history' group whose major selling point is that they perform medieval jousts on motorcycles rather than on horseback. More than just a show, the troupe is a way of life, a figurative Arthurian roundtable based on an equality of race, colour, class, sexuality and gender unavailable in the mainstream society they have left behind. For Billy, this is a space free from moral or ethical compromise, as he prefers to live 'hand-to-mouth' on the road than accept the corrupt rule of law and commercialism that epitomises his view of the United States. During the film's opening performance, Billy rejects the advice of Morgan, 'the infamous black knight' (Tom Savini), to pay a bribe to a local deputy sheriff threatening foreclosure. As a result, Billy is thrown in jail and made to watch as his friend Bagman (Don Berry) is savagely beaten in the adjacent cell. In spite of the pain, Bagman laughs off this assault, strengthened by the sense of community that awaits their release, a community he regards as an unimpeachable 'Camelot' fortified by Billy's idealism.

This community is, however, on the verge of collapse. Aside from the constant threat of financial destitution, Billy's rising dogmatism is alienating him from the group. He believes that theirs is a spiritual existence and his most trusted advisor is a magician and former medical doctor called, appropriately enough, Merlin (Brother Blue). After Billy loses in battle in the film's opening (in the film these jousts are unscripted, though strongly safeguarded and based on principles of fair play), he retires to camp and recalls to Merlin his dream of a 'black bird'. For Billy, this bird is a mythical entity that he is sure will lead to his destruction. In the meantime, the visceral, death-defying spectacle of their performances[85] attracts the attention of the sleazy talent agent Bontempi (Martin Ferrero). Bontempi's offer of representation is brought to Billy through the troupe's lawyer Steve (Ken Hixon) and promises to double their income and supply expensive new costumes and cycle equipment. Billy is incensed by this offer and rejects it, leading to the following exchange:

> STEVE: It's money, Billy. It's all to do with money. Money makes the world go round, even your world.
> BILLY: No, it's just getting too tough. It's tough to live by the code. I mean, it's real hard to live for something that you believe in. People try it and then they get tired of it, like they get tired of their diets. Or exercise. Or their marriage. Or their kids. Or their job, or themselves. Or they get tired of their God. You can keep the money you make off this sick world, lawyer, I don't want any part of it.

If this monologue appears to place Romero's ideological distaste for the mainstream directly into the mouth of his protagonist, it is followed by a clear-headed and compassionate response by Bagman, who argues:

> BAGMAN: The way I see it is this: you got two separate fights. The one for truth and justice and the American way of life and all that. That's gotta

take a backseat to the one for staying alive. You gotta stay alive! Man, you can have the most beautiful ideals in the whole world, but if you die, your ideals are gonna die with you. The important thing is we gotta stay together, we gotta keep the troupe together. And if keeping the troupe going means that we have to take some of this promoter's money, then I say let's take it and get some sleep.

Unable to shake off these words, later that night Billy burns Bontempi's business card and rouses a startled Bagman from his sleep:

BILLY: There's not two different fights. There can't be two different fights. You got to fight for your ideals, and if you die, your ideals don't die. The code that we're living by is the truth. The truth is our code, I can't let people walk on that idea – I can't!

In a Billy as Romero reading of the film, this rejection of compromise can be seen as further evidence of the independent filmmaker's steadfast determination to do the same. In truth (the opaqueness of Billy's response notwithstanding), this rhetoric is delivered by a character whose commitment to 'the code' borders on fanaticism. The film positions Billy as a zealot from the beginning, introduced stripped naked and self-flagellating in devout imitation of the knights he idolises. His behaviour is erratic and contradictory. At one point, he demands that 'no one goes anywhere in this outfit without my permission', then later breaks up a group meeting he deems undemocratic because not all of the troupe are in attendance. As his girlfriend Queen Linet (Amy Ingersoll) tells him, 'everybody here made a conscious, adult decision to be here. To be with you. When you go crazy, you force them to rethink that decision', a proclamation that becomes true when Morgan and his crew leave with Bontempi. At his most self-righteous, Billy refuses to give an autograph to a wide-eyed young fan, later screaming at Linet, 'I'm not trying to be a hero! I'm fighting the dragon!'

In his *Cinéaste* review of 1981, critic Ed Sikov also identified Billy as a Romero surrogate. But unlike those peers who celebrated the romanticism of this indie knight king, Sikov argued that this characterisation suggested Romero as a filmmaker with 'profound reservations' regarding his role as 'cult leader'.[86] In Billy's pageantry (parading around modern-day Pennsylvania dressed as a mythical king), Romero could be seen to address the artificiality of his standing as 'king of the independents', an identity that is faintly absurd and largely self-constructed. The monarchical infrastructure of his onscreen knights also recalls the controls he fought for, and won, at Latent Image. The film's reproach of Billy's dictatorial leadership suggests Romero may not have been entirely reconciled with his evisceration of Latent's egalitarian infrastructure. Asked about this self-criticism, Romero concedes this is 'only because of the Ed Harris character. And I felt that way about myself, that I was being too demanding or that I didn't need to stick that closely to a code.'[87]

As Romero's comments imply, Billy need not be understood as Romero's onscreen avatar in an absolute sense. In its focus on community, *Knightriders* is an ensemble and, unlike their king, the troupe is well aware of the real-world concerns that surround them, knowing that overheads must be paid, bikes maintained and that an ear of corn costs 75¢ each (in contrast, Steve chastises Billy for not knowing how much 'gas is selling for, or two-by-fours, or hamburgers or anything else'). They enjoy the freedom the commune offers but treat the mythos with irreverence. Morgan, who accidentally took his name from a female character from Arthurian legend, is the most outspoken, joking that he 'was never into this King Arthur crap anyway'. And as the film progresses, Morgan moves to the centre of the narrative. Though he is narcissistic, adulterous and ambitious (he openly desires Billy's throne), Morgan the black knight is far from the antagonist of legend; he is simply Billy's opposite, material as opposed to spiritual and willing to make compromises where necessary.

It is Billy's extremism and devout suffrage that pushes Morgan to leave the troupe and start a more commercial enterprise with himself as king, rejecting Billy's crown as a 'crown of thorns'. In Morgan's subsequent career, Romero indulges in an unfiltered attack on mass culture (re Hollywood), reiterating every known stereotype concerning the moral and artistic bankruptcy of the mainstream industry. As a performer, Morgan is decked out in a glittery new armour and in a degrading photoshoot is made to pose in nothing more than a metal codpiece and black cloak – 'think medieval sex', the photographer yells at him. Off camera, Morgan and his followers dive headlong into a world of hedonism: poolside parties, drinking, drugs and motel room groupies. Morgan's relationship with a bourgeois journalist (Amanda Davies) is quickly revealed as superficial, for her nothing more than a brief interlude until her more affluent partner gets back in town. The shallowness of this existence is erosive, climaxing with in-fighting ('bad craziness' as one-character calls it) and a violent motel room punch up that leaves Morgan morally and spiritually adrift.

At this moment, headlights appear on the highway and Sir Lancelot-proxy Alan (Gary Lahti) rides in from the darkness, come to remind Morgan that 'there can only be one king at one time. That's the law.' Morgan thus returns and is welcomed as a prodigal son, gladly allowed to challenge for the kingship and encouraged by Billy most of all. His ultimate victory is hard fought and, after being crowned king, Morgan rejects the deal with Bontempi, telling the agent, 'y'know those contracts? Burn 'em, baby' (something Romero was unable, or unwilling, to do in reality). Now without a throne, Billy takes to the road, seeking out and humiliating the corrupt cop who beat Bagman and handing his broadsword to the autograph-seeking fan he previously refused.

'CAMELOT IS A STATE OF MIND'

Figure 3.1   A new direction for both Laurel and its biker-knights in *Knightriders* (1981).

In a final moment of transcendence, Billy imagines himself a real knight errant riding on horseback. Lost in this reverie, he loses sight of the road and collides with an oncoming truck. The film closes with the troupe gathered at Billy's funeral, saying a final goodbye before being led by Morgan on to another town (see Figure 3.1).

In this conclusion, a singular correlation between Romero and Billy is somewhat confusing. Examined literally, does Billy's death point towards a future for Laurel Entertainment without Romero's totemic presence? This is, of course, entirely possible and would in fact come to pass in the mid-1980s. Yet at this early stage in the company's development, with its IPO reaffirming independence and generating more creative possibilities than ever before (including this, his first non-horror film in almost a decade), this seems an entirely pessimistic disparity. Sikov regards the film's use of allegory as equally perplexing, and is specifically unsure what to make of the 'oblique symbolism' of a silent Native American biker with a black bird painted on his armour who becomes Billy's squire in the second half of the film.[88]

Taken in the context of Laurel's corporate development, Billy's 'last ride' and the presence of his squire and the black bird become more lucid. Handing over his crown can be seen as the moving from one stage to the next, the dogmatic idealism once necessary to their independence now replaced by Morgan's pragmatic and more flexible approach to survival beyond the mainstream. If it's easy to see parallels between Morgan and Rubinstein, Morgan is also Romero, a man who has seen first-hand the way the mainstream works (Laurel's own flirtations with Hollywood and a then active relationship with

Warner) and found his determination to remain independent renewed. Although the *Knightriders* troupe is often deemed a stand-in for Romero's own group of collaborators,[89] their measured response to Billy's fanaticism allows Romero as screenwriter to discuss and redefine his own ideas about independence, written during a time when massive infrastructural changes were taking place at the company he co-founded. In the above exchange between Billy, Steve and Bagman, as Romero's reservations about growth and professionalisation are made plain, so, too, is a realist acceptance that this process might be necessary.

Onscreen, the knights can only move forward when zealous leadership has been buried. In this sense, Billy is not Romero, but a representation of something symbolic. This is emphasised by the character's affinity with magic and the foreshadowing of the black bird. As his physical leadership becomes increasingly problematic, what he represents remains fundamental to the troupe, a dream to be remembered and kept in mind, though not to the point of destruction. Merlin reminds us that magic is not something otherworldly or mystical, 'magic's got to do with the soul', an internalised desire for self-fulfilment and independence that Billy ultimately passes down to the group.

After Billy's death, his now knighted squire returns to the group, standing among the collective as a silent reminder of the former king's ideals. At this moment, it is tempting to regard Billy as a literal representation of the 'independent spirit' critics repeatedly point us to in their analysis of this sector. And how Romero articulates this spirit is fascinating, becoming part of a wider image management and reorganisation of Laurel's corporate identity. *Knightriders* foregrounds authenticity, ridiculing mass culture and presenting an at times genuinely romantic vision of a life apart from everyday compromise. But it is still a film about compromise and the way compromise can be made while remaining true to a fundamental principle. As Laurel's professionalisation threatened to pull it away from Romero's authentic-independent identity, *Knightriders* became a broader mediation of (or, at the very least, a meditation on) that changing identity. *Knightriders* begins by showing an independent ideology at its most pious and ends with the most radical representative of this creed buried and left behind. The subsequent decision to move forward pragmatically, with Billy's ethos, or spirit, still in mind, is therefore entirely justified.

Conclusion

By 1982, Laurel was no longer a 'seat-of-your-pants' regional independent. The company's IPO transformed it into a professionalised production unit with a formalised system of corporate governance, demonstrating responsibilities to shareholders, stronger ties to bicoastal centres and a binding contract with a distributor-exhibitor. Professionalisation offered a base from which to produce auteur-driven, non-genre independent film, yet sat at odds with Romero's image as a cult filmmaker. Rhetoric surrounding cult and the independent auteur is therefore both inadequate and of value, limited in terms of theoretical analysis (where identity is complex and, to a degree, self-consciously managed), while useful for firms or filmmakers looking to craft a saleable (anti)brand. Seen in the context of Laurel's corporate changes, the film *Knightriders* becomes a fascinating articulation on Romero's evolving industry status, relocating his 'radical' identity within a pragmatic model for long-term survival. However, as we have seen, the film industry, and the independent sector in particular, was far from constant. Though Romero may have made peace with Laurel's need to grow, additional adjustments, both internal and at large, would have considerable ramifications for his ideas of agency and his place within the firm.

Notes

1. Rosenkrantz et al., 1980, p. 1.
2. Laurel Entmt., 1980, p. F-6.
3. See 'Companies, Going Public', 2014.
4. Bragg, 2009, p. 7.
5. Laurel Entmt., 1980, p. F-6.
6. Gedajlovic et al., 2004, p. 903.
7. Ibid., p. 904.
8. Lien and Li, 2014, p. 352.
9. According to financial experts Bharat A. Jain and Omesh Kini, one-third of post-IPO companies are expected to fail outright. See Jain and Kini, 1999, p. 1282.
10. Ibid., p. 1293.
11. Harmetz, 1982, p. H25.
12. '*Dawn of the Dead* in $1,300,000 Gross at 65 N.Y. Sites', 1979.
13. 'Romero-Rubinstein "*Knights*" for UA-Overseas', 1979, p. 6.
14. Ibid., p. 26.
15. Ibid., p. 26; 'Romero's "*Dawn of the Dead*" Non-Theatrically to C5', 1979.
16. Rosenkrantz et al., 1980, p. 15.
17. Block, 2012.
18. Jenkins, 2003, p. 285.
19. Sarris, 2007.
20. Heim, 2002, p. 14.
21. Laurel Entmt., 1981, p. 8.
22. See Lien and Li, 2014, p. 347; Keasey and Wright, 1993, p. 291.
23. Filatotchev, Toms and Wright, 2006, p. 260.
24. Laurel Entmt., 1981, p. 6.
25. Ibid., pp. 11–15.
26. Gabrielsson, 2007, p. 689.
27. Ibid., p. 688.
28. Dekker et al., 2015, p. 531.
29. Laurel Entmt., 1980, p. F-7.

30. Laurel Entmt., 1984b, pp. 8–9.
31. Cook, 2015.
32. Dubensky, interview with the author, 16 June 2016.
33. Menne, 2019, pp. 13–14.
34. Also incorporated into a separate legal entity was Laurel's studio space and equipment. In 1981, the firm installed a brand new $150,000 post-production facility all owned by the subsidiary Laurel-Communications, Inc. See Laurel Entmt., 1981, p. 1. Aside from studio space, the firm's 247 Fort Pitt Blvd. base housed fifth-floor offices, which by 1984 cost the company $900 on a month-to-month basis. Not included was 'the area beneath the stairway at a monthly rental of $50 [and] the area opposite the utility sink and bathroom at $50 per month'. See Laurel Entmt., 1984d, p. 2.
35. Laurel Entmt., 1981, p. 15.
36. See Schein, 1983, pp. 24–5 and Daily and Dalton, 1992, p. 27.
37. Wasko, 2003, pp. 41–2.
38. Lammi, interview with the author, 19 April 2018.
39. Romero et al., 2013.
40. Karr, 2014, p. 14.
41. Rosenkrantz et al., 1980, p. 18.
42. Reed, 2018, p. 3.
43. Larson, 1977, p. 14, original emphasis.
44. Vella and Melewar, 2008, p. 8, original emphasis.
45. Simões, Dibb and Fisk, 2005, p. 153.
46. Bharadwaji and Menon, 1993, p. 23.
47. Ibid., pp. 31–2.
48. Vella and Melewar, 2008, p. 9.
49. See Blank, 1980, p. 10; Honeycutt, 1980.
50. Burke-Block, 1981.
51. Tompkins, 2014, pp. 207, 208.
52. See Yakir, 1981, p. 45.
53. Lamont, 1981, p. 16.
54. Tobias, 2004.
55. Quoted in Jacobs, 1980, p. 28.
56. Buckingham, 2009, p. 25.
57. Moran, 2002, p. 66.
58. See Cook, 2000, p. 308.
59. Coppola's ambition with American Zoetrope was to create an autonomous production unit centred around young, up-and-coming filmmakers. Despite the company's tumultuous history, it admirably still survives to this day, remaining an important figure in the history of American independent cinema. For more on Zoetrope's early history, see Chaillet and Vincent, 1985, pp. 29–30.
60. In their collaborations on *Strange Behavior* (Laughlin, 1981) and *Strange Invaders* (Laughlin, 1983), the director-writer partnership of Laughlin and Condon showcased a fondness for genre and 1950s science-fiction pastiche. How *Cat People* fit into this proclivity is unknown. Condon later became famous as the director of *Gods and*

Monsters (1998) and *The Twilight Saga: Breaking Dawn Part 1* and *Part 2*, released in 2011 and 2012 respectively.
61. 'WB Has Domestic "*Creepshow*" Rights', 1982, p. 3.
62. Fitch, 2014.
63. Martin, 1981a, p. 33, original emphasis.
64. Bill Condon corroborates this frustrating repetition of 'meetings and schedules' on *Cat People*. See Swires, 1983, p. 43.
65. Rosenkrantz et al., 1980, pp. 18–19.
66. Laurel Entmt., 1981, pp. 8, F-12.
67. 'Laurel Entertainment Out of Development Stage as Cash Flows', 1982, p. 4; 'WB Has Domestic "*Creepshow*" Rights', 1982, pp. 3, 32.
68. Laurel Entmt., 1983b, p. 15.
69. 'Laurel Entertainment Out of Development Stage as Cash Flows', 1982, p. 4.
70. Laurel Entmt., 1982a, p. 4.
71. Laurel Entmt., 1981, p. 5.
72. Caldwell, 2008, p. 206.
73. Harmetz, 1982, p. H15. The title of this article is drawn from a quote by Rubinstein and amusingly situates the Laurel partners as two parts of a bodily whole – as if American cinema's most famous producer-director had been revived, bisected and sent off to work in separate offices on the east coast.
74. Ibid., p. H15.
75. Ibid., pp. H15, H25.
76. Crawley, 1982a, p. 48.
77. Crawley, 1982b, pp. 36–7.
78. Ibid., p. 36.
79. King, 2009, p. 30.
80. Harmetz, 1982, p. H15.
81. Bernardini, 2010, p. 177.
82. Gange, 1987, p. 108.
83. Martin, 1981, p. 66.
84. Blank, 1980, p. 10; Alexander, 2010, p. 46.
85. In many ways this parallels the attention-getting violence that became a Romero trademark in films such as *Night of the Living Dead*, *The Crazies* and *Dawn of the Dead*.
86. Sikov, 1981, p. 32.
87. Romero, interview with the author, 7 April 2016.
88. Sikov, 1981, p. 33.
89. See Stevens, 2013, p. 13. Adding to this interpretation is the fact that a number of Laurel's behind-the-camera personnel appear onscreen playing the knights, including John Harrison, Christine Forrest and special effects guru Tom Savini.

4. THE ONCE AND FUTURE KING: AGENCY AND THE LIMITS OF CONTROL, 1981–1985

Agency is said to refer to the autonomy of an agent to enact choice within specific political, cultural and/or social conditions. In this sense, a study of agency can be seen as a study of power relations. Analyst Kris R. Cohen says that a political framework is the dominant one when it comes to this subject, yet at the same time recognises that our concept of agency is also dependent upon the disciplinary lens through which we choose to view it.[1] Beyond political sociology, Thomas Schatz calls for an examination of human agency in relation to media industries, specifically asking if there is space for individual authorship among the 'industrial machinery' and external intermediaries that are increasingly centralised by this critical subfield.[2] Laurel Entertainment's auteurist manifesto may seem like an answer in the affirmative, but, as we have seen, George A. Romero's auteur status was complex, part of a wider negotiation with numerous internal and external players, from the marketplace to partnerships with the likes of Warner Bros. and UFDC. While this chapter explores agency in regard to these associations, I will also apply 'agency theory' as a particular principle of economics, allowing a clearer understanding of the 'agency relationship'[3] between Laurel's co-founders and the changing individual objectives that culminated in Romero's departure from the company in 1985.

MONGREL(S): PORTFOLIOS AND PROJECT DEVELOPMENT

Through their engagement with the press, George Romero and Richard Rubinstein defined Laurel Entertainment as an equal partnership between disparate individuals. This allowed them to project a corporate identity of professionalism and anti-establishment cult authenticity, seemingly without contradiction. How this compartmentalisation of creative and commercial interests worked on a practical level is less clear. On paper, Romero was the firm's creative supervisor and was initially in charge of Laurel's projects in development. Beyond *Knightriders*, his desire to make more films outside of the horror genre was visible in the diverse itinerary of projects listed in Laurel's Sale of Common Stock Prospectus. Most remarkable on this list was a proposed adaptation of Thomas Bell's *Out of This Furnace*, a classic working-class drama that follows three generations of 'ethnic Slovak' immigrants living in Braddock, Pennsylvania from 1881 to the 1930s.[4] Laurel optioned *Out of This Furnace* on 19 May 1981, securing the worldwide film and television rights until 1 April 1984.[5] This option was later renewed for an additional twelve-month period and an unnamed Emmy award-winning writer was hired to draft the screenplay.[6]

In the early 1980s, an adaptation of *Out of This Furnace* would have neatly aligned with the emergent independent cinema 'movement', placing Romero more firmly within the canonical sector. Diane Jacobs observed that at the 1979 New York Film Festival, four of the six new independent films screened were set in the rural outdoors (*Northern Lights, Alambrista!, Heartland* and *Gal Young 'Un*), and three of those in the past.[7] Like *Heartland* and *Gal Young 'Un*, the third part of Bell's novel centres on a female protagonist and explores issues of gender and independence against a developing American landscape. *Out of This Furnace*'s look at labour organisations and immigration is also similar to *Northern Lights*, which focused on Scandinavian workers and the formation of a rural worker and farmer alliance in 1915 North Dakota. Indie documentaries *Harlan County U.S.A.* and *Free Voice of Labor: The Jewish Anarchists* (Fischler and Sucher, 1980) also dealt with unionisation and worker rights.

The critical support these films received did not always make them an easy sell for distributors, emerging in a period where 'no clearly defined speciality film market existed'.[8] On Richard Pearce's *Heartland*, the absence of star names (either in the cast or behind the camera), onscreen action and 'youth appeal' culminated in a lack of interest that allowed distributor Levitt-Pickman to leverage a significant percentage of profits away from the filmmakers.[9] Rosen and Hamilton write that the *Heartland* filmmakers were 'naïve about distribution, trusting that if they made a good film, an advantageous distribution deal would inevitably follow'.[10] *Northern Lights* also struggled to find a distributor, leading the filmmakers to distribute the film themselves.

The acquisition of *Out of This Furnace* was then highly speculative, yet in keeping with the firm's creative and commercial schema. On one hand, the project reinforced Romero's agency as the firm's creative supervisor, part of a longed-for and decisive break away from his typecasting as a cult horror auteur. On the other hand, Laurel's industrial growth allowed it to develop several projects simultaneously. *Out of This Furnace* was just one of a number of films in development, including those more firmly rooted in genre. In many ways, this recalls the 'portfolio of films' strategy identified by Pokorny and Sedgwick, where the major studios would produce and release an eclectic range of films in the hope that one hit would compensate for the rest. Laurel simply adapted this portfolio strategy to the independent sector on a reduced scale, focusing on project development instead of production.

When projects were not part of a pre-arranged development deal with a distributor (such as *Cat People* with Warner Bros. or *Necronomicon* with Luigi and Aurelio De Laurentiis), Laurel had to meet development costs itself, resulting in potential financial losses if these properties did not move into production. Moreover, as a production company only, making films was still Laurel's primary source of income. In 1982, the firm's total non-concurrent story development costs were approximately $191,153, falling slightly to $187,018 in 1983.[11] The $541,577 received from *Creepshow*'s sale to Warner demonstrated that if just one of these projects went forward, then it had the potential to offset the development costs of all the other projects combined. Placing a film like *Out of This Furnace* on the books was therefore advantageous to both partners, expanding creative opportunities as they spread risk across a diverse portfolio of projects.

This technique of financing film packages directly through the company was achieved through the capital generated by the IPO and granted greater creative freedom down the line. Rubinstein told Aljean Harmetz:

> Taking seed money [from the studios] puts us in an employer-employee relationship . . . if we finance the development ourselves, we can approach the industry later as a partner. We always have three to five projects in development. It makes good business sense, like holding out a deck of cards and asking, 'Which one do you want to finance?'[12]

Laurel's diverse range of projects in development solidified independence, enabling the company to hold off on a deal with financers, film-to-film, until production requirements had been met, including production budget, payment and final cut. The firm's IPO gave it bargaining power and the capacity to pursue projects under optimal conditions. It gave Laurel the agency to say 'no'. As an example, producer William Teitler spoke of his disappointment when it came to the Laurel project *Beauty Kills*, written by *Tales from the Darkside* and *Beetlejuice* (Burton, 1988) screenwriter Michael McDowell. Teitler recalls an offer of $2.9 to $3 million from MGM to produce the film. Rubinstein ultimately held out for $4 million and the studio passed.[13] To date, the film, like a number of Laurel projects from this period, remains unproduced.

In the press, Rubinstein emphasised Romero's agency as creative leader. In reality, outside of his own directorial projects, Romero was relatively hands-off in constructing the firm's portfolio. A number of these projects were in fact assembled and sourced by 'a core group of four individuals who regularly review and report on unsolicited material submitted to management'.[14] If the material was deemed suitable, senior management would then decide if they wanted to take out an option, usually on a short-term basis of one or two years with the potential for renewal. Economically, this made sense. Bringing in external properties was a means of rapidly enhancing the portfolio. Buying them short-term also meant that Laurel could option these properties at a reduced premium and, if all sources of investment were exhausted, the company could abandon the project and transfer funds to a new acquisition.

After these properties were acquired and expanded into attractive packages (a screenplay/treatment, poster art and promotional material), Laurel would attempt to sell them at national and international film markets. On 4 May 1983, Laurel advertised all of its latest projects in development in *Variety*'s annual Cannes Film Festival special, a bumper edition that also served as a catalogue of product on sale and included the hotel addresses and contact numbers for those producers in attendance. Laurel's updated portfolio included *Day of the Dead*; *Creepshow 2* (Warner Bros. were at that stage scheduled to distribute worldwide); Stephen King's *The Stand*; Thomas Block's 1979 suspense novel *Mayday*; Michael Palmer's novel *The Sisterhood* (1982); *Calling the Shots* by Carole Lucia Satrina (about a New York City policewoman); *The Match* (a coming-of-age sports drama written by James Sadwith); *Dolls* (a 'horror/fairy-tale' mystery by Steve Nelson and not to be confused with Stuart Gordon's 1987 film of the same name); *Imagine That!* (a children's fantasy written by John Harrison); and an adaptation of Mary Shelley's *Frankenstein*.[15]

Prominent among this roster was a mysterious single-page illustration, later unveiled as *Copperhead* (and eventually re-titled *Mongrel: The Legend of Copperhead*),[16] a comic book adventure film in co-production with Marvel Comics. In this partnership, Laurel was to package and produce *Copperhead* as a motion picture. At the same time, Marvel would pursue 'the publishing and merchandising aspects of the project'.[17] Laurel had been after a Marvel property for some time but was frequently outpriced when it came to more popular characters such as *The Fantastic Four* and *The Incredible Hulk*. Indicatively, in the mid-1980s, the Cannon Group purchased the theatrical rights to Marvel's *The Amazing Spider-Man* for a reported $225,000 plus a percentage of gross revenues.[18] This roughly equalled Laurel's collected story development costs for fiscal 1984.[19] Laurel instead decided to create an original character in collaboration with Marvel's then editor-in-chief Jim Shooter and artists drawn from the company's famous 'bullpen'.

In 1983, Marvel was a subsidiary of the conglomerate Cadence Industries and though far from the Disney powerhouse it is today, the company was still the largest worldwide publisher of comic books, selling a reported 5.8 million comics a month in the US and Canada alone.[20] Despite this identified audience and, more to the point, the box office success of DC Comics' *Superman: The Movie* (Donner, 1978) and *Superman II* (Lester, 1981), Marvel had thus far been unsuccessful in transferring its core properties to the big screen. In 1983, *The Human Torch* at Columbia Pictures, *Spider-Man* with Roger Corman and a live-action *X-Men* film by Canadian company Nelvana Ltd. all stalled, causing Marvel figurehead Stan Lee to situate *Copperhead* as their most fully developed filmic project.[21]

Shooter and Romero began working on the idea around 1982 and Shooter delivered a detailed treatment on 20 July 1983. By October, Romero had expanded this into a screenplay under the title *Copperhead Conquers the Warhawks*. The story is set in a post-apocalyptic future (Romero gives the exact date as 2068) where much of the world has been decimated by nuclear war. Tensions between East and West remain high and ground warfare continues across the globe. In the totalitarian United States, the war economy booms, but ordinary citizens are left impoverished and desperate, resulting in an emergent rebellion led by the mysterious Jericho. The US government determines to squash this domestic threat once and for all and enlists square-jawed war hero Adam York for an experimental project known as the Mongrel programme. York's body and mind are enhanced by robotic technology, transforming him into a state-owned 'mongrel' of machine and man. But as the cyborg sheriff of the nation's new capital Philadelphia, York comes face-to-face with the government's oppression of its citizens, quickly realising that his real enemies are the very people that created him.

In this story of a synthetic law enforcement officer whose body (but not whose soul) is co-opted by a brutal capitalist state, readers will no doubt be reminded of Paul Verhoeven's *Robocop* (1987), made some four years later. While the similarities are striking (Romero's script contains the same sense of biting satire and extreme violence that made *Robocop* famous), *Copperhead* is first and foremost a comic book movie.[22] As Romero described it, the film was a 'typical introduction of a superhero – how he comes into his powers – and will take him through his first series of adventures'.[23] The Copperhead character is very much a hybrid of popular Marvel heroes Captain America and Iron Man, displaying the enhanced 'super soldier' characteristics of the former and the technological capabilities of the latter. This said, Marvel and Laurel had one greater, seemingly inescapable influence that drove production. As Marvel artist and *Copperhead* conceptual designer Bob Layton put it, the film was to be 'Romero's *Star Wars*'.[24]

Shooter's treatment coincided with the release of George Lucas's third *Star Wars* movie *Return of the Jedi* (Marquand, 1983), which by July had earned over $200 million at the domestic box office. *Copperhead* was clearly intended to capitalise on this success, depicting epic battle sequences, an array of spaceships and creatures and robots (from giant killers to sassy domestic droids), and a narrative that concerns a band of plucky rebels taking on an evil empire. And just in case potential investors missed these similarities, both treatment and screenplay were littered with references to Lucas's blockbuster. *Copperhead*'s all-seeing central computer Equator is given a voice like 'Darth Vader', while the government's base is described as a vast structure not unlike a grounded 'Death Star'.[25] Strategically, Romero and Rubinstein were no doubt alert to Lucas's desire to use his *Star Wars* trilogy as a platform for greater industrial independence,[26] and to the role ancillary markets played in this agenda. If all had gone to plan, *Copperhead* would have been the first film in a franchise, with each part generating an 'amazing amount of revenue from lunch boxes, animated television series, toys, clothing, video games, and bubble bath'.[27]

On the surface, such a large-scale, multi-platform fantasy project seems out-of-step with movements in the independent sector elsewhere. As Louis Malle's *My Dinner with Andre* (1981) and Wayne Wang's *Chan is Missing* (1982) exhibited the commercial appeal of speciality independents, distributors such as UA Classics, Universal Classics and Orion Classics provided an additional platform for the advancement of this sector.[28] By 1982, however, despite having *Out of This Furnace* on their roster, Romero had come to feel that rising production costs made the chances for success on a small speciality film like John Sayles's *Return of the Secaucus Seven* (1979) 'very, very slim'.[29] Verifying Romero's estimation, in the early 1980s inflationary forces such as a 45 per cent increase in the price of colour film stock, alongside a willingness from the major studios to back larger-scale, special effects-heavy films, resulted in an increase in production costs in the United States.[30]

And Laurel was not the only company adapting to this trend. Stephen Prince reports that, in the wake of *Star Wars*, 'without question, the decade's most popular genre was science fiction and fantasy, furnishing more blockbusters during the period than any other genre'.[31] At the top end were films like Columbia's *Krull* (Yates, 1983), which cost $47 million, and *Return of the Jedi*, which cost $32.5 million. Mid-range films included Paramount's $17 million *Star Trek III: The Search for Spock* (Nimoy, 1984) and Universal/Lorimar's $15 million *The Last Starfighter* (Castle, 1984). Notwithstanding the expense, and a demonstrable growth in speciality independent film production, focus on science fiction and fantasy was not restricted to studio blockbusters and in the lower budget and independent arena existed films like MGM's $8 million *The Beastmaster* (Coscarelli, 1982), Cannon's $6 million *Hercules* (Cozzi, 1983) and New World Pictures' $2 million *Battle Beyond the Stars* (Murakami, 1980).

Production of such material by Cannon and New World et al. recalls the market-orientated exploitation practices of the 1960s and 1970s, 'defining what customers want and ensuring that the company's activities are arranged in a way which will achieve customer satisfaction'.[32] If science fiction and fantasy films were in the 1980s what biker and sexploitation films used to be, then this product was now placed within a more eclectic production roster. In *Variety*'s 1983 Cannes special issue, independent producer-distributors Cannon, New World, Carolco Pictures, Lorimar and Hemdale Film Corporation all showcased diversity. Cannon, in particular, boasted a mammoth 42-page eager-to-please spread that seemingly had it all. Alongside fantasy fare like *Hercules*, the firm had major 80s movie stars (from Charles Bronson to Roger Moore); exploitation sequels such as *Exterminator 2* (Buntzman, 1984); horror in *House of the Long Shadows* (Walker, 1983); erotica (personified by *Emmanuel* star Sylvia Kristel); and even speciality independents, notably John Cassavetes's 1984 *Love Streams*.[33]

In 1987, Todd McCarthy in *Variety* disclosed that the number of independent films released in a twelve-month period ending 31 May was up by 44 per cent from the previous year, which itself had been a six-year high in regard to the number of indie films hitting the market.[34] Of the 277 independents made during this period, Cannon and New World led the way, releasing forty-two and twenty-eight films respectively, which combined to just over 25 per cent of the overall total. Atlantic Releasing, Shapiro Entertainment, Vestron Pictures, Concorde Pictures and Charles Band's Empire Pictures were in near proximity,[35] with each focusing output on exploitation, horror, genre fare, mass-appeal features and the occasional speciality or so-called 'quality' indie. The independent sector recognised by the trades was deeply heterogeneous and speciality distributors stood alongside their market-orientated peers. As 'quality' films began to prove profitable, they were placed on the roster of both types of distributor; in the latter type, they were part of an expansive portfolio that catered to a diverse range of audiences and markets. In this context, Cannon and canon sat happily side-by-side.

For Laurel, the decision-making behind the firm's choice of products was part of a manifold internal and external agency. As the professed creative-leader, Romero pushed for a diversity of product that would expand his efficiency beyond the low-budget horror genre in which he felt 'trapped'. This portfolio of products, often identified by a story acquisitions department answering to Romero and Rubinstein, served to spread risk across a range of projects. Large-scale endeavours such as *Copperhead* showcased professionalism and reveal Laurel's (unrealised) ambition to become a larger corporate entity. High-profile partnerships with external parties such as Marvel were also attention getting (featuring in a *New York Times* profile) and exhibited legitimacy to potential investors and shareholders.[36] Most importantly, Laurel recognised the agency of the marketplace above all else, allowing inflated negative costs and zeitgeist trends to dictate its choice of projects.

Given Hollywood's current obsession with Marvel superheroes, Laurel's *Copperhead* may appear to some to have been ahead of its time. In fact, by 1985 it was actually slightly too late in terms of marketplace trends. Michael A. Hiltzik of the *Los Angeles Times* reports that by 1985 'Hollywood was bored with superheroes'.[37] This was most evident in the disappointing domestic box office gross of Cannon's *Superman IV: The Quest for Peace* (Furie, 1987), which earned little over $15 million on a $17 million production budget. Cannon, New World and Carolco all struggled to attract monies for their own Marvel projects in the mid-1980s.

Alsop, Bertelsen and Holland write that while a person or group may be able to choose options, the effective realisation of these choices is largely determined by the institutional context, or 'opportunity structures' within which they live or work. Formal institutions such as the rules of law, regulatory frameworks, private organisation and the marketplace dictate the success or failure of these choices.[38] For Alsop et al., there are three principal indicators of empowerment or agency:

1. Whether an opportunity to make a choice exists (*existence of choice*).
2. Whether a person or group actually uses the opportunity to choose (*use of choice*).
3. Whether the choice brings about the desired result (*achievement of choice*).[39]

The Laurel partners may have established a shared agency when it came to their portfolio of films, but in the final count they were disempowered by the formal institutions that surrounded them. 'Achievement of choice' was often far beyond their control.

Of the twelve films Laurel advertised in *Variety*'s 1983 Cannes special, only three went into production. And of these projects, *Day of the Dead* was already scheduled as part of a deal with UFDC, while *The Stand* and *Creepshow 2* (Gornick, 1987) were made after Romero's departure. Why the majority of these films failed to attract investment is due to a multitude of factors, including the insignificant financial returns of *Knightriders* and *Creepshow*, the scope of Laurel's ambitions on projects like *Copperhead*, the company's own agency to reject an unfavourable deal, changing marketplace trends and so on. As Rubinstein justified to shareholders in the wake of these disappointments, 'it is entertainment industry experience that only a small percentage of projects that enter the development stage are subsequently produced, and Laurel cannot predict which, if any, of its projects in development will come to fruition'.[40] Largely restricted by institutional 'opportunity structures', other external intermediaries would soon encroach upon Romero's agency elsewhere, alienating him from the company he co-founded.

Method and Restrictions

Retrospectively, it is tempting to position *Knightriders* as the zenith of Romero's agency as Laurel's co-founder. *Dawn of the Dead*'s box office seemed to unlock a space of unlimited creative potential, emboldening Romero to write and direct a 146-minute semi-autobiographical non-genre film on which he retained final cut. Tony Williams views this as a common industrial practice that permits stars and directors to parlay the success of one film into the production of a more personal, if less economically assured, follow-up project. He cites Francis Ford Coppola's *The Conversation* (1974), made in the immediate wake of *The Godfather* (1972), and Martin Scorsese's *The Last Temptation of Christ* (1988), which followed his Paul Newman vehicle *The Color of Money* (1986), as evidence of this pattern. To Williams, these films see practitioners 'break away from generic and star vehicles to produce creative statements free from economic constraints'.[41]

In terms of production, *Knightriders* was typical of Laurel's reported creative practices in that Rubinstein remained hands-off. Even with David Vogel acting as line producer, Romero's on-set creative control was apparently absolute. This is supported by John Harrison, who later directed Laurel's *Tales from the Darkside: The Movie* (1990). Harrison recollects:

> [Rubinstein] would never sit down with George and tell him how to write a scene or how to shoot a scene or how to cut the movie. He protected George ... what he used to say to all of us was, 'I've been able to build the box. What you do inside the box is okay. But you can't get outside the box'. In other words, 'I've got the money, I've set up the production, I've got the distribution in place, now go off and make the movie. Don't come back with a movie that costs 10 per cent more than it was supposed to' ... He wanted to provide the resources and then he would let the filmmaker go ahead and do it.[42]

Ed Lammi covered the majority of the organisational production tasks on *Day of the Dead* and also noticed this permissive approach to filmmaking, recalling that Rubinstein only appeared on set once a week to check on progress and authorise spending.[43] It is in this sense that Laurel followed 'Sarris's auteur theory of direction', providing a supportive platform for creative autonomy.

As Laurel prepared an adaptation of Stephen King's 1983 novel *Pet Sematary*, Romero and Rubinstein co-signed a legally binding memorandum that laid out the particulars of the former's directorial contract. As seen in Figure 4.1, this detailed Romero's financial terms, his credit and his approval rights on a number of 'creative matters'. This memorandum gives a fascinating insight into the way Romero's agency was expressed in legal terms. Clauses deemed essential to the so-called auteur were formalised and the contract safeguarded his on-set

Parties: George A. Romero ("GAR") and Laurel Entertainment, Inc. ("Laurel")
Subject: "*Pet Sematary*"

A. *Commitments*

   Laurel commits to GAR as Director of picture on work for hire basis, GAR commits to direct picture (barring illness or uninsurability of Romero). Commitments provided for by this paragraph will expire on January 19, 1986, unless pre-production commences on or before that date.

B. *Financial*

   Fees: Greater of (i) $375,000 or (ii) 50% of the first $750,00 received for GAR/Richard P. Rubinstein/Stephen King services and 15% over $750,000 (to aggregate $500,000 ceiling), excluding any money paid to Steve King.

   Profit Participation: 5% of profits (as defined for Steve King) received by Laurel, excluding any money paid to Steve King.

C. *Creative Matters*

   GAR to have right to approve (but shall not unreasonably withhold approval of) the following provided, however, that the rights of approval must be exercised consistently with budget and scheduling requirements, and consistent with a running time for answer print of not more than 120 minutes and an MPAA rating not more restrictive than R. Approvals are additionally subject to any rights of completion guarantor and Stephen King's rights of approval.

   a. set designer and sets
   b. costume designer and costumes
   c. 1st asst. director and staff
   d. composer and or music
   e. sound recordist
   f. post production and sound personnel
   g. editor
   h. special effects
   i. lighting director
   j. director of photography
   k. 'final cut'

   If he desires, GAR may supervise post-production (but without additional compensation).

D. *Credit* As appropriate and customary.

The parties intend to execute a more formal agreement but, by signing this memorandum, intend to be bound hereby notwithstanding that a more formal document is not signed.

Figure 4.1 *Pet Sematary* Memorandum of Agreement, 20 March 1985 (abridged from Laurel Entertainment, Inc., 1985b, pp. 1–3).

independence, his choice of collaborators and final cut. These terms were, however, dependent on the running time, an MPAA rating and, most intriguingly, were 'subject to any rights of completion guarantor and Stephen King's rights of approval'. Mention of King here divulges his growing importance to Laurel as 'a substantial creative and financial partner',[44] marking him as far more than just another novelist from whom Laurel had optioned work. On paper, King had power to undermine Romero's decision-making, though there is no evidence that this was ever wielded. That the rights of a completion guarantor are also foregrounded is telling, suggesting an additional non-creative intrusion into Romero's sacrosanct space on set.

On *Knightriders*, Romero's on-set freedom was supported by partners UA Corporation and UFDC, both of whom allowed Laurel to proceed independently once the screenplay and key creative personnel had been agreed upon. Former UA Senior Vice-President and Head of Worldwide Productions Stephen Bach records that once UA executives signed off, the production partner became responsible for delivering the project on time and on budget. The production would then operate without direct supervision from UA in an apparent atmosphere of 'autonomy and creative freedom'.[45] UA built a reputation as a patron of the auteur filmmaker, exemplified by Woody Allen's multi-picture deal with the company. As Allen told *Fortune* magazine, 'they see the picture when I'm ready to give it to them'.[46] Tino Balio observes that despite the 'legal safeguards built into the financing-distribution contracts, the company bet on the person, the integrity of the producer to make the picture as mutually agreed. UA's producers, with few exceptions, had the right to the final cut.'[47]

This may have worked (thus far) for UA, but on *Knightriders* UFDC was far from pleased with the final result. Prior to *Knightriders*' release, Romero was confident in his ability to get a return on his investor's money, but at the same time admitted he could not identify a target audience for the film, claiming 'it's not yet defined and demographics don't always apply'.[48] Although initial reviews were favourable, UFDC was unconvinced about the film's profit potential and decided on a limited release in New York, Florida and California in spring 1981, before poor returns saw it withdrawn entirely. UFDC was equally stung by a troubled production which saw adverse weather conditions and a threatened SAG strike take *Knightriders* 30 per cent over schedule and 5 per cent over budget.[49]

Production problems on *Knightriders* unfortunately came at a time of broader industrial change. In the late 1960s, director-auteurs had been lauded as the saviours of Hollywood; now the studios were looking to curtail their influence. Shortly after announcing the company's partnership with Laurel, UA began reshoots on *Heaven's Gate* (Cimino, 1980) and, as Jack Kroll writes, 'everyone knows about Michael Cimino's *Heaven's Gate* . . . the biggest fiasco in film history, dollar for dollar, shooting day for shooting day, length of run for length of run ... ego for ego'.⁵⁰ By 1985, Cimino's film had earned only $2 million in rentals on a cost of $36 million. In his own post-mortem on *Heaven's Gate*, journalist Michael Dempsey attributes the film's failure to a series of mitigating factors, including declining ticket sales and corporate mismanagement, adding that Cimino's rampant ego presented studio hierarchy with an opportunity to oust the director as 'filmmaking's linchpin'.⁵¹

Reports indicate that *Heaven's Gate*'s production was problematic, slowed to a lethargic pace by Cimino's perfectionism and the inexperience of producer Joann Carelli. Filming dragged on from 16 April to 4 October 1979 (with reshoots in April and June 1980), leading UA to insert its own production manager Derek Kavanagh to oversee filming, a move antithetical to the distributor's traditional hands-off approach.⁵² As rumours of Cimino's hubris played out in the press,⁵³ the studios took collective measures to safeguard against a repeat of this so-called 'fiasco'. Legal expert Mark C. Phillips says that as a direct consequence of *Heaven's Gate* (alongside Hollywood's increasing reliance on outsourced independent production companies) the studios came to use completion guarantees with greater frequently.⁵⁴ As Steve Mangel, the head of International Film Guarantors (IFG) in Hollywood, tells us, a completion guarantee

> assures whoever is financing the production, whether it's a bank or an individual, that the film will be made and delivered within the time period specified; that it won't cost them anymore than the original investment; and that in a worst case scenario – production is shut down – it's a guarantee that they can get their money back ... Knowing what goes on – on a day-to-day basis—is the key to monitoring.⁵⁵

A completion guarantee (or completion bond) is now common in independent film production,⁵⁶ typically provided by a third-party bonding company who place a representative on set to undertake the monitoring identified by Mangel. This representative, or guarantor, is there at every stage of the production to ensure that the original script and financial agreements are all complied with.⁵⁷ Most studios have the capital to self-bond and provide this service internally.⁵⁸ The higher risk associated with independent production, however, frequently necessitates additional third-party supervision.

According to Michael Gornick, UFDC only began to worry about Laurel after the box office disappointment of *Knightriders*.⁵⁹ Nevertheless, the concurrent fallout of *Heaven's Gate* indicates that this nervousness was part of a wider industrial shift. Laurel cannot have been helped by a *Variety* review on 8 April 1981 that called *Knightriders* 'the most egregious case of auteurist self-indulgence since "*Heaven's Gate*"'.⁶⁰ Regardless of the scheduling and cost overruns on this film, UFDC were slow to place a completion guarantor on its next Laurel co-venture. *Creepshow* was instead to be Laurel's first fully unionised production and the distributors trusted that this greater formalisation would provide the required assurances.

To guide the production, Laurel, through its Laurel-Show subsidiary, hired professional first assistant director Richard Hawley to work alongside Romero. The first assistant director (or first AD) is on hand to coordinate the logistical side of directing and to communicate these requirements to the rest of the crew. It is their responsibility to keep filming on schedule and to control on-set discipline, but Hawley's formal orthodoxy was found to be incompatible with Romero's improvisational style. He was replaced by second assistant director Carl Clifford, who was then also deemed unsuitable for the same reason. Finally, Rubinstein surmised that an internal colleague familiar with Romero's methods would be better suited and he placed John Harrison in the role.[61] In spite of Harrison's best efforts (and those of other unit and production managers), *Creepshow* began to drift over-schedule and UFDC insisted that Laurel employ external manager David Ball to monitor production. Ball was, and is, a self-titled 'bondable' producer, film accountant and freelance representative for completion guarantors. He had previously worked for the Hassaneins as production manager on *Cattle Annie and Little Britches* (Johnson, 1981) and felt strongly that good film art could only emerge from a robust and well-organised governance onset: 'it's the business that allows the art form and not the other way around', he stated.[62]

Ed Lammi says that on *Creepshow* (and then later on *Day of the Dead*), Ball was there to watch the 'hot costs' – that is the unplanned components that can cause the budget to swing, such as overtime hours, additional transportation, catering, number of extras, and so on.[63] Ball was credited as co-producer on *Day of the Dead* but was for all intents and purposes a completion guarantor representative, keeping the film on schedule, on budget and with the power to take over production if necessary. Ball remembers Romero's frustration at having 'Salah's man' on set and, in turn, he was unimpressed by Laurel's lax organisational skills. 'When they went into the proper world of filmmaking, they had to learn discipline. It was my unenviable task of having to teach it to them', he later said.[64] Mark C. Phillips writes that this tension is typical of a relationship between the independent filmmaker and the guarantor, where 'one seeks artistic freedom, while the other attempts to keep that freedom within the bounds of fiscal propriety'.[65] Once Ball took over governance of the set, Romero's loose, improvisational shooting style essentially became a thing of the past.

In a *Cinefantastique* article intended to coincide with *Creepshow*'s US release, Paul Gange wrote, 'Romero's crew is still basically a group of neighborhood friends having fun together; no one watches the time clock, no studio chief peers over Romero's shoulder'.[66] This is essentially a fiction. In the wake of the overruns on *Knightriders* and wider institutional changes, UFDC demanded tighter controls over production, limiting Romero's agency and on-set decision-making.

Even as Rubinstein endeavoured to remain hands-off, from a business perspective he had no other choice than to allow external intermediaries a say in Laurel's production method. In point of fact, Rubinstein appreciated David Ball and later rehired him independently of UFDC to produce *Creepshow 2*. Though the completion guarantor is oft-neglected in the study of independent film production, the presence of this figure in relation to Laurel Entertainment, both on set and within Romero's contractual terms (where the guarantor's approval rights superseded that of even the director), indicates the institutional significance of this intermediary between filmmaker and financier.

If Romero resented the creative interference of UFDC and its representatives, Laurel's partnership with the distributor was also lacking financially. As part of the equity agreement between firms,[67] on each production UFDC was entitled to a distribution fee, recovery of distribution expenses and a recoupment of negative costs, all taken from the distribution income of that particular film. Laurel was to receive 50 per cent of the remaining net profits, unless the previous film in this contract, as was the case with *Knightriders*, failed to recoup enough revenue to cover these distribution costs. As Laurel's financial statement made clear, the *Knightriders* deficit, as of 31 March 1983, resulted in a reduction of the firm's net profit participation on *Day of the Dead* to 25 per cent of the first $5.5 million.[68]

Romero later blamed UFDC for *Knightriders*' box office failure, claiming the distributor was more interested in its $35 million production *Lion of the Desert* (Akkad, 1980) – released almost concurrently on 17 April 1981 – than it was his independent drama about the troubles of a Pennsylvanian Renaissance fair.[69] In fairness to UFDC, *Knightriders* was a difficult sell. The film's abandonment of genre rendered Romero's valued identity as an 'indie horror' auteur redundant and, lest the film be misunderstood as horror, the advertising made no mention whatever of *Dawn of the Dead* or any of his previous films. A revised poster only went as far as to add 'from the master of action and suspense' to the campaign. At best, Romero's carefully constructed brand image was an inconvenience; at worst, it was a perceived liability. By breaking the business wheel that had been so successful on *Martin* and *Dawn* (which carefully balanced genre, authorship and cult to create an attractive marketplace brand) Laurel appeared far from a fiscal guarantee and UFDC became visibly skittish about future collaborations.

The Laurel-UFDC co-production intended to follow *Knightriders* was the science fiction comedy *Shoo-Be-Doo-Be-Moon*. According to Gornick, the project was 'like a 50s monster film; it has elements of the movies we grew up with. There are special effects involving spaceships and aliens.'[70] Tom Dubensky remembers artists constructing a scale model of the film's alien antagonist, designed to look like a pile of spaghetti and complete with a retractable penis, this appendage part of the screenplay's ribald humour.[71] Unwilling or unable to finance the film, UFDC took the project to Cannes, but efforts to raise the necessary funds came to nothing. In Laurel's fiscal 1981 annual report to shareholders, Rubinstein conveyed that *Shoo-Be-Doo-Be-Moon* was postponed and by 1982 the distributor had withdrawn entirely, leaving Laurel to seek financing elsewhere.[72] The company's fiscal 1982 report stated, 'in the event that new financing is found . . . [Laurel] must arrange to refund to the distributor, with interest, the production advances, which the Company has received with respect to the project which amount is $137,873, excluding interest'.[73] New financing never materialised and by 1983 *Shoo-Be-Doo-Be-Moon* was no longer on Laurel's development portfolio.

For UFDC, *Creepshow* represented a far safer bet because of the clearer brand association with genre and the 'talent packaging' of Romero and Stephen King. Indeed, Romero's brand identity was always of primary importance to UFDC and in 1985 the firm's advertising executive Terry Powers stated, 'the appeal of a horror film such as [*Day of the Dead*] becomes vastly increased the minute the name George Romero appears in the opening credits'.[74] Still locked into an 18 January 1985 production start date, UFDC and Romero could not come to an agreement on *Day of the Dead*'s budget. In line with projects such as *Copperhead*, Romero envisioned an epic conclusion to his zombie trilogy, featuring a huge cast of protagonists (living and dead) fighting for survival above and below ground on a tropical island compound. An early draft of the screenplay begins on the streets of a post-apocalyptic Florida (as a ragtag group of survivors dodge zombies and engage in a dramatic gunfight with pirates) and ends with the entire island destroyed in a massive explosion. 'The first script was like *Raiders of the Lost Ark* with zombies', recalled special make-up effects technician Tom Savini.[75]

Determined to top *Dawn of the Dead* in terms of action and violence, Romero pushed for an unrated feature that would deliver the onscreen bloodshed anticipated by his brand identity. In one self-conscious passage in an early draft of the screenplay, as the undead descend upon their victims, Romero gleefully intones, 'this is it, gore fans. The gross finale. The intestine-tugger. THE ZOMBIES GET THEIR SUPPER. THEY FEAST . . . like Romans at an orgy'.[76] When the budget for this version was estimated at around $9 million, UFDC balked. According to Richard Hassanein, 'by *Day of the Dead* it became more and more difficult for theaters to play movies that were not rated, so we couldn't gamble our money on not getting an R rating'.[77] Laurel held firm to produce Romero's vision, agreeing to scale back to around $7 million. UFDC still refused to budge, instead offering half that amount for an unrated version of the film.

Associate producer Ed Lammi was hired in June 1984 for a mooted October start date and was surprised by the lengthily pre-production schedule. Lammi soon understood that this was because of the unresolved discrepancies between the screenplay and budget, telling Richard Rubinstein something he already knew, '"you're not going to make this picture for that budget"'.[78] Lammi says

Figure 4.2   The apocalypse on a scaled-down budget in *Day of the Dead* (1985).

that he and Romero spent the summer of 1984 scaling the film down, at one point making a final plea to Salah Hassanein for a $7 million budget. Salah agreed, providing the film was rated R, to which Romero refused, telling Hassanein, 'if I scale back to an R-rated movie my fans would abandon me'. As Lammi observes, 'Salah knew his market' and Romero felt he knew where his cult appeal rested, resulting in an entirely new version of *Day of the Dead* written for a top-to-bottom budget of $3.6 million (see Figure 4.2).[79]

Even with these compromises, *Day of the Dead* was not the box office success hoped for. As Laurel's fiscal 1986 10-K report told shareholders, 'although *Day of the Dead* remains to be exploited in a number of markets, Laurel does not expect any potential profits to be material'. Indeed, profit shares from all of Laurel's films with UFDC after *Dawn of the Dead* had 'not been substantial'.[80] Laurel's relationship with UFDC, despite resulting in three completed feature films, was something of a disappointment. The partnership steadily encroached upon Romero's sovereign production space, denying him agency to fulfil his creative ambitions, and for little financial reward. Romero's frustrations were then heaped onto the shoulders of Laurel and Richard Rubinstein, where he deemed the company's professionalisation a failure. Speaking to *Fangoria*'s R. H. Martin in a colourful interview conducted in 1985 shortly after his partnership with Laurel was terminated, Romero said:

> I found that, within Laurel, I couldn't take as many chances . . . I sat on my ass for three years between *Creepshow* and *Day of the Dead*. And I think that, had I been an individual facing the problems that faced

me with the first script for *Day of the Dead*, I would have told them to shove it. Because of the responsibility that I had to Laurel's stockholders, I wasn't able to do that, couldn't take that kind of chance. I want to be able to do my own projects, take my own risks, without that kind of fiscal responsibility. What I'm doing [by leaving] is buying myself a certain amount of freedom.[81]

If anything, Laurel's partnership with UFDC reaffirmed the limits of control available in the independent sector, where agency was ultimately dictated to by the marketplace and external intermediates and partners.

Agency Theory, Self-interest and Divorce

Laurel Productions of Pennsylvania began as a single-purpose platform for George Romero's creative agency. As the company transformed into Laurel Tape & Film and the Laurel Group, Richard Rubinstein's plans appeared in alignment with these interests. By 1985, this initiative had failed. When the company expanded to become the publicly run Laurel Entertainment, the firm's objectives shifted, now aligned to the demands of shareholders and the day-to-day necessities of managing a profitable enterprise with responsibilities to a permanent staff of employees. During this period, Romero made the decision to step back from the minutia of running the company, declining re-election as chairman of the board and resigning as secretary in 1983 to focus on the firm's creative output. Officially, Romero was still a majority shareholder and retained joint ownership of the company. In practice, he ceded managerial control to his more business-savvy cohort. This separation of ownership and control can create 'agency problems in the decision process'[82] of the firm and in this case prompted Romero's departure.

Agency theory has become a key system of analysis in business studies, shedding light on corporate governance and the control and management of the firm. Following the work of Stephen A. Ross, an 'agency relationship' usually exists between at least two persons designated the agent and the principal. The agent's role is to work on behalf of the principal in regard to all decision-making.[83] However, agency theory argues that these agents/managers tend to act self-interestedly, pursuing their own short-term goals (be this financial or in terms of career advancement and so on) that are not necessarily aligned with the interests of the principal.[84] For Michael C. Jensen, agency theory is based on the 'simple tautology [that] cooperative behavior between human beings is viewed as a contracting problem among self-interested individuals with divergent interests'.[85]

Issues of agency theory are far from straightforward and Kathleen M. Eisenhardt draws a distinction between what she calls 'positive agency theory' and 'principal agent research'. The latter looks for a formal theory regarding the principal-agent paradigm based on logical deductions and mathematical proof. The former is a 'less mathematical' approach that looks to specific situations where the agent and the principal may reveal conflicting objectives, and how corporate governance can act to restrict the agent's apparent 'self-serving' behaviour.[86] Jensen and Meckling, though likewise focused on positive agency theory, add normative agency theory to the mix, an area of analysis that prescribes how contracts and corporate incentives can be structured to ensure that the agent behaves in a manner that will benefit the principal's welfare.[87] Notwithstanding these discrepancies in approach and method, Eisenhardt understands that at 'the heart of agency theory' lie the conflicting goals that arise when individuals participate in a cooperative endeavour.[88]

Even without these discrepancies, agency theory is an imperfect model in the context of this investigation. The relationship between Romero and Rubinstein was not, strictly speaking, a contractual one between a principal and an agent. Rather, it was a partnership between two principals with equal shares in the company they co-founded – that is, in its final form, Laurel Entertainment. The intricacies of principal-agent research and the applied methods that proliferate this field also surpass the range of this humanities-focused enquiry. Keeping this in mind, Laurel's hierarchal valuation of the so-called auteur nevertheless brings issues of agency to the fore. Equal partner though he may have been, Rubinstein repeatedly proclaimed to 'believe in the auteur, the captain of the ship',[89] self-consciously positioning himself as an agent in the service of Romero's creative principal. But was this really the case, or were there conflicting goals at the heart of Laurel's dual leadership organisation?

As has been made clear, Laurel's production output was limited by the opportunity structures dictated by external forces. A number of economic theorists measure agency through an individual's ability to achieve their goals, suggesting that agency theory is about more than just control and self-interested behaviour; it is about implementing a desired outcome.[90] An agent's inability to reach set goals suggests a lack of power, and a lack of power is inconsistent with ideas of individual agency. Agency is therefore only quantifiable through the successful achievement of choice.[91] In terms of film production, the Laurel partners were disempowered from realising their goals by larger institutional forces.

This said, Alsop et al. write that 'empowerment is based on tackling the differences in capabilities that deny actors the capacity to make transforming choices'.[92] Rubinstein's capabilities, his human capital, had been developed through television production, and in 1983, with his partner taking a backseat in regard to wider leadership responsibilities, he had sufficient control to move the company back in this direction.

Rubinstein's entrepreneurial interest in television began with Ultimate Mirror, an SME through which he expressed a desire to democratise small-screen production. Immediately after forming Laurel Tape & Film, Rubinstein again pursued this interest, leading the company to produce the tax-shelter-funded series *The Winners*. In 1983, as Laurel looked to obtain financing for big-screen fantasy epics, Rubinstein turned once more to television with the series *Tales from the Darkside*. The series was intended as a spin-off from *Creepshow*, until rights issues with UFDC and Warner Bros. pushed Laurel to create an original entity. Like *Creepshow*, *Tales from the Darkside* was an example of anthology storytelling, in this case emulating the science fiction/horror format of popular network shows *Alfred Hitchcock Presents* (1955–1962) and *The Twilight Zone* (1959–1964). Each *Darkside* episode was fabricated as a self-contained story often based on the work of a high-profile writer, including Clive Barker, Robert Bloch, John Cheever, Harlan Ellison, Frederik Pohl and, of course, Stephen King. *Darkside* was, in fact, at the forefront of a return to anthology storytelling in the 1980s and 1990s, followed by Steven Spielberg's *Amazing Stories* (1985–1987) for NBC and new iterations of *The Twilight Zone* (1985–1989) and *The Outer Limits* (1995–2002). As can be seen, Laurel not only followed trends during this period; they were also instrumental in establishing them.

And typically for Rubinstein, the series was atypical of traditional television production, sidestepping the national broadcast networks in favour of first-run syndication (that is, releasing the show directly on local television stations across the US, rather than on a single network). *Darkside* was developed with TV producer Jerry Golod and financed by Lexington Broadcast Services (LBS) and Tribune Broadcasting Company. Each episode cost approximately $124,000 and this amount never altered throughout its four seasons. In view of the minimal budget set aside for production, David Vogel declined to produce the series, instead acting in a supervisory capacity as Executive in Charge of Production. The role of producer went to William Teitler, a relative newcomer whose background included television commercial work and corporate documentaries. According to Teitler, Rubinstein told him that '"because you've worked on commercials then you know what quality is, and because you've worked on documentaries then you know how to do things inexpensively"'.[93] On Teitler's suggestion, production was split between New York and Los Angeles, a cost-effective move that also allowed the show to draw upon established bicoastal talent pools. Teitler oversaw production on the east coast and T. J. Castronovo oversaw production in the west.

Although Romero penned the pilot episode, 'Trick or Treat' (Balaban, 1983), he was relatively uninvolved when *Tales from the Darkside* went to series, contributing only three additional teleplays. The feature film spin-off *Tales from the Darkside: The Movie* also had a segment written by Romero, entitled 'The Cat from Hell' and based on an original story by Stephen King. However, this was simply a leftover from *Creepshow 2* and Romero otherwise had nothing to do with this feature. In terms of the series specifically, creative development was handled by Vogel and the show's story consultant Tom Allen. When Vogel left to produce Spielberg's *Amazing Stories*,[94] Teitler took over this role. For Romero's part, he expressed annoyance at the show's cheapness, finding it an unworthy distraction to Laurel's primary agenda. 'I wanted to continue to make films . . . Richard just wanted to go TV. He just wanted to do whatever he could to try and boost the stock. It was hopeless'.[95]

Rubinstein and his *Tales from the Darkside* partners were unconcerned about Romero's lack of interest in the series, accepting that his brand identity was perhaps the most essential contribution he could make. On 20 July 1983, Laurel took out a one-page ad for the pilot in *Variety*, emphasising Romero as executive producer and writing in the banner, 'the modern master of the macabre who packed movie theatres with *The Night of the Living Dead* [sic], *Dawn of the Dead*, and *Creepshow*, is bringing his talent for terror to television'.[96] In Romero's employment agreement with Laurel dated 19 June 1983, the importance of his brand value was made clear, formally acknowledging the rights of distributor LBS to add 'George Romero Presents' to the *Tales from the Darkside* title if they so requested.[97]

Romero's contract also stressed that if the pilot went to series, and Romero was no longer an employee of Laurel Entertainment, then the company would still be entitled to use his name in connection to the show, granting Romero 5 per cent of the net proceeds 'regardless of whether or not he is acting as Executive Producer'.[98] Since this contract was written while the pilot was in production, it was assumed that Romero would act as the story editor and the agreement bestowed upon him approval rights over directors, writers and scripts, 'subject to budgetary limitations and to contractual delivery obligations'.[99] He ultimately declined these responsibilities, leaving *Darkside*'s overall management to Rubinstein.

As we already know by now, Laurel's division of creative and economic responsibilities was complex. Rubinstein and Romero publicly accentuated this disparity as a means of establishing a clear yet multifaceted corporate identity. A closer look at their employment contracts also proves that they were legally bound to these roles. For his part, Romero was contracted to 'participate in and supervise' the creative aspects of the company's business.[100] Rubinstein, meanwhile, had 'such authorities, duties and responsibilities in respect of the conduct of the business and operation of the company as are provided in the by-laws of the Company'.[101]

Returning to Jensen and Meckling's definition of normative agency theory, if these contracts seemed to benefit Romero's artistry and his welfare as the principal, they also provided a means through which Rubinstein could control all of the company's activities. As business leader, Rubinstein was charged with finalising agreements between all of Laurel's creative and technical personnel, be they professional advisors, producers, writers, directors, performing artists, distributors or others.[102] Rubinstein overruled his partner's concerns about a move back into television and Laurel's activities during this period strongly reinforced his agency. Apparently self-interested in returning to a medium in which he displayed both passion and expertise (human capital), *Darkside*'s four-season run exhibited Rubinstein's control in determining creative output. In accord with Alsop et al.'s indicators of empowerment, Rubinstein's management of *Darkside* displayed the existence of choice (in his exclusive decision to move into television production), the use of choice (based on the talent available and economic capabilities) and an overall achievement of choice (production of a financially viable product). These factors were apparently unavailable to Romero, on this production and more widely speaking.

Rubinstein's decision to push forward on *Tales from the Darkside* without Romero's full endorsement had additional negative ramifications for his partner. In *Variety* on 3 June 1981, Rubinstein discussed plans to encompass a more dynamic range of creative personnel, telling reporter Stephen Klain that the company was actively on the lookout for 'newer talents, or writers who might be more recognized from other media'.[103] If this seemed to refer to screenwriters and partners such as Stephen King, Rubinstein later told *Variety* that Laurel was 'starting to acquire material that is not exclusively for George . . . we're not looking for financing strictly contingent on George directing'.[104] The article goes on to say that while Romero intended to direct *The Sisterhood*, he may not have time, and that *Imagine That* would be directed by screenwriter Harrison on a budget of under $2 million.[105]

Laurel's fiscal 1985 Form 10-K makes clear that *Tales from the Darkside* was intended to encourage, nurture and develop relationships with new writers and directors. In the first season alone, the company employed thirteen directors and seventeen writers.[106] Of those directors listed, a number were drawn from Romero's production team, including Harrison, Gornick, Warner Shook (an actor who had appeared in *Knightriders* and *Creepshow*) and Tom Savini. This was all 'part of Laurel's growing plans to bring new talent up through the ranks'.[107] In the case of Gornick, his ambitions to surpass his role as staff director of photography created disharmony. After directing two episodes from *Darkside*'s 1984 first season (notably 'The Word Processor of the Gods' based on a story by King), Gornick found he enjoyed the responsibilities associated with being on-set creative leader. In turn, he was reluctant to join the production of *Day of the Dead* in his customary role as DP, only taking the position because his employers demanded it.[108]

From the days of Latent Image, Romero's open-door policy provided a training ground for regional creative talent. Such development, however, appeared conditional and Gornick suggests that Romero resented the aspirations of his DP, feeling that *Darkside*'s talent farming interfered with, rather than facilitated, Romero's own creative process.[109] On the other hand, Rubinstein felt that encouraging personnel to reach their maximum potential made good business sense. He understood that, at this juncture, Laurel's survival would depend on the production of motion pictures. To make profits, the company needed to reach the retail market more often, a factor made more likely with a wider stable of in-house creative talent.[110] *Tales from the Darkside* employed approximately seventy additional individuals during production, creating strength in depth and moving Laurel closer to producing, as intended by Rubinstein, 'more than one motion picture simultaneously'.[111]

In the meantime, as Romero's feature film projects stalled, during fiscal year 1984 company revenue 'consisted primarily of license fees earned for the television pilot of "*Tales from the Darkside*"'.[112] The decision to extend *Darkside* into a series created additional income and LBS paid a reported $2.4 million for the first season. This was a healthy amount, even if a large percentage was undoubtedly fed back into production. By 31 March 1985, Laurel had received partial payment of $902,000 of the total licence fees for season two. In January of the same year, Laurel entered into an agreement with Embassy Telecommunications, Inc. for the foreign television rights to the first season of *Darkside*. From this deal alone, Laurel recorded accounts of approximately $394,000, with accrued liabilities of approximately $245,000.[113] Rubinstein's motivation for moving back into television, self-interested or not, concerned the economic wellbeing and long-term survival of the firm as a whole.

Jocelyn J-Y. Desroches et al., in an empirical analysis of SMEs in relation to growth, draw upon the work of J. C. Laufer to argue that owner-managers and innovators/entrepreneurs actively cultivate the growth of their firms as a means of self-accomplishment. 'The artisans, on the other hand, do not want their firm to grow, and are extremely concerned with maintaining their personal autonomy.'[114] How true this sounds of Rubinstein and Romero. Building a company around Romero's creativity may have been, at the outset, convenient for each partner, yet as the company expanded, their individual interests moved out of alignment. Once again, this is not uncommon in business practices, and economists have noted that the value of an original founder can diminish over time.[115] This is often the case when wider corporate demands and obligations to stakeholders move away from the founder's intentions. Zahra and Filatotchev write that as growth occurs, the founder's 'opportunism and entrenchment' can amplify, often requiring a transference of control. In this instance, 'a robust system of governance and accountability is needed to put a "straitjacket" on founders' opportunism'.[116]

Romero's employment contract for 1983 attempted to do just that. A pivotal clause stated that,

> except as otherwise herein provided, Romero shall devote to the performance of his obligations under this agreement such time, energy and attention as is reasonably necessary of a full-time employee in his position, and he shall use his best efforts for the profit, benefit and advantage of the Company.[117]

However noble his dogged pursuit of auteurist filmmaking, by 1985 it did not appear to fulfil this part of his contract. Agency theory assumes that all parties in a business transaction are fundamentally self-interested, an agent seen to put their own incentives ahead of those of the firm. If we accept that all parties in a business endeavour behave in this manner, then Rubinstein's self-accomplishing endeavours at least catered to stakeholders at every level, including himself, his shareholders, the firm's employees, external business partners and his founder-partner. Romero's self-interests, for the most part, looked primarily to his own creativity.

As stated, though agency theory is an imperfect model when applied to Laurel, this perspective allows us to consider self-interested behaviour in relation to Laurel's corporate activities. The Laurel principals differed in their fundamental responsibilities to the holistic corporate entity they had formed; Rubinstein was interested in collective growth, Romero in individual accomplishment. Romero's agency problem was that he lacked the opportunity structures or level of control to achieve his primary goal. When this became apparent, he retreated from the company. Rubinstein later conceded that focusing business activities around his partner's creative output alone was no way to run a business,[118] made less practical as the company continued to expand while Romero's self-determined incentives remained entrenched.

After declining to renew his contract terminating on 19 June 1985, Romero was immediately re-contracted by Laurel as a consultant (if requested) and as the director of Stephen King's *Pet Sematary*.[119] In this sense, the company's agency problem was resolved. Control was transferred to Rubinstein in a more complete sense, empowering him to act as the company's sole principal. In the end, it is unclear if Romero was ever utilised in the capacity of creative advisor and *Pet Sematary*, as we shall see, was eventually passed to another filmmaker. Either way, Romero's new contract of employment essentially made him little more than another agent working for the company, his self-interested behaviour now carefully tempered and managed. Understandably, Romero's departure had a dramatic impact on Laurel's corporate identity and future business relations. Although Rubinstein was now free to lead the company in whichever direction he pleased, the massive waves of consolidation about to hit both Hollywood and the industry at large would have additional, unexpected consequences for Laurel Entertainment.

CONCLUSION

An investigation into agency and agency theory from a sociopolitical and economic perspective considers the multifaceted interactions and institutional levels of control that impact, and to a large degree dictate, auteurist activities in the independent sector. Externally, issues of creative agency are a result of constant negotiations between stakeholders, where, simply put, financial success appears the best means of sustaining total autonomy. Industry trends also play a part and the demands of the marketplace have the final say in determining output. Laurel's strategy of developing a portfolio of films in development for an array of markets (including potentially game-changing blockbusters such as *Copperhead*) was shrewd, if of limited success. Finally, a consideration of agency theory and issues of self-interest challenges the uncritical valorisation of the auteur filmmaker in independent cinema analysis. As seen in this close evaluation of Laurel's growth, Rubinstein's careful nurturing of a multitude of internal talent strengthened the firm's infrastructure and economic potential, in the process supporting a diverse array of creative practitioners in the independent sector. Romero, on the other hand, wanted Laurel to remain focused on his own creative agency. After all, if agency theory is about self-interest then, fittingly, so too is the politics of the auteur.

NOTES

1. Cohen, n.d.
2. Schatz, 2014, p. 40.
3. Jensen and Meckling, 1976, p. 308.
4. Though ostensibly a horror film, Romero's *Martin* is something of an epilogue to *Out of This Furnace*. Also set in Braddock, the film reveals the same immigrant communities some forty years after Bell's novel concludes. In *Martin*, the surrounding steel mills, so central to Bell's text, have now closed and it is this absence of industry that creates the graveyard landscape through which Martin wanders.
5. Laurel Entmt., 1981, p. 4.
6. Laurel Entmt., 1982a, p. 2.
7. Jacobs, 1979, p. 59.
8. Rosen and Hamilton, 1990, p. 108.
9. Ibid., p. 112.
10. Ibid., p. 108.
11. Laurel Entmt., 1982b, p. 12; Laurel Entmt., 1983c, p. F-13.
12. Harmetz, 1982, p. H15.

13. Teitler, interview with the author, 21 April 2018.
14. Laurel Entmt., 1982a, p. 3.
15. Laurel Entmt., 1983a, pp. 61–9; see also Laurel Entmt., 1983c, pp. 5–7.
16. Since each title contains the name *Copperhead*, I will refer to it as such throughout this work.
17. Laurel Entmt., 1983b, p. 3.
18. Hiltzik, 1998.
19. Laurel Entmt., 1984e, p. F-13.
20. Harmetz, 1983.
21. David, 2011.
22. Coincidentally, *Robocop* got his own Marvel comic on 28 July 1987.
23. Harmetz, 1983.
24. Burlingame, 2014.
25. Romero, 1983, pp. 16–17.
26. Sherman, 1980, p. 53.
27. Harmetz, 1983.
28. See Tzioumakis, 2013a, p. 3.
29. Hanners and Kloman, 1982, p. 75.
30. Prince, 2002, p. 20.
31. Ibid., p. 288.
32. Blythe, 2014, p. 7.
33. 'The Cannon Group', 1983, pp. 17–59.
34. McCarthy, 1987, p. 3.
35. Ibid., pp. 3, 34.
36. Laurel Entmt., 1983b, p. 3.
37. Hiltzik, 2002.
38. Alsop, Bertelsen and Holland, 2006, p. 13. In keeping with the diverse range of scholarship drawn upon in this investigation, Alsop et al.'s text was published by the World Bank and addresses issues of global poverty and developmental intervention. Though the opportunity structures addressed in this work are therefore apart from those in film production, the framework for analysis is applicable.
39. Ibid., p. 17, original emphasis.
40. Laurel Entmt., 1986, p. 7.
41. Williams, 2015, p. 105.
42. Harrison, interview with the author, 22 March 2018.
43. Lammi, interview with the author, 19 April 2018.
44. Harmetz, 1984.
45. Bach, 1986, p. 49.
46. Schuyten, 1978, p. 131.
47. Balio, 2009, pp. 345–6.
48. Burke-Block, 1981.
49. Harmetz, 1982, p. H25.
50. Kroll, 1981, p. 58.
51. Dempsey, 1981, p. 53.
52. See *Final Cut: The Making and Unmaking of Heaven's Gate*, 2004.

53. Particularly damaging was Les Gapay's 'Unauthorized Progress Report' (1979) in the *Los Angeles Times* and a *Today Show* interview that personally attacked Cimino for the film's spiralling budget.
54. Phillips, 1992, p. 109.
55. Quoted in Boyle, 2001.
56. Gates, 2013, p. 106; Cones, 2013, p. 80.
57. Phillips, 1992, p. 112.
58. Lammi, interview with the author, 19 April 2018.
59. Axl and Jscott, 2013.
60. Cart, 1981.
61. Harrison, interview with the author, 22 March 2018.
62. Ball, interview with the author, 25 January 2016.
63. Lammi, interview with the author, 19 April 2018.
64. Ball, interview with the author, 25 January 2016.
65. Phillips, 1992, p. 98.
66. Gange, 1982, p. 17.
67. In regard to film production, equity financing is essentially where an investor provides the money and the financial risk. The investor must then receive back all of their investment before the production company and/or filmmakers can start to share in the profits. As seen above, Laurel's equity agreement with UFDC was tied to a multi-picture contract and not just the financing/profits of a single film.
68. Laurel Entmt., 1983c, p. F-12.
69. Romero, interview with the author, 7 April 2016.
70. Blank, 1979.
71. Dubensky, interview with the author, 16 June 2016. The film was later re-titled *Invasion of the Spaghetti Monsters* in view of the alien's outward appearance.
72. Laurel Entmt., 1981, p. 3; Laurel Entmt., 1982b, p. 14.
73. Laurel Entmt., 1982b, p. 14.
74. 'UFD's Hassamein [sic] "Interested only in Commercial Feature Films"', 1985.
75. Daniel, 1988, p. 7. The Florida opening of *Day of the Dead* remains in the finished film, albeit on a reduced scale.
76. Romero, 1984, pp. 82–3.
77. Karr, 2014, p. 19.
78. Lammi, interview with the author, 19 April 2018.
79. Ibid.
80. Laurel Entmt., 1986, p. 6.
81. Martin, 1985, p. 47.
82. Fama and Jensen, 1983, p. 321.
83. Ross, 1973, p. 134.
84. Dekker et al., 2015, p. 518.
85. Jensen, 1983, p. 331.
86. Eisenhardt, 1989, pp. 59–60.
87. Jensen and Meckling, 1976, pp. 309–10.
88. Eisenhardt, 1989, p. 63.
89. McCarthy, 1983, p. 31.

90. Drydyk, 2013, p. 251; Alkire, 2008, p. 14.
91. Alsop et al., 2006, p. 18.
92. Ibid., p. 15.
93. Teitler, interview with the author, 21 April 2018.
94. Another fantasy anthology show, only this time with a budget of around $800,000–$1 million per half-hour episode.
95. Romero, interview with the author, 7 April 2016.
96. Laurel Entmt. and LBS, 1983, p. 97.
97. Laurel Entmt., 1984b, p. 2.
98. Ibid., p. 14.
99. Ibid., p. 2.
100. Ibid., p. 2.
101. Laurel Entmt., 1984c, p. 2.
102. Ibid., p. 3.
103. Klain, 1981, p. 6.
104. McCarthy, 1983, p. 6.
105. Ibid., p. 31.
106. Laurel Entmt., 1985c, p 5.
107. Gange, 1983.
108. Karr, 2014, p. 60.
109. Ibid., p. 60.
110. Laurel Entmt., 1984a, pp. 2–3.
111. 'Laurel's First Profitable Year', 1983, p. 8.
112. Laurel Entmt., 1984e, p. 16.
113. Laurel Entmt., 1985c, p. F-12.
114. Desroches et al., 1991, p. 16.
115. Jayaraman et al., 2000, p. 1222.
116. Zahra and Filatotchev, 2004, p. 895.
117. Laurel Entmt., 1984b, p. 5.
118. Rubinstein and Martin, 2004.
119. Laurel Entmt., 1985c, p. 31.

5. LAST STAND: MERGERS, ACQUISITIONS AND THE SMALL BUSINESS ENTERPRISE, 1985–1994

'Mention Laurel Entertainment, the Pittsburgh-based movie company, and one name comes to mind – George Romero,' wrote journalist Ron Weiskind in October 1984.[1] This may have been so, but as we have seen, Laurel's success owed as much to Richard Rubinstein's stratagem as it did his partner's auteurist output. When the company's totemic figure stepped down in June 1985, Laurel faced a period of change in which its corporate identity and production output would need to be redrawn. 'Change' defined Laurel's activities from Romero's departure onward, augmented, as now seems familiar, by macro-level industrial goings-on as much as internal adjustments. In the 1980s, a series of mergers and buyouts had a seismic impact on Hollywood and the surrounding media landscape, part of a larger global business trend dubbed 'merger mania' by marketplace analysts.[2] In the late 1980s, a first wave of industry-wide mergers and acquisitions (M&A) offered the solidity Laurel long desired. A second wave in the early 1990s resulted in dissolution. By assessing these developments, this chapter offers a ground-level perspective on M&A activity, providing a rare case study of one of the many small to medium business enterprises swept up, or swept away, by these waves of media consolidation.

Pre-merger: Syndication and Library Assets

From the company's first feature film in the mid-1970s, Laurel's identity hinged on Romero's cult auteur status. After his exit, on the surface little appeared to change. Advertising material for *Creepshow 2* and *Tales from the Darkside*:

The Movie continued to foreground Romero's involvement. *Creepshow 2* posters emphasised the value of writers King and Romero as 'masters of the macabre', presenting an image of a ghoulish figure pointing directly towards their above-the-title names. Romero's termination of contract agreement made clear the importance of his brand name, ensuring its indefinite usage in the marketing of the *Tales from the Darkside* television series. In 1987, Romero was still contracted as a creative consultant and had begun preparation to direct Laurel's *Pet Sematary*, affirming his lingering significance to the company he co-founded.

Even when accounting for Romero's name value, attracting production monies remained a challenge. Warner Bros. retained first refusal rights on *Creepshow 2* as late as 31 March 1986,[3] finally putting the project in turnaround where it was picked up by Roger Corman's New World Pictures on a reduced budget. Monies for *Pet Sematary* were similarly unforthcoming, and Laurel eventually allowed Paramount Pictures to option the project outright. In this agreement, Rubinstein stayed on as *Pet Sematary*'s producer and Paramount honoured Laurel's original contract with King to write the screenplay and to situate production in his hometown of Maine, New England. Otherwise, this was not formally a Laurel production. The company received no credit on the final print (beyond individual credits for Rubinstein and Mitchell Galin) and Paramount's in-house producer Ralph S. Singleton oversaw the day-to-day responsibilities of production.

Paramount's scheduling clashed with Romero's reshoots on *Monkey Shines* for Orion Pictures and he was replaced by up-and-coming director Mary Lambert. Laurel vice president of production Michael Gornick claims the decision to go ahead with Lambert at the helm was made because Romero 'wasn't saleable as the director of this project'.[4] How much truth there is to this statement is not known and Romero's rights of first refusal on *Pet Sematary* casts some doubt on Gornick's remarks. This said, Romero's diminishing box office appeal probably resulted in few sleepless nights at Paramount when he proved unavailable. For Romero's part, he felt betrayed by the decision to move ahead without him and vowed to permanently 'call it a day' when it came to working with Rubinstein.[5]

On its April 1989 release, *Pet Sematary* received only lukewarm reviews in the press. Vincent Canby in the *New York Times* felt the story of a mystical animal graveyard with the powers to resurrect the dead strained credibility, concluding that the film's penchant to over-contextualise the fantastical elements (through dialogue and 'ominous music') attested to a lack of trust in the audience.[6] Rubinstein was so aggravated by Canby's review that he wrote an angry retort to the *Times*' letters pages on 21 May 1989:

> The major problem here is that [Canby] incorrectly labels the picture as a thriller. '*Pet Sematary*' is a horror movie, and it is a genre convention

that horror movies telegraph their plot way ahead and the characters aren't smart enough to stay out of trouble. This approach hasn't seemed to bother the fans.[7]

If Rubinstein's justifications for the suggested failings of the plot are something of a backhanded compliment to horror fans, it is intriguing to see him reinforce Laurel's genre identity so ardently, something he may have felt was imperative in the wake of Romero's departure.

Laurel's *Creepshow 2* and *Tales from the Darkside: The Movie* faired only marginally better with the critics, with Michael Gornick's direction on the former compared unfavourably to Romero's on the first *Creepshow*.[8] Anthony Kaufman reminds us of the importance of 'artistry' when it comes to canonical independent cinema, which forms for him one of three key points of reference alongside financing and production contexts.[9] With Romero absent, it can be argued that Laurel never reached the same level of artistry that it had under his stewardship. Such value judgements are, of course, entirely subjective (Romero was himself no stranger to scathing reviews), and it is not my intention to organise Laurel's pre- and post-Romero phases into good art vs. bad art paradigms. What we can say with a little more certainty (and even here there is contention) is that the filmmakers who stepped into Romero's shoes lacked his penchant for auteurist filmmaking, either from the classical Sarris model (despite showing technical competence, *Creepshow 2*, *Pet Sematary* and *Tales from the Darkside: The Movie* lack the 'distinguishable identity' of their directors) or from a commercial perspective.

In the defence of these filmmakers, the firm positioned them as peripheral figures. Deference to King's artistry was evident in his deal on *Pet Sematary*, while interviews with *Creepshow 2* producer David Ball and Laurel's creative director Mitchell Galin reveal an almost awe-like admiration for the novelist.[10] King's agency was picked up on by Canby in his *Pet Sematary* review, referring to the novelist/screenwriter as 'the film's auteur as well as author'.[11] Directors Harrison, Lambert and Gornick were essentially employed to translate a blueprint of a script to the big screen. More so, Gornick and Harrison were in-house collaborators, chosen as much for their reliability as their artistic talents. Granting that these filmmakers were allowed a degree of creative latitude on set,[12] their artistic worth was secondary to the company's wider endeavours. From a commercial standpoint, Laurel still had Romero and King as the firm's masters of horror, or 'auteur-as-commodity',[13] even if, as far as Romero was concerned, that was in name only.

After the departure of Romero and David Vogel in the mid-1980s, Laurel's creative governance was handed to former television producer Mitchell Galin, who joined the company as vice president of production in April 1985. On paper, he shared this title with Gornick. In reality, he was a company leader second only to Rubinstein. Galin had previously served as director of development and production supervisor for Robert Halmi, the famed 'miniseries king' and so-called 'biggest TV movie producer in the world'.[14] Under Galin's tenure, Robert Halmi, Inc. (which sold to Hallmark Cards in 1994) produced such lavish television movies as *The Phantom of the Opera* (Markowitz, 1983) and *China Rose* (Day, 1983), both for CBS.

By 1986, Laurel's executive corporate officers were therefore as follows: Rubinstein remained president and treasurer; Virginia M. McGuire was controller of the company and vice president of finance and secretary; and Gornick and Galin were vice presidents of production.[15] On 29 July 1987, McGuire, Gornick and Galin were appointed to senior management level and Diane Vilagi to vice president of production administration.[16] That same year, former Warner Bros. employee Charles Jeffrey Caiman rounded off the group of corporate officers as vice president of television and Laurel listed fifteen members of staff employed on a year-round basis.[17]

Galin's immediate responsibility on joining Laurel was to oversee production of seasons three and four of *Tales from the Darkside*, which remained the company's most reliable source of revenue. *Darkside* was now being broadcast on a reported 125 local stations across the US, mostly programmed in late-night timeslots. Rubinstein favoured this scheduling, since he felt that this was when 'horror buffs are most likely to watch and when there is less original programming to compete for viewers' attention'.[18] The series had continued to increase in value well after the production of the pilot episode and in fiscal 1984 television licence fees accounted for 60 per cent of Laurel's revenue. By fiscal 1986, these licence fees accounted for approximately 85 per cent of the revenue.[19] On 24 June 1987, George Anderson reported that Laurel's net income was approximately $1.5 million, the main source of which was *Tales from the Darkside*.[20]

As mentioned in Chapter 4, accepting that much of the series revenue went back into production, the programme did at least generate a more reliable source of monies than Laurel's feature film output. *Darkside* further benefited from its economical approach to production, and William Teitler recalls an 'inherently organised ... automobile-style assembly line'.[21] Production encompassed exactly four days (consisting of no more than ninety shots) and ran concurrently with pre-production on the following episode. Post-production was overseen by Teitler, working with two film editors on alternating episodes, each episode taking approximately four weeks from start to finish. Given that the show was a 'lean operation with small overheads', a decision was made to produce seasons three and four consecutively, bypassing the start-up costs associated with yearly renewal.[22] With the crew already in place, and studio space in New York and Los Angeles rented, Laurel pressed forward to complete both seasons (totalling forty-two episodes) in a five- to six-month period, after which, the firm's commitment to syndicators LBS and Tribune was finished. The show broadcast its last episode in July 1988.

This push to generate more episodes was about more than licensing fees and saving on start-up costs. Todd Gitlin records that in television 'the real money was in syndication', where a series moves beyond its network home to run repeatedly on multiple channels for an unlimited period of time.[23] Notwithstanding the fact that *Darkside* was pre-syndicated, additional episodes still equalled additional revenue. Famed television producer Aaron Spelling, the man behind hit shows *Charlie's Angels* (1976–1981) and *Dynasty* (1981–1989), said that a minimum of sixty-six episodes was required for 'successful domestic repeat syndication of network or first-run syndication programming'.[24] This number allows a scheduling strategy known as strip programming, where stations can establish a consistent audience base by broadcasting a series five days a week in the same time slot. With sixty-five episodes, a show can air for thirteen weeks straight (former media executive Jeffrey C. Ulin tells us that this is half a network season), while added episodes and repeats can extend this run to an entire broadcast year.[25] As a first-run syndicated package, *Darkside* was ready-made for such distribution. Teitler says that although the creative participants endeavoured to produce the best episodes possible, on a business level *Darkside* was essentially 'syndication fodder'.[26]

With this so-called 'magic number'[27] for repeat syndication reached, it made little sense to renew *Darkside* beyond season four (bringing the total number of episodes to 90). Laurel then determined to produce a second anthology programme that could repeat the trajectory of its older sibling and, in 1987, fashioned two pilots for first-run syndication in collaboration with LBS and Tribune. The first, *Moment of Fear*, intended to downplay the supernatural in favour of Hitchcockian suspense. The second, *Night Rose*, focused on eroticism and was picked up on an exclusive basis by premium cable service HBO, who then lost interest when executives deemed John Harrison's pilot 'too pornographic'.[28] With neither show attracting much attention, Galin edited together a 'scissor reel' of *Darkside*'s most iconic monsters and pitched it to Tribune as a new anthology horror series that placed such creatures at the forefront.[29] *Monsters* (1988–1991), as it was later called, displayed an identical model to *Darkside* and Tribune immediately fast-tracked it into production, placing it on the air the same calendar year that *Darkside* concluded. The show spanned three seasons and seventy-two syndicated episodes.

Aside from these financial incentives, Laurel 'benefited from its involvement in television series production as a result of the opportunity to develop relationships with many writers and directors in both New York and Los Angeles'.[30] A consequence of this focus on bicoastal television production was that Laurel's Fort Pitt Blvd base was rendered surplus to requirements. Rubinstein had maintained offices in New York from Laurel's inception and all of the firm's corporate officers would now join him there. The creative staff were also relocated to New York and, since this space was 'suitable and adequate for its present needs', Laurel ended the lease on its Pittsburgh offices in July 1987.[31] When *Creepshow 2* commenced principal photography in September 1986, it became the first Laurel feature film to shoot entirely outside of Pennsylvania, filming in Arizona and Maine respectively. If Romero's exit formally ended the company's auteurist focus, Laurel's status as a thriving regional film base away from bicoastal centres was now also a thing of the past.

The demise of Laurel's regional status was a profound change for a firm whose geographic location had been key to its formative identity. Yet this went unnoticed in the press and, given the gradual relocation to New York, made little difference in terms of the company's productivity. Pittsburgh had made sense for a number of reasons, based on its corporate status, knowledge of tax shelter schemes, distance from Hollywood unions, informal locus of eager (and therefore cheap) talent and the facilities accumulated by Romero and Latent Image. For Romero, Pittsburgh had been a separation from mainstream modes of production – literal and figurative. Now this was at an end. In some ways, relocation to New York was itself an ideological shift towards a more standardised corporate governance, a shift that had begun with the firm's IPO in 1979. Laurel's growth demanded closer relations with larger, established partners and a commitment to regional production now made little sense.

Laurel's focus on television was another modification of the firm's identity; a change that unlocked significant revenue. Since production began, *Darkside* had been licensed to numerous foreign territories and in 1986 took advantage of the booming home video market to license the video cassette rights for its first season to overseas and domestic distributors.[32] Laurel's back catalogue, of course, included feature films, and in 1986 the company reported that 25 per cent of its revenue came from the licensing of domestic cassette rights to 'a single major motion picture distributor'.[33] Feature films were therefore not entirely put to one side and, as the $450,000 in fees received for *Creepshow 2* demonstrated, could still generate income.[34]

On 9 May 1986, Laurel acquired the assets of the California-based limited partnership Angeles Cinema Investors. These assets consisted of cash, four feature films and the 'amounts due or to become due' in respect to these films in the future. The films acquired were *Blue Skies Again* (Michaels, 1983), *Irreconcilable Differences* (Shyer, 1984), *Scandalous* (Cohen, 1984) and *Swing Shift* (Demme, 1984), this latter film starring Goldie Hawn, Kurt Russell and Ed Harris. Laurel's report to shareholders made it clear that the domestic theatrical release of all four had been 'completed'[35] and, with the exception of *Irreconcilable Differences*, that they had all been box office disappointments.

The worst offender was the sports comedy *Blue Skies Again*, which returned a paltry $46,603 at the domestic box office. The question then arises as to what Angeles Cinema Investors was and why Laurel would purchase four films it knew to be exhausted theatrically.

Angeles Cinema Investors was one of a number of venture capital vehicles investing in feature films in the early 1980s. Distinct from the limited partnerships of Laurel's 1970s tax shelter projects, these investors expected to turn a profit, though typically did not receive more than 10 to 15 per cent annually on their invested capital.[36] In industry speak, it was known as 'dumb money', dominated by the folly of 'deep-pocketed dentists, oil tycoons and other wealthy individuals eager for a piece of the glamourous, but high-risk, game of film production'.[37] Sale of Angeles Cinema's assets to Laurel promised at least some returns on an ill-advised business venture. For Laurel, beyond the added liquidity, the ancillary value of Angeles Cinema's films was not totally exhausted, and Laurel now viewed such markets as a key part of its advancement.[38] More so, acquisition of these properties, when placed alongside the feature films directed by Romero and the *Tales from the Darkside* television series, represented 'a significant step towards Laurel's long-term goal of building a "library" of motion pictures and TV programs with continuing residual values'.[39] In this transformative stage, what Laurel wanted was quantity. Quality, if not discounted, was no longer a leading concern.

Owning 'substantial library assets' has long been an integral part of the major studios' infrastructure,[40] and in the 1980s and 1990s theorists observed a move towards the consolidation of library ownership. In their article 'Who Owns the Movies?' (1994), Elliot Forbes and David Pierce write that

> Wall Street loves libraries and weighs them heavily in valuing stock; banks and other lending institutions readily accept them as collateral; and the cash flow generated by their exploitation sometimes sustains companies through otherwise tough periods. And with the constant development of new media, film libraries have historically appreciated in value over time.[41]

Constructing a substantial library of content was at the root of M&A activity during this period. As per Stephen Prince, media mogul Ted Turner's acquisition of MGM/UA in 1986 hinged on the studio's library of classic films, providing 'an outstanding bank of programming in perpetuity' and a steady stream of content for Turner's small-screen broadcasting outlets.[42] Operating on a much-reduced scale, Laurel's acquisition of Angeles Cinema Investors' assets enhanced the firm's marketplace potency across platforms. Given what was to come, one wonders how much of this activity was really about making the company itself an attractive target for acquisition.

In 1987, the *New York Times* predicted a 'tough season' for independent production companies, attributed to a dissipating enthusiasm around home video and pay television and the continuing rise of production and market costs.[43] During this period, the Cannon Group faced worsening financial difficulties and in August 1988 competitor De Laurentiis Entertainment Group, Inc. filed for Chapter 11 bankruptcy.[44] By 1991, leading independent companies Atlantic Releasing, Empire International, Vestron, Cinecom and Weintraub Entertainment Group were defunct. Orion Pictures filed Chapter 11 bankruptcy in December 1991. That this 'tough season' coincided with the reports of independent film's prosperity detailed in Chapter 4 illustrates the uncertainty and risk/risk-reward that frequently surrounds this sector.

When reviewing Laurel Entertainment for potential acquisition, auditors for Spelling Productions summarised that 'as an independent entity, the prospects for Laurel's growth are limited by the increasingly difficult time it, like other small independent entertainment companies, is experiencing in raising capital'.[45] The problems in financing feature films notwithstanding, Laurel was also facing difficulties with its small-screen partners. During the production of *Tales from the Darkside*, relations with Jaygee Productions soured and, on 31 March 1988, Jaygee filed a complaint against Laurel for breach of contract. Chief among its concerns was a lack of payment on net proceeds, lack of profit participation on the upcoming *Tales from the Darkside: The Movie* and a lack of profit share on the sister show *Monsters*, a programme Jaygee determined to be a direct spin-off from *Darkside*. Jaygee sought general damages of no less than $800,000 and punitive damages of no less than $3 million.[46]

The above episode reinforced Laurel's financial vulnerability and the need to identify 'friendly' partnerships in future enterprises. From an M&A perspective, business professor Robert F. Bruner labels so-called 'friendly' companies the 'white knight', that is, buyers who purchase a target with an eye towards synergic relations and/or strategic partnerships and who agree not to dismantle the company or lay off employees.[47] Laurel's mounting library of assets certainly made it attractive to acquiring firms. For Laurel, a volatile independent landscape, not to mention the financial threats from former partners, made a protective 'white knight' guardian desirable. From the evidence at hand, it seems likely that acquisition was, at the very least, on Laurel's mind during this period.[48] And whether actively courted or not, Laurel suddenly had an opportunity to cultivate such a relationship. Rubinstein and Galin were friendly with Jules Haimovitz, an expert in 'restructuring the business profile' of entertainment companies.[49] Haimovitz joined Aaron Spelling Productions in December 1987 and by the middle of 1988 had arranged a merger between the two companies. A third company in this partnership, Worldvision Enterprises, Inc., offered a solution to Laurel's longstanding distribution woes.

Merger and Acquisition

In the entertainment industry, the 1980s merger wave is said to have begun in 1985 when media baron Rupert Murdoch's News Corp. purchased 20th Century Fox, nothing less than 'one of the most important mergers in industry history' according to Schatz.[50] Management consulting firm McKinsey & Company reported that, from 1988 to 1989, $80 billion was committed to 'big takeovers' in the entertainment industry,[51] including publisher Time Inc.'s merger with Warner Communications (costing $14 billion), and Japanese electronics giant Sony's acquisition of Columbia Pictures ($4.7 billion), both in 1989. *Variety*'s Richard Gold noted that these mergers created a snowball effect where M&A became 'essential to the competitive survival of American enterprise in the emerging global entertainment communications marketplace'.[52]

Kolev, Haleblian and McNamara see this as part of a wider movement spanning multiple industries and continents, influenced by permissive legal environments, favourable economic conditions (including recovery from an economic recession) and financial innovations such as junk bonds.[53] In this context, economists observe that the stock market tends to negatively value unrelated diversification between joining firms, and in the 1980s the Reagan administration's 'hands-off' approach to same-industry mergers, which diminished challenges from anti-trust authorities, resulted in an exponential growth of such synergies.[54] Michael Lubatkin equated the confidence in same-industry mergers to a so-called merger contingency framework, where 'the better the strategic fit between the acquiring and the acquired firm (that is, the more the respective environments of the two firms have unifying features) the greater the potential value created by the merger'.[55] Synergy between firms was thus part of a sound strategic plan, bringing together complementary resources that facilitate more effective operations.[56]

Prince situates the entertainment industry within this macroeconomic trend, as large-scale conglomerates initiated a process of what he has called 'deconglomeration', that is, shedding dissimilar firms for a more precise alignment of internal operations.[57] Prior to the 1980s M&A wave, the owners of the major studios typically had 'no experience of – and little interest in media entertainment'.[58] This was epitomised by Gulf and Western (a conglomerate that once specialised in clothing, auto parts and manufacturing) and its purchase of Paramount in 1966.

Looking at what makes an effective same-industry synergy, economists begin with a simple question: 'what problem does this [merger] solve, or why do we need it?'.[59] Mergers are frequently broken into distinct types (see Table 5.1), and the 1980s entertainment industry often combined vertical and horizontal integration. This granted firms ownership and control over each stage of production, distribution and sales output, simultaneously enabling them to sell product

Table 5.1 Types of merger (see: 'Types of Mergers: Different Types of M&A in the Corporate World', n.d.).

Merger Type	Characteristics	Media Industry Examples
Horizontal	Between firms in the same industry with competing production output. Offers lower costs and larger capabilities (economies of scale).	AIP merged with production company Filmways in 1979. Filmways was similarly acquired by Orion Pictures in 1982.
Vertical	Between firms in the same industry but at different levels of the supply chain.	UK film company The Rank Organisation owned exhibitor Odeon Cinemas from 1941 to 2000.
Conglomerate	Unrelated firms in entirely different industries. A *pure conglomerate* merger is between firms with nothing in common; a *mixed conglomerate* merger offers product and/or market extension.	Coca-Cola Co.'s acquisition of Columbia Pictures in 1982.
Product Extension	Between firms offering different but related products/services in the same market. Such products can complement each other and/or be consumed simultaneously.	The Viacom-Paramount merger in 1994 brought together a host of related media products (see Figure 5.1).
Market Extension	Firms that offer the same products/services but in entirely different markets. Allows a greater geographical reach.	India's Eros International merged with US firm STX Entertainment to become Eros STX Global Corp. in 2020.

across different media platforms – film, television shows, books, music, videogames, toys and so on.[60] Smaller business enterprises hoped to ride this wave, fearing that failure to do so would see them cut adrift. In 1988, the Hollywood-based production company Heritage Entertainment, Inc. acquired Landmark Theatre Corp.'s chain of domestic theatres, admitting to shareholders that the wider trend of consolidation was behind this purchase. Heritage cited Aaron Spelling's acquisition of Laurel Entertainment as a precedent that its shareholders would be wise to follow.[61]

In a 1989 proxy statement to shareholders, Aaron Spelling Productions recorded that Laurel's east coast concentration 'on the lower budget, first-run television syndication market as well as on feature films' would horizontally compliment the firm's own production of prime-time network television on the west coast, providing 'significant flexibility in producing programming in all budget ranges'.[62] Aside from this market extension, Laurel's accumulating portfolio of content matched Spelling's objective to expand significantly its library of entertainment programming.[63]

What these SEC reports left out was that Spelling's future was uncertain. The company had recently ended a seventeen-year exclusive contract with ABC television, prompting the *Wall Street Journal* to call Spelling a 'lackluster performer . . . no longer a major power in prime-time television'.[64] The acquisition of Laurel was one part of Spelling Production's attempt to strengthen its position. In July 1988, the company announced a merger with Great American Communications Company (GACC), combining Spelling Productions with GACC's Worldvision Enterprises, Inc. under the organisational framework (or holding company) Spelling Entertainment, Inc. Worldvision was a leading television distributor with an extensive library of programming, including Hanna-Barbera's range of children's animation, from *The Flintstones* to *Scooby-Doo*. As future Spelling president Peter Bachmann stated, Worldvision's library 'generates a very stable cash flow that helps underwrite its operations and new productions'.[65] More importantly, it gave Spelling a guaranteed distribution outlet. The deal was worth a reported $65.4 million in cash, plus stock options of around $118 million for GACC owner Carl Lindner Jr, granting him a 49 per cent controlling interest in the company. Partnership with Worldvision added a large degree of self-sufficiency to the firm's operations, and Laurel would provide another source of programming to be distributed through this network.

From an SME perspective, Worldvision could 'generate revenues internally',[66] meaning Laurel no longer had to worry about sourcing distribution for its small-screen output. With these incentives in mind, and Laurel's reported losses of $211,000 on sales of $3.5 million in fiscal 1988,[67] the company agreed to become a wholly owned subsidiary of Spelling Entertainment. The deal was finalised on 1 March 1989 at a total purchase price of approximately $12 million. This consisted of $7.1 million cash (which included related expenses) and approximately 734,000 shares of Class A Common Stock with a market value of $4.9 million.[68] For Laurel's 2,600,847 shares of common stock, former shareholders received a combination of $1.70 in cash per share and approximately .282 of a share of Spelling stock.[69]

Though the benefits were clear, this merger definitively ended Laurel's fifteen-year tenure as an autonomous production company. As with its exit from Pittsburgh, Laurel's evolving identity made this transition relatively unproblematic for the firm. Michael Z. Newman reminds us that ideas of independent 'autonomy, authenticity, and distinction'[70] have, of course, never been as absolute as consumers might like, particularly as the 1980s and 1990s M&A waves saw 'media conglomerates offer their own alternative to themselves, bringing in even those consumers who might be contemptuous of their very existence'.[71] This said, Laurel no longer offered even a notional projection of the autonomy-authenticity that had been so important to both the canonical sector and Romero's own 'cult auteur' image. The firm's self-conscious desire to cultivate an anti-establishment brand left with Romero and, in 1989, Laurel's identity, as confirmed by Spelling's report to its shareholders, was simply that of an east coast producer of low-cost television and film product. As far as the company's growth was concerned, legitimising cultural notions of autonomy-authenticity were now irrelevant. Maintaining the firm's autonomy in terms of real-world working practices was of greater urgency.

As a wholly owned subsidiary of Spelling Entertainment, Laurel's board of directors was disbanded and replaced by one consisting of Aaron Spelling, Jules Haimovitz, Spelling chief operating officer (and former senior vice president of Viacom) Ronald Lightstone and Rubinstein. Senior management remained unchanged and Rubinstein entered a five-year employment contract that guaranteed his services as president and chief officer until March 1994. The contract promised a yearly salary of $300,000 (to increase by $25,000 each year) and numerous benefits and stock options.[72] Rubinstein told *Variety* that a large part of his corporate responsibilities had now come to an end, freeing him to return to the minutia of day-to-day production activities.[73] Although Laurel was now irrevocably beholden to a parent company, the firm was otherwise self-driving. Galin claims that Spelling was entirely hands-off when it came to its east coast unit, granting Laurel the freedom to formulate its own productions provided 'the [financial] numbers made sense'. According to Galin, Laurel still 'had the authority to make the deal'.[74]

But what deals was Laurel now attempting to make? Film production was still on the agenda and Spelling was impressed with the $57 million box office on *Pet Sematary*, on which Laurel retained profit participation.[75] A sequel to *Tales from the Darkside: The Movie* was also in the works, alongside an adaptation of Stephen King's *Thinner*, originally published under his pseudonym Richard Bachman in 1984.

In November 1990, Spelling initiated Spelling Films International, a fourth wholly owned subsidiary under CEO Ian Jessel. This unit was added 'to acquire and distribute feature films for international theatrical, television and home video release'[76] and in 1992 contributed to the financing and release of indie films *The Player* (Altman), *Storyville* (Frost) and *Twin Peaks: Fire Walk with Me* (Lynch). Rather than a boon to the Laurel partners, Spelling Films reported that only one or two films would be made in-house, with the rest sourced from third-party co-ventures.[77] Once again, this was about library building, emphasised in September 1993 when Worldvision acquired 150 movies from the struggling Carolco Pictures. Properties in this deal included blockbusters *Total Recall* (Verhoeven, 1990), *Terminator 2: Judgement Day* (Cameron, 1991), *Basic Instinct* (Verhoeven, 1992) and the *Rambo* trilogy (1982–1988). As for Laurel, if the firm wanted to continue to make feature films, it still had to source third-party financing independently. Even under this new corporate umbrella, money for features was difficult to obtain and the firm's agency, in regard to the existence of choice, remained limited to surrounding opportunity structures.

Tales from the Darkside: The Movie originated before the Spelling merger and was once again optioned by Paramount Pictures, again with Rubinstein and Galin producing. *Thinner* was not completed until well after Laurel's closure and the firm made no other theatrical features in the interim. Instead, Worldvision gave them a direct line of access into television. Spelling encouraged activity on the small screen, readily introducing Rubinstein and Galin to network executives as a new 'potential supplier'.[78] Early 1990s television seemed like fertile ground and Amanda Lotz reports that new technologies (remote control, video recorders and analogue cable systems) and a growth in the number of channels 'expanded viewers' choice and control', combining to facilitate an 'explosion of content providers'.[79] As these factors created opportunities for independent television producers, another fortuitous development was about to make Laurel's transition into small-screen production even more attractive.

Stephen King's *The Stand* and Corporate Identity

In 1988, Lorimar-Telepictures Corporation signed an 18-month deal with Laurel to finance and distribute *The Stand*, moving a step closer to Rubinstein's 'vision' of the property as a major theatrical motion picture.[80] In King's post-apocalyptic novel, a weaponised virus is accidentally released from a US military facility, creating a plague-like 'super-flu' that quickly disseminates 99.4 per cent of earth's human population. In the wake of civilisation's collapse, the sci-fi premise gives way to fantasy, as disparate survivors across the United States begin to dream of either a 108-year-old African American prophet of God called Mother Abigail or the demonic 'Walkin' Dude' known as Randall Flagg. These figures are beacons, symbols of light and darkness, dividing humanity between the 'just plain folks' who make the pilgrimage to Abigail in Boulder, Colorado and the human detritus instinctively drawn towards Flagg in Las Vegas. As the 'Boulder Free Zone' rebuilds its own democratic system of law and order, Flagg's malevolent presence looms, leading a band of Abigail's followers on a quest to rid the world of evil, once and for all.

After eight years and five drafts, King came to feel that his novel could not be condensed into a single feature. In January 1988, Lorimar hired screenwriter Judith Rascoe to try where he had failed.[81] Lorimar was thereafter subject to a hostile takeover by Warner Bros. and the project wound up in the hands of the company's new parent. Rubinstein and Warner replaced Rascoe with Rospo Pallenberg, who in January 1991 delivered a third draft of the screenplay. Pallenberg was in many ways a logical choice when it came to abridging *The Stand*, having previously collaborated with John Boorman on the Arthurian fantasy *Excalibur* (1981) and on an unfilmed three-hour version of J. R. R. Tolkien's *The Lord of the Rings* (1954–1955). In the February 1991 issue of *Cinefantastique*, Rubinstein praised Pallenberg's adaptation, while the writer himself joked that the difficulties of translating the book to film had led him to briefly consider the miniseries format instead, if only 'on a *bad day*'.[82] These words ended up being somewhat prophetic.

In November 1990, ABC had a sizeable hit with the $12 million miniseries adaptation of Stephen King's *It*, produced by WBTV and directed by Tommy Lee Wallace (after original director George A. Romero withdrew). Although King was not actively involved in the production of *It*, he was increasingly interested in television. He had been impressed by ABC's cult series *Twin Peaks* (1990–1991), which aired in April of that same year, convinced that the David Lynch-produced show had opened the door to more offbeat and adult modes of small-screen address.[83] Accordingly, King started working on an original teleplay called *Golden Years* (1991) about an elderly janitor who begins to age in reverse. Given Laurel's heightened agency in small-screen production, and its ongoing work on *The Stand*, the company made a natural partner and *Golden Years* went ahead with a short-order first series of seven episodes with monies from distributor Worldvision and CBS, providing Laurel with its first ever network co-production.

King remained an important asset to Laurel and, in turn, he found Rubinstein to be a sympathetic partner. Through the single purpose entity Laurel-King, Inc., the firm held options on a number of King's stories (and at one point asked him to host and oversee an anthology series called *The Stephen King Playhouse*) and frequently granted him the right of first refusal to adapt his own material. When ABC suggested modifying *The Stand* into a miniseries (with WBTV as partner), King used the opportunity to reassert his control over the production, penning a faithful 366-minute update of his own work and personally selecting Mick Garris as director. King had worked with Garris on the film *Sleepwalkers* in 1992 and felt he would be willing to 'serve as a conduit for the script . . . Mick understood that this was going to say *"Stephen King's The Stand"* and not *"Mick Garris' The Stand"*'.[84] Rubinstein happily acceded to King's decision-making, seemingly well aware that his own preference for a more seasoned filmmaker was secondary to King's brand potential. ABC's senior vice president Judd Parkin shared this valuation, confident that King's name alone would be enough to recoup monies through television advertising sold at $150,000 per 30-second spot.[85]

The *Stand's* total budget was $28 million, Laurel's largest to date, and Galin says that ABC paid a 'very healthy license fee' for the initial distribution rights.[86] Laurel raised additional monies through Worldvision's foreign pre-sales, or, more accurately, a projection of what foreign pre-sales would be. Rubinstein liked to boast that the company did not use deficit financing on these network projects,[87] although it seems that significant monies were sourced in this way. In deficit financing, the licence fee usually provides only a percentage of the budget, meaning programmes would be made by the production company at a loss. The remaining percentage would then be sourced through secondary markets, including overseas broadcast rights, home video and so on. *The Stand* appeared in the UK on Sky TV in September 1995 and was then released on a double VHS set by Warner Home Video. Indeed, Spelling Entertainment's annual report highlighted that, in fiscal year 1992, Worldvision released thirteen titles to the rental market, including *Beverly Hills, 90210* (1990–2000), *Golden Years* and *Tales from the Darkside*.[88]

While the relative ease with which *The Stand* obtained small-screen financing suggested new directions, the text itself contains themes and iconography most associated with Laurel of old, from the depiction of a biological weapon turned on US citizens (*The Crazies*) to images of widespread social collapse (Romero's '*Dead* series'). Despite Broadcast Standards and Practices, graphic horror also plays its part, with no shortage of wide-eyed corpses and acts of violence (the most striking of which is a crucified man wearing a crown of thorns made from hypodermic needles) to maintain Laurel-King's credibility with genre fans.[89]

A number of these aspects were, of course, taken from the source novel, but King's teleplay adds further embellishment by paraphrasing, consciously or otherwise, scenes from Romero's back catalogue. In a pivotal sequence in *Day of the Dead*, pilot John (Terry Alexander) argues that any hope for the future will depend upon a total abandonment of America's past (that is, the viewer's present, represented onscreen by the records, tax reports and 'negatives for all your favourite movies' that are buried with the survivors in an underground research shelter). In *The Stand* 'Episode 3: The Betrayal', King adapts this scene into the following exchange between sociology professor Glen Bateman (Ray Walston) and Midwest farmer Ralph Brentner (Peter van Norden):

> GLEN: The plague took the people, but it couldn't take the gadgets, could it? No, they're all still out there. Everything from electric can openers to cobalt bombs, just waiting for someone to come along and pick 'em up. And the scavenger hunt starts today.
> RALPH: Hell, Professor. What's so bad about puttin' the rocks back in people's scotch?
> GLEN: It's the old way. And the old way was a death trip.

In the novel, Glen does not frame things quite so directly. Although he confesses to a deep fear of technology, and that mankind's attempts to rebuild society might again lead to catastrophe, he also sees value in the past. Glen wants to 'ratify the *spirit* of the old society' and, as he tells the group, 'the technological society has walked off the court, so to speak, but they've left all the basketballs behind. Someone will come along who remembers the game and teach it to the rest again.'[90] It is Harold Lauder, a morally questionable teen who eventually joins Flagg's disciples, who is the more sceptical, replying 'just because the Gordian knot has been cut for us is no reason for us to go to work and tie it back up'.[91] By 1994, King seemed more inclined to agree with both his antagonist and George Romero. Like his novel, King's teleplay is ultimately about American community values, but it is interesting to see him reconsider *The Stand*'s themes, if only briefly, through the prism of Romero's more revolutionary politics.

Similarities to Romero's work are unsurprising, particularly in light of the director's original connection to the project (optioning a novel that shared his own interests and preoccupations) and his active involvement with *The Stand* throughout the 1980s. King would, in fact, have been working on the original screenplay as Romero wrote, rewrote and shot *Day of the Dead*. If *The Stand* then seems like an archetypal Laurel/Romero production, it is important to record that equally present were the facets that were redefining Laurel's identity in its post-Romero, post-merger phase, primarily: the concentration on prestige small-screen production, the foregrounding of the Stephen King brand and the absence of a director-auteur at the project's centre. If not exactly a hybrid text, as Laurel's *Martin* had been, *The Stand* is a manifestation of a firm in transition, suggesting a consistency as Laurel moved from one distinct period of activity to another. The horror fandom that Rubinstein thought so important to Laurel's success was catered for here (and he continued to directly address such consumers in fan magazine *Fangoria* and *Cinefantastique*), as were the networks, television advertisers and new corporate partners that now shaped Laurel's existence.

And it was these latter influences that now transpired to be the most dominant. After *The Stand* evolved from big-screen production to small-screen miniseries, films moved to the background and when *Golden Years* and *Monsters* ended their respective runs, Laurel turned exclusively to miniseries and movies-for-television (MFT). As Spelling Entertainment told shareholders in 1990, 'Laurel believes this is a logical area of expansion; television movies occupy a natural middle ground between Laurel's theatrical motion picture and television series businesses'.[92] Given his significant experience in MFT production at Robert Halmi, Mitchell Galin was well-equipped to lead the company in this direction.

The agreement with CBS on *Golden Years* stipulated that the network was 'required to order from Laurel an MFT by a date certain or pay a penalty of $100,000'.[93] It was on this account that CBS commissioned Laurel's *Precious Victims* (Levin, 1993), a 'true-life' drama based on the double kidnapping of two new-born babies in Jersey County, Illinois in the 1980s. On the small screen, production begot production and, under Spelling's and Worldvision's patronage, from 1991 to 1994 Laurel entered into an unprecedented period of activity, producing *Golden Years*, *Precious Victims*, *The Stand* and *The Vernon Johns Story* (Fink, 1994). A two-part adaptation of Stephen King's *The Langoliers* (Holland) also entered production during this period, premiering on ABC on 14 May 1995, some six months after Laurel started closing down its offices.

MFTs such as *Precious Victims* and *Vernon Johns* were hardly groundbreaking fare and topical telefilms 'based on a true story' had long been an MFT staple. *Variety* mischievously placed *Precious Victims* in the 'baby suspense genre', ridiculing 'all the kidnapping and child custody battles collecting on primetime's doorstep'.[94] Rote though these productions may have been, Galin says that of all his work for the company, he is proudest of *Vernon Johns*, claiming its civil rights story of a minister (played by James Earl Jones) preaching equality in 1950s segregationist Alabama was representative of the kind of socially conscious media that he aspired to produce.[95] *Vernon Johns* revealed Galin's creative agency, as he acquired projects for which he had an affinity and produced them in a medium in which he had evidenced human capital. These projects also finally moved Laurel beyond genre, able actively to 'broaden its focus' to produce a diversified production slate.[96] This was something the firm had struggled to achieve under Romero's creative leadership.

By focusing on network television, Laurel's identity, already seen to be transitional, became a mirror of its parent. Above, we have seen how corporate leaders and economists favour M&A synergies between related companies, stressing the importance of sameness and a merger contingency framework. Even so, such partnerships still hinged on difference. In Laurel, Spelling had identified three areas of divergence that could extend its marketplace reach, based on: (1) geographical separateness; (2) specialisation in 'high quality yet cost-effective production of fantasy and horror projects'; and (3) the production of first-run syndicated television that could be rapidly mass produced.[97] De Bernardis and Giustiniano's work on organisational identities after an M&A event argues that, while corporate ambiguity in the marketplace is detrimental, holding firms can manage 'multiple identities under a shared group identity' to achieve success in multiple markets.[98] Nonetheless, Laurel's and Spelling's identities began to collate.

Laurel's business offices remained on the east coast, yet other 'areas of divergence' were dissipating. Fantasy and horror product was still important, if no longer centralised, and the production of first-run syndicated programming ended with *Monsters*. Sameness between corporations may be a leading instigator in pursuing a merger, but in Laurel's case this facsimile continued to develop after the event, demonstrating a moving together of identities as the firms operated in tandem. In fact, the term 'moving together' is actually inexact. For Spelling, merger was about consolidation and library building, its programming continuing much as it had before. Change was therefore primarily identifiable in the subsidiary and not the parent.

To a large extent, Laurel's transformation was organic. Galin's agency as creative leader (coupled with the interests and marketplace value of key creative partner Stephen King) made a movement into network television a natural progression. Laurel benefited from television production long before it merged with Spelling and a sustained engagement with this medium revealed a savvy recognition of 'strategic momentum', that is, 'the tendency to maintain or expand the emphasis and direction of prior strategic action in current strategic behavior'.[99] Nevertheless, by the early 1990s, Laurel was not the same firm Spelling had acquired. The use of shared resources played a part in this transformation. Singh and Montgomery discern the value creation behind the 'combination of human capital (specialized) and physical assets' post-merger.[100] Worldvision's and Spelling's resources made Laurel's appropriation of network programming the path of least resistance, augmenting the parallels between the parent and its subsidiary.

Laurel is, of course, just one case study and further empirical work needs to be done to see how common this pattern is of subsidiaries taking on the characteristics of a parent post-merger. With this in mind, analysis of independent cinema does volunteer other examples of this behaviour, particularly in Disney's procurement of Miramax in December 1993 and Ted Turner's purchase of New Line Cinema the following January. For these acquiring media conglomerates, this was about reaching new market segments or, in the case of Turner, of continuing to expand the library of programming for his television networks.[101] Like Laurel, New Line's and Miramax's internal governance remained autonomous. Justin Wyatt observes that 'the most impressive difference [post-merger] given their new affiliation was a greater access to funds and more latitude in production decisions'.[102]

Change was actually more dramatic than this. In *Indie, Inc.*, Perren looks closely at Miramax in its pre- and post-Disney phases, finding that this latter era facilitated greater control over development, access to the parent's marketing/distribution resources and an ability to keep talent (stars, producers and directors) under its umbrella, behaviour not dissimilar to that of a major.[103] At post-merger Miramax and New Line, mass appeal, star-driven properties such as Miramax's *The English Patient* (Minghella, 1996) and New Line's *The Lord of the Rings* trilogy (2001–2003) now sat alongside so-called 'edgy' fare with greater frequency. Perren writes that after the Disney takeover, Miramax became '"hybrid" in nature', enabling films like *Pulp Fiction* (Tarantino, 1994) to receive award nominations from the Academy and from supposed counterpoint events such as the Independent Spirit Awards, evincing an expansive marketplace reach.[104] Post-merger, the portmanteau term 'indiewood' was used to best describe Miramax's and New Line's transformed identities.

The extent of Miramax's emulation of Disney went even further and on 16 September 1993 the Weinstein brothers launched the subdivision Miramax Family Films. Miramax planned to produce low-cost (around $6 million per film) fantasy films with an eye towards the family market. As Bob Weinstein told the *Los Angeles Times*, 'we have the best parent company in the world when it comes to marketing family films, so we'd be crazy not to take advantage of that'.[105] Films released under this corporate banner included the Irish coming-of-age drama *Into the West* (Newell, 1992), *The Neverending Story III: Escape from Fantasia* (MacDonald, 1994) and the talking-pig movie *Gordy* (Lewis, 1995). Perren records that Miramax Family Films was closed when it provided 'too much overlap with Disney product'.[106]

In Laurel's case, merger was not with a large entertainment conglomerate. Yet like Miramax, Laurel was driven by a pragmatic utilisation of wider available resources, logical decision-making, human capital and strategic movement to mirror the behaviour of its parent. De Bernardis and Giustiniano suggest that a firm's identity is most salient during periods of change, growth or retrenchment, citing the loss of a sustaining element or the effects of M&A.[107] In 1985, Laurel had change forced upon it, instigated by the departure of its co-founder/creative leader. The firm's identity moved in line with the capabilities of its new parent, facilitating a more diverse range of output than ever before. From this point forward, Rubinstein told journalists that Laurel's 'primary business is TV'.[108] However, as the 1990s progressed, this corporate conversion did not protect the firm from the wider industrial changes amassing on the horizon. Laurel may have ridden the storm, but another wave was about to hit.

'Have a Good Holiday, by the Way We're Shutting You Down'

Merger with Aaron Spelling Productions and Worldvision was mutually beneficial for all parties. Under the Spelling Entertainment umbrella, Laurel increased its output, producing a diversified range of small-screen material that recontextualised (if, due to a relationship with Stephen King, never entirely abandoned) the firm's reputation for genre product. Worldvision's access to national and international markets, not to mention ancillaries such as home video, shored up distribution and unlocked a consistent and repeatable source of income. Having been introduced to network executives, Laurel became a steady supplier of content, much to the satisfaction of its partners. Taken collectively, in fiscal 1989 Spelling Entertainment reported revenues of approximately $48.2 million. In fiscal 1990, the first full year of joint operations, this combined revenue totalled $134.8 million.[109]

Behind the scenes, things were less stable. Almost immediately after it was established, Spelling Entertainment was put up for sale. Aaron Spelling's ABC television shows *Dynasty* and *Heartbeat* (1988–1989) were reportedly haemorrhaging viewers and, in what would later prove an embarrassing comment made to the *Los Angeles Times*, Spelling pronounced, 'I can honestly say that I don't know what the networks want anymore'.[110] Clare L. Drew's 1990 article 'The Selling of Spelling' was ruthless in appraising the firm, writing off Spelling's 'fumbled attempts at a comeback' and dismissing his company as little more than an 'ailing conglomerate'.[111] Drew conceded that the firm was in its infancy, and that the 'asset value' of Laurel and Worldvision promised a more consistent revenue.[112] Be that as it may, pressure to sell was being applied by major shareholder Carl Lindner Jr, owner of Great American Broadcasting and 49 per cent of Spelling Entertainment's stock. Lindner's own financial losses necessitated streamlining his overall holdings, and as one Lindner executive stated, the Spelling shares 'were great assets, but not core assets'.[113]

Subsequent activity was rapid. On 6 May 1991, Great American sold 14 million shares of Spelling Entertainment Class A common stock (and 250,000 shares of cumulative preferred stock) to the Charter Company, a Florida-based conglomerate with interests in oil operations, banking and land development. Charter changed its name to Spelling Entertainment Group, Inc. in October of the following year and instantly began selling off its non-entertainment-driven assets in an attempt to enhance synergy. A reported $25 million in cash was obtained from its oil operations, which was in turn pumped back into television programme development.[114] In this case, the parent self-consciously merged its identity with that of the subsidiary.

Charter's parentage was short-lived and on 31 March 1993 Blockbuster Entertainment attained 48 per cent of Spelling common stock. Blockbuster then acquired additional common stock from third parties and as of 25 March

1994 owned 70.5 per cent of the company's outstanding stock.[115] Blockbuster's ascent since opening its first video rental superstore in Dallas in 1985 had been dramatic, taking advantage of the home video boom to transform itself into a formidable entertainment industry player. By 1989, Blockbuster was the leading home video rental chain in the United States, drawing in a revenue of $663 million in that fiscal year alone. Now with more than 3,500 stores globally, under entrepreneur Wayne Huizenga's leadership Blockbuster instigated plans for expansion. Purchase of Spelling Entertainment was high on Huizenga's list of priorities, as he viewed the acquisition of a media content provider the next logical step towards controlling production as well as distribution.[116]

A month prior to this acquisition, Blockbuster purchased a stake in production-distribution company Republic Pictures Corporation for $25 million, obtaining its library of 1,400 feature films and 3,000 television episodes. In September 1993, Blockbuster instigated a merger between Spelling and Republic in a 'stock swap' valued at around $140 million. Through Spelling, Blockbuster harboured plans to produce straight-to-video content that would bypass the cinemas and go directly into its stores, a move that led Robert Alexander of Alexander and Associates, Inc. to call Blockbuster 'the first modern studio . . . instead of making productions for the big screen, they'll be concentrating on production for the electronic screen at home'.[117] This platform would have been ideally suited to Laurel's middle-ground between film and television, but the company was an increasingly small cog in a multiplatform machine. What had started as a partnership of companies on the east and west coast (with a distributor in between), now included a film production unit, another production-distribution unit (Republic and Worldvision merged into one distribution entity in April 1994) and its home entertainment-focused parent.

In January 1994, Blockbuster merged with Sumner Redstone's Viacom Inc., a transnational media conglomerate whose principal segments of operations included network and cable television, entertainment and broadcasting. The merger came during another global propagation of M&A activity in the 1990s, which included Disney's purchase of Miramax and Ted Turner's acquisition of New Line. In terms of the entertainment industry, this 1990s M&A wave is often conflated with activities from the surrounding decades, placing News Corp.'s acquisition of Fox in 1985 as the start of a wave of industry-wide consolidation that went into the 2000s.[118] Paramount's merger with Viacom in 1994 is therefore placed at the mid-point of this activity.

Business scholarship, however, considers the M&A activity of the 1990s as an entirely separate global cycle from the one preceding it. Kolev et al. point us towards five waves of M&A activity, occurring intermittently from the late nineteenth century to the mid-2000s. The 1990s wave is defined through a number of contextual factors, including enlarged economic globalisation, cross-border acquisitions, a disappearance of hostility and, crucially here, and in stark contrast to the 1980s, an emphasis on stock and stock swapping to complete acquisitions.[119] Rappaport and Sirower posit that in 1988, approximately 60 per cent of the value of large deals priced over $100 million was paid for in cash, while under 2 per cent was paid for in stock. A little over a decade later, the number of large deals completed using stock swaps (which included Spelling's merger with Republic) had risen to 50 per cent, with only 17 per cent now done with cash.[120] Accepting that there is a clear through line between M&A waves in the 1980s and 1990s (they both focus on synergy and on couplings between comparable partners), the difference had a pronounced impact on the future of the industry, not least of all in terms of Laurel Entertainment's longevity.

The Blockbuster-Viacom merger was financed by an exchange of stock worth $8.4 billion and was actually part of a wider strategic movement to finance Viacom's acquisition of Paramount Communications. In September 1993, the *New York Times* reported that Viacom proposed a $8.1 billion merger agreement with Paramount that followed this 'stock-swap' trend and called for just $1.09 billion in cash to be paid to Paramount shareholders.[121] A stock-swap transaction, rather than an outright purchase with cash, has several disadvantages, leading to an over-valuation of stock while implying that the venture is embedded in risk. As Rappaport and Sirower write, acquiring firms might propose a stock-swap transaction as a way of 'hedging their bets' or if they do not have adequate cash resources to make a cash offer, but 'a really confident acquirer would be expected to pay for the acquisition with cash so that its shareholders would not have to give any of the anticipated merger gains to the acquired company's shareholders'.[122] Adequate cash resources, or lack thereof, was indeed the case with Viacom. Sensing an opportunity, QVC chairman Barry Diller entered a counteroffer of $9.5 billion for Paramount, now placing Viacom's plan in jeopardy.

As QVC and Viacom entered into a bidding war, Viacom recognised that they needed cash. In September, Blockbuster agreed to invest $600 million (in exchange for convertible preferred stock) to bolster Viacom's bid. Bidding against QVC pushed Paramount's price to over $10 billion and Viacom, as a heavily leveraged firm, had trouble borrowing money. Blockbuster, on the other hand, had 'strong cash flows and no debt',[123] making them an ideal partner. In January 1994, Viacom's partnership with Blockbuster turned into a merger.

Less than one month later, the Paramount board unanimously voted for Viacom's bid of $107 per share, giving Redstone's firm 50.1 per cent of the company. Law professor Clark W. Furlow describes this as a two-step transaction. Since Viacom was only able to raise the cash for a tender offer for just over half of Paramount, this would be followed by a so-called 'squeeze out merger' for the remaining shares, exchanged for a mix of Viacom's equity and debt securities. Furlow writes, '[a]t the end of the process, Paramount's stockholders would have received a mix of cash, debt securities and shares of the combined enterprise'.[124]

Variety's Paul Noglows summarised the Viacom–Paramount deal as 'one of the longest (10 months), costliest (Paramount cost Viacom about $10 billion plus $62 million in advisement fees) and ugliest (the rival suitors bounced in and out of court) takeover battles in U.S. corporate history'.[125] For Viacom, it was worth it. Now sitting alongside Walt Disney and Time-Warner as one of the largest mass media and entertainment conglomerates in the United States, Viacom's acquisition of Paramount allowed it, in the words of Peter Bart, to not only 'control the destiny of [its] own product in the marketplace, but [its] competitors' as well'.[126] As the dust settled, Viacom emerged with a majority interest in a dizzying array of media subsidiaries, including MTV, Nickelodeon, VH-1, Showtime, Paramount Pictures and Paramount Television (Figure 5.1). It was only logical that some of these subsidiaries would now be surplus to requirements.

Viacom, via Blockbuster, now owned approximately 78 per cent of Spelling's Common Stock and the new parent began to look over its subsidiary with a critical eye. By this juncture, Spelling had regained its marketplace credibility with the Fox Network's *Beverly Hills, 90210*, but due to the large overlap with Paramount Television, Viacom simply did not need the content that Spelling was providing. In 1995, Viacom put Spelling up for sale with an estimated market value of between $1.2 and $2 billion, a price that was judged a gross overvaluation by some television executives.[127] Without a serious offer, Viacom took Spelling off the market the following year. According to Sallie Hofmeister of the *Los Angeles Times*, Viacom instead started 'paring the company down' and in 1998 closed Spelling Films International.[128]

This 'paring down' had in fact begun much earlier, when Viacom asked why, in the wake of a 'mega-merger' with Paramount, they needed Laurel Entertainment. From Viacom's perspective, Laurel was nothing more than a minor east coast subsidiary then specialising in unfashionable MFT product.[129] More than that, Laurel's sacrosanct autonomy, which extended beyond production to include internal organisational structures (staffing, benefits, workplace bonuses and so on), was deemed ill-suited to a holistic, top-to-bottom business organisation.

Galin remembers Viacom bringing 'specific rules about how things were done' and Laurel's bonus structure proved a major point of contention.[130] Viacom wanted restrictions on the type of bonuses Laurel awarded to its employees (something they applied universally across all subsidiaries); Rubinstein and Galin felt that any economic cap on rewarding success would limit Laurel's competitiveness in the marketplace. This applied especially to attracting and maintaining high-quality staffing. Laurel's resistance to its new parent's management techniques positioned the company as 'a square peg in a round

	Viacom	Paramount	Blockbuster
Cable Network Programming	MTV, MTV Europe, VH-1, Nickelodeon, Showtime, the Movie Channel, FLIX	USA Network, Madison Square Garden Network	
Retail Distribution			3,500 video stores in 49 states and nine countries
Motion Picture and Television Production	8,500 syndication library including films, programs for broadcast television and first run syndication	Paramount Pictures library of approximately 890 films; Paramount Television network programs	Library of over 12,000 hours of TV shows and films, including Spelling, Laurel and Republic Pictures
Cable Television Systems	Viacom Cable: 1.1 million subscriptions		
Television and Radio Broadcasting	Five network-affiliated stations (three CBS and two NBC) and fourteen radio stations	Four independent and three Fox-affiliate stations	
Publishing		Simon and Schuster, Silver Burdett Ginn, Prentice Hall Imprints	
Interactive/Multimedia	Joint venture with Paramount to develop and publish interactive software	Joint venture with Viacom	Largest wholesaler and retailer of interactive computer games
Cinema Chains	Parent company National Amusements own 800 cinemas in the US and the UK	Famous Players, Cineamerica, joint venture United Cinemas International	

Figure 5.1 The Viacom–Paramount merger, 1994 (abridged from 'Viacom–Par Merger: What's in It', 1994, p. 185).

hole' according to Galin or, as Rubinstein apparently once joked, little more than a 'rounding error' as far as Viacom was concerned.[131]

On 23 November 1994, the day before Thanksgiving, the Laurel offices received a fax from Viacom informing them that the company would be closed. As Galin glibly summarised, the fax basically said, 'have a good holiday, by the way we're shutting you down'.[132] Even though Rubinstein and Galin's contracts guaranteed a fair settlement, lengthy legal negotiations were fought to get more than the rudimentary two-weeks redundancy payment offered to its staff. The eventual compensation included a guarantee that Laurel staff would be hired back by Viacom on later projects on a freelance basis. As part of the exit plan, the divorcing companies had to determine what to do with those Laurel projects in various stages of development and production. Though the exact details are unclear, it seems that projects already in active production remained at Spelling, such as the feature film *Stephen King's Thinner* (Holland, 1996, distributed by Paramount with Rubinstein and Galin staying on as producers). Projects in earlier stages of development left with the Laurel partners. Ownership of syndicated television shows *Monsters* and *Tales from the Darkside* stayed with Viacom in an agreement that gave Rubinstein and Galin the exclusive rights to future projects with Stephen King.[133]

As Laurel shut down, Rubinstein and Galin entered into a production deal with ABC to once again produce MFTs and miniseries programming. ABC gave the partners overhead money to open new offices and to hire a scaled-back workforce of only a few full-time assistants. Under the terms of the agreement, production was more prescribed and some decision-making needed approval from their patron.[134] On 20 March 1995, the partnership formalised as New Amsterdam Entertainment, Inc., named after New York's original moniker. Production began on the MFT *Kiss and Tell* (Wolk) soon after, airing on ABC on 15 January 1996. This was followed with a feature film adaptation of Stephen King's *The Night Flier* (Pavia, 1997), distributed by New Line. In 2000, New Amsterdam produced miniseries adaptations of Frank Herbert's *Dune*, directed by John Harrison, and its sequel *Children of Dune* (Yaitanes, 2003) for the Sci-Fi Channel. As before, feature films remained an aside and Rubinstein told *Variety* that event television would 'continue to be a cornerstone of New Amsterdam'.[135] Such was the consistency between Laurel and New Amsterdam's output that writer Frederick C. Szebin thought that Laurel had simply changed its name.[136]

From a macro-industrial viewpoint, closure of Laurel's offices was simply a by-product of the widespread M&A consolidations of the 1980s and 1990s. The 1990s wave of stock-swap transactions had made Paramount an obtainable goal for Viacom, yet competition with rival corporations raised the price and resulted in 'surprise' partnerships[137] that Redstone and Viacom's board of directors might otherwise have not considered. In Viacom's acquisition of Blockbuster, the latter firm's subsidiaries were barely, if at all, acknowledged and as the Viacom–Paramount media empire arose, numerous internal SMEs were rendered inconsequential. At a micro-industrial level, Laurel's merger with Spelling initially provided security in a hostile independent landscape, only to later negate the firm's agency in determining its own system of internal governance. After Romero's exit, Rubinstein had to navigate a series of potentially fatal corporate changes, his skill evident in Laurel's consequent growth and the speed and consistency in which a second production company emerged when Laurel's survival proved untenable. Indeed, New Amsterdam continued to operate, in some capacity, into the twenty-first century, and Rubinstein never let go of his hard-fought independence.

Conclusion

This chapter has provided a rare glimpse into M&A from the perspective of a small or medium enterprise, nuancing an understanding of such activities in the entertainment industry. Economists and media industry theorists have long been attentive to the importance of sameness between firms when it comes to industry synergy. This ground-level exploration elaborates on this reading to argue that successful mergers can instigate a more pronounced mirroring between firms, where collated resources and knowhow result in the acquired firm taking on key characteristics of its parent – in the process, narrowing differentiation and altering its corporate identity. Laurel's 1994 miniseries *The Stand* can be seen as an artistic manifestation of this transitory identity. Additionally, we have seen how analysis can benefit from the key distinctions between M&A waves already identified by business scholars, in this case those that altered the global business landscape in the 1980s and 1990s. Accepting that there are important overlaps, this was far from one continuous wave and the switch from cash to stock payments resulted in 'surprise' mergers that had a lasting impact on the industry at large. Ironically for Laurel, after over twenty years as an independent SME, it was closer ties to the mainstream industry that finally proved the firm's undoing.

Notes

1. Weiskind, 1984.
2. Lubatkin, 1983, p. 218.
3. Laurel Entmt., 1986, p. 9.
4. Axl and Jscott, 2013.
5. Jones, 1990, p. 19.
6. Canby, 1989.

7. Rubinstein, 1989.
8. Harrington, 1987.
9. Quoted in Nikolic, 2017, p. 3.
10. Ball, interview with the author, 25 January 2016; Galin, interview with the author, 23 May 2018.
11. Canby, 1989.
12. Harrison, interview with the author, 22 March 2018.
13. Martin, 2004, p. 96.
14. Rutenberg, 2000.
15. Laurel Entmt., 1986, pp. 15–16.
16. 'Executives in Turnaround', 1987.
17. Laurel Entmt., 1987b, pp. 11, 24–5.
18. Farber, 1986.
19. Laurel Entmt., 1986, p. F-19.
20. Anderson, 1987.
21. Teitler, interview with the author, 21 April 2018.
22. Ibid.
23. Gitlin, 1994, p. 57; One of television's most famous syndicated shows is NBC's *Seinfeld* (1989–1998), which has earned over $3 billion in syndication revenues, see Horton, 2019.
24. Spelling Entmt., 1989a, p. 10.
25. Ulin, 2019, p. 262.
26. Teitler, interview with the author, 21 April 2018.
27. Ulin, 2019, p. 262.
28. Laurel Entmt., 1987b, p. 4; Harrison, interview with the author, 22 March 2018.
29. Galin, interview with the author, 23 May 2018.
30. Laurel Entmt., 1988, p. 4.
31. Laurel Entmt., 1987b, p. 12.
32. Laurel Entmt., 1986, p. 4.
33. Ibid., p. F-19.
34. Laurel Entmt., 1987a, p. 5.
35. Laurel Entmt., 1986, pp. 10–11.
36. Vogel, 2020, p. 141.
37. Kelly, 2006.
38. Aaron Spelling Prod., 1989, p. 77.
39. Laurel Entmt., 1986, p. 4.
40. Vogel, 2020, p. 97.
41. Forbes and Pierce, 1994, p. 43.
42. Prince, 2002, pp. 71–2.
43. Fabrikant, 1987, p. L37.
44. Put simply, Chapter 11 allows a debtor to reorganise and come up with a plan to repay its creditors.
45. Aaron Spelling Prod., 1989, pp. 25–6.
46. Laurel Entmt., 1988, pp. 13–14.
47. Bruner, 2004, p. 848.

48. Companies are often coy about publicising their desire to become an acquisition target, particularly in the independent sector where ideas of autonomy and authenticity are central. See the recent 'will they, won't they' courtship between indie production company A24 and Apple in Lang, 2018 and Marotta, 2018.
49. Sharkey and Freeman, 1998, p. 20.
50. Schatz, 2008, p. 22.
51. Micklethwait, 1989, p. 4.
52. Gold, 1989.
53. Kolev, Haleblian and McNamara, 2012, p. 23.
54. Shleifer and Vishny, 1991, p. 53.
55. Lubatkin, 1987, p. 40.
56. Lubatkin, 1983, p. 218.
57. Prince, 2002, p. 60.
58. Schatz, 2008, p. 18.
59. Altman, 2015.
60. Micklethwait, 1989, p. 6.
61. Heritage Entmt., 1989, p. 32.
62. Aaron Spelling Prod., 1989, p. ix; a proxy statement (Form DEF 14A) is a mandatory SEC document that all public firms must file before a shareholder vote. It bestows comprehensive information on the topic at hand, be it a change of the board of directors or a proposed M&A.
63. Spelling Entmt., 1990, p. 2.
64. Rundle, 1988.
65. Littleton, 1998, p. 54.
66. Cohn, 1989.
67. Segal, 1988, p. 26.
68. Spelling Entmt., 1989c, p. 5.
69. Spelling Entmt., 1989b, pp. 5–6.
70. Newman, 2009, p. 34.
71. Ibid., p. 17.
72. Aaron Spelling Prod., 1989, p. 29.
73. Cohn, 1989.
74. Galin, interview with the author, 23 May 2018.
75. Spelling Entmt., 1989a, pp. 12, 13.
76. Spelling Entmt., 1990, p. 9.
77. 'Spelling Ent. Forms Intl.', 1990, p. 50.
78. Galin, interview with the author, 23 May 2018.
79. Lotz, 2014, pp. 25, 26.
80. Wood, 1994, p. 20.
81. Laurel Entmt., 1988, p. 7.
82. Wood, 1991, p. 29, original emphasis.
83. Applebome, 1991, p. H25.
84. Warren, 1994a, p. 30, original emphasis.
85. Goldman, 1994.
86. Galin, interview with the author, 23 May 2018.

87. McClellan, 1993.
88. Spelling Entmt., 1992, p. 7.
89. In interviews, King frequently derided what he called 'Standards and Practices bullshit', claiming *The Stand* pushed as far as it could against the network censorship mandates of the day. See Warren, 1994, p. 42. However, the show was very much part of a wider industry drive to meet modern sensibilities and to compete with cable television. This was led by adult-minded programmes such as Fox's *Married ... With Children* (1987–1997) and ABC's *NYPD Blue* (1993–2005). See Kolbert, 1993, pp. H1, 31.
90. King, 1978, p. 347, original emphasis.
91. Ibid., p. 532; In one passage from the novel, the Boulder-Free democratic committee is accused of being 'the old way' and the old ways, we are told, are Flagg's ways. Ibid., p. 698. Yet this committee, and the people behind it, are ultimately a force for good in rebuilding a new America.
92. Spelling Entmt., 1990, p. 9.
93. Spelling Entmt., 1991, p. 4.
94. Loynd, 1993.
95. Galin, interview with the author, 23 May 2018.
96. Spelling Entmt., 1990, p. 8.
97. Ibid., p. 8.
98. De Bernardis and Giustiniano, 2015, p. 351. Simplified, the organisational identity of a firm comprises the 'central and enduring attributes' that make a firm or organisation distinct from its competitors. See Whetten, 2006, p. 220.
99. Amburgey and Miner, 1992, p. 335.
100. Singh and Montgomery, 1987, p. 378.
101. See Tzioumakis, 2013b, p. 64; Wyatt, 1998, p. 84.
102. Wyatt, 1998, p. 84.
103. Perren, 2012, pp. 91–2.
104. Ibid., p. 92.
105. Eller, 1993, p. B9.
106. Perren, 2012, p. 104.
107. De Bernardis and Giustiniano, 2015, pp. 336–7.
108. Cohn, 1989.
109. See Spelling Entmt., 1989a, p. 33; Spelling Entmt., 1990, p. 12.
110. Finke, 1989, p. 3.
111. Drew, 1990, p. 26.
112. Ibid., p. 28.
113. Thomas, 1995.
114. Heimann, 1992.
115. Spelling Entmt., 1993, p. 2.
116. Arnold, 2005, p. 46; even then there were warning signs that the video rental market might not last forever. Of particular concern was emergent video-on-demand (VOD) technologies that would later have a dramatic impact on Blockbuster's future and that of the industry at large. See Torres, 1991; Brown, 1993.
117. Grossman and Stern, 1993.

118. Schatz, 2008, pp. 26–7.
119. Kolev et al., 2012, p. 25. Their chapter offers more information on how these five waves are characteristically differentiated.
120. Rappaport and Sirower, 1999, pp. 147–8.
121. Quint, 1993.
122. Rappaport and Sirower, 1999, p. 154.
123. Fabrikant, 1994, p. D1.
124. Furlow, 2009, p. 534.
125. Noglows, 1994, p. 11.
126. Bart, 1994.
127. See Hofmeister, 1995, pp. D1, D5.
128. Hofmeister, 1998.
129. Goldman, 1994.
130. Galin, interview with the author, 23 May 2018.
131. Ibid.; Dubensky, interview with the author, 16 June 2016.
132. Galin, interview with the author, 23 May 2018.
133. Ibid.
134. Ibid.
135. 'New Amsterdam Riding New Dawn', 1996.
136. Szebin, 1996, p. 31.
137. Lippman and Bates, 1994.

EPILOGUE: LIFE AFTER DEATH

In order to make sense of current media industry practices and future directions, Paul McDonald argues that researchers must 'contextualise these contemporary phenomena, recognizing how the signs of continuity and change witnessed in the media industries of today arise from complex and contested histories'.[1] By engaging with a media industry studies framework that scrutinises past developments and contexts, we gain a greater historical understanding of American film production away from the established bicoastal centres. Laurel Entertainment, Inc. may have been neglected from previous critical accounts, but a close analysis of the firm across four decades reveals the complex interplay of creative and economic concerns that exist for independent practitioners. Though independent cinema is frequently distilled as 'the province of the auteur',[2] this work has shown the numerous factors that dictate the production of media goods in this sector, from the marketplace to the relationships between individual stakeholders. Placing Laurel and its methods within the broader history of the American film industry offers a fuller comprehension of decision-making, artistic incentives and business planning away from Hollywood.

But while the previous chapters have demonstrated Laurel's value to our understanding of a heterogeneous American independent cinema landscape, it is also worth taking a moment to note the firm's more direct impact on filmmakers and the industry at large. Indeed, a number of film workers who began with Laurel went on to become leading industry players at varying levels of production. David E. Vogel, for instance, forged a career pathway that took him from Laurel executive to president of the Walt Disney Motion Picture Group. *Day of the Dead* producer Ed Lammi became Executive Vice President of Production for Sony Pictures Television. *Tales from the Darkside*'s William Teitler is now a respected producer on Hollywood blockbusters such as *The Polar Express* (Zemeckis, 2004) and the *Jumanji* franchise (1995–present). Laurel's most famous alumnus (after Romero) is arguably special effects wizard Tom Savini, whose work revolutionised the field in the 1980s. Savini's assistant Greg Nicotero founded Hollywood's go-to special effects company KNB and is an executive producer on hit shows such as AMC's *The Walking Dead* (2010–2022) and Shudder's *Creepshow* revival.

That these figures became embedded in mainstream production only emphasises the difficulty of long-term survival in the independent sector. Others, such as John Harrison, Pasquale Buba and Nicholas Mastandrea, endeavoured to freelance between sectors as opportunities arise, while the work of collaborators such as Christine Forrest Romero became less frequent (though she was recently announced as a producer on Lynne Ramsay's Stephen King adaptation *The Girl Who Loved Tom Gordon*). Filmmakers Tom Dubensky and Tony Buba, however, remain doggedly committed to independent regional production and have collaborated on important work such as *Struggles in Steel: The Fight for Equal Opportunity* (1996) and *We Are Alive! The Fight to Save Braddock Hospital* (2012). Both Rubinstein's and Romero's search for independent production was also long lasting, but unlike Dubensky and Buba they eventually left Pittsburgh behind. For Romero, his partnership with Peter Grunwald at Romero-Grunwald Productions took him to Toronto, where he permanently relocated and directed three more zombie films and the outstanding *Bruiser* (2000). In 2018, he also, posthumously, became a children's author, with the release of his *The Little World of Humongo Bongo*.

Though both Romero and Rubinstein left Pittsburgh, their influence on the city remains. In addition to the above-the-line film workers mentioned above, Tony Buba credits Laurel (alongside public broadcaster WQED) with developing a base of professional crew members in Pittsburgh.[3] In 1990, the newly formed Pittsburgh Film Office (PFO) began a proactive bid to attract 'runaway' Hollywood productions into the area, becoming an industry leader thanks to Pennsylvania's film tax credits and the region's already established talent base. Films such as *The Dark Knight Rises* (Nolan, 2012), *Fences* (Washington, 2016) and *Ma Rainey's Black Bottom* (Wolfe, 2020) have taken advantage of these benefits over the last decade. PFO director Dawn Keezer claims the office has brought in approximately $1.5 billion to the local economy, with film producers always remarking upon the 'depth' of Pittsburgh's crew.[4] Like Buba, Keezer attributes this depth to the seeds planted by George Romero and *Night of The Living Dead*.[5]

Laurel can, of course, take a lot of the credit for cultivating this talent base, even if the firm's contribution remains overshadowed by Romero and the production of his (in)famous first feature. In this sense, Laurel was the victim of its own success in building a brand around George A. Romero. But as noted, 'George A. Romero's independent cinema' really denotes a collective rather than an individual, something I'm sure the ever-modest Romero would have readily agreed with. And though Rubinstein was quick to take Laurel out of the region after Romero's departure in 1985, he remained committed to supporting up-and-coming filmmakers. In the early 1990s, Rubinstein launched the Laurel Entertainment Award for Screenwriting Excellence in association with film schools at Columbia University and NYU Tisch School of the Arts. While the award may have been somewhat self-interested on Laurel's part (allowing the firm to cultivate low-cost contacts with promising new talent), winners Jeffrey Stanley and Andrew Stein both acknowledge it bolstered their career prospects. Stein claims the announcement of the award in the trade papers helped him attract an agent, and he also went on to work at Laurel as a script reader.[6]

Laurel and Romero's influence can also be seen on regional practitioners across the US. In Austin, Texas, Robert Rodriguez and his producer-partner Elizabeth Avellán initiated the full-service film facility Troublemaker Studios, a firm that mirrors Laurel in a number of ways. Troublemaker owns its own studio space; it has benefited from partnerships with major independent distributors (like Laurel with UFDC, Troublemaker entered into a multi-picture deal with Miramax in 1998); and the firm has frequently expanded beyond its founder-auteur to accommodate additional filmmakers and ancillary products. Rodriguez claims that the independent production of *Night of the Living Dead* inspired his decision to eschew Hollywood for a 'community of likeminded filmmakers who can come up with a whole other process using less money and more imagination'.[7]

Glass Eye Pix is a New York-based production company founded by writer-director Larry Fessenden and, like Rodriguez, Fessenden cites *Night of the Living Dead* as a kind of spiritual guide.[8] Glass Eye Pix began as little more than a brand for Fessenden's own directorial efforts (such as the *Martin*-inspired vampire film *Habit* in 1995) but has now expanded, in the words of Greg Newman at distribution partner MPI Media Group, to fill 'a niche market for the elevated, smart genre film'.[9] Glass Eye Pix and its low-budget production arm ScareFlix have produced early work by Kelly Reichardt and Ti West, as well as breakthrough genre films such as *Stake Land* (Mickle, 2010). To date, Glass Eye Pix is a privately run enterprise, keeping budgets for each project between $300,000 to $1 million by drawing monies from a diverse array of sources. This includes MPI, equity investors, profits from previous releases and self-financing. These monies have allowed the firm to retain a small staff, yet Fessenden admits that he has been the 'primary benefactor of Glass Eye Pix over the years, which makes it an unsustainable enterprise'.[10]

Despite the long-term uncertainty of Fessenden's 'no-budget model',[11] it is shared by a number of filmmakers who resist the traditional 'graduation process' that is said to take indie filmmakers into the so-called adult world of big-budget, star-driven studio productions. Glass Eye Pix's partner on *Depraved* (Fessenden, 2019) was Forager Film, a Chicago-based production company founded by acclaimed filmmaker Joe Swanberg, Eddie Linker and Peter Gilbert. According to Forager collaborator Alex Ross Perry, Swanberg's firm demonstrates 'that the golden rule of filmmaking career trajectory – "always move onwards and upwards" – was outdated and of no use to those of us who had come up together through films with budgets that barely reached five figures'.[12] Whether this can be sustained long term, or if, like a number of Laurel's high-profile alumni, the assurances of mainstream production will prove too enticing, remains to be seen.

In the meantime, as in the early days of Latent Image, Forager has kept costs down by destabilising traditional job divisions and utilising a more egalitarian production strategy. This approach manifested in Swanberg's shared directorial credits on *Nights and Weekends* (2008, with Greta Gerwig) and *Autoerotic* (2011, with Adam Wingard).[13] Baltimore-based filmmaker Matthew Porterfield has also experimented with egalitarian production, and on films like *Putty Hill* (2010) rejected 'the division of labor and totalitarian authorship characteristic of most film productions, even those made on the smallest scale, still beholden to a model developed off the Pacific coast and commodified in the dead shadows of Manhattan'. If Porterfield felt this represented a 'fresh approach to American regional cinema', it had the virtue of already being tested in Pittsburgh a few decades earlier.[14]

Laurel's overall influence on these firms and filmmakers is hard to measure. Each, in their own ways, recall Laurel's pragmatic and ideological concepts regarding independent cinema, balancing auteur filmmaking with low-cost genre product and innovative production practices to achieve corporate success. As mentioned in the introduction, we must be careful when making broad claims about the organisational behaviour of similar or competing SMEs. The internal corporate activities of a firm are based on a series of mitigating factors, including intent, opportunity structures, business orientation and attitudes towards risk. This case study on Laurel Entertainment sheds light on the nature of these mitigating factors, but how these factors change across time, and how individual firms across the industry react to them, is impossible to infer without closer inspection of their infrastructure. Indeed, the value of this work is in its transportable multimethod approach. By drawing upon business and economic theory, this work has presented a new paradigm with which to undertake an investigation into film production practices in the United States and more widely. Applying this methodology to contemporary non-Hollywood production companies such as Troublemaker, Glass Eye Pix, Forager Film, or even larger-scale indies such as Blumhouse Productions may take us in exciting, and entirely unexpected new directions.

EPILOGUE

As for a final word on Laurel? Well, as an interesting postscript, though its offices closed in the mid-1990s and production has long ceased, the firm has not quite been buried. After Viacom acquired the CBS Corporation in 1999, and then split with it in 2006, the divorce package passed a large portion of Viacom's television library assets to CBS. Since Laurel was now identified as a TV company,[15] the firm ended up at CBS as part of this deal. CBS subsequently released the entire *Tales from the Darkside* series on DVD and in 2015 went as far as to commission a new pilot overseen by Stephen King's son Joe Hill. As noted, CBS was also behind the recent remake of *The Stand*. In December 2019, a new period of entertainment industry M&A activity saw Viacom and CBS reattach as ViacomCBS. Laurel Entertainment (now an LLC without a registered staff) was itemised as one of ViacomCBS's 1,098 domestic and international subsidiaries. This list includes companies both active and dormant and Spelling Entertainment is also accounted for here.[16] If the analogy were not so pointed, it would be tempting to say that Laurel, after leading a long and varied life, now counts itself as one of the undead – long deceased, but somehow still living.

NOTES

1. McDonald, 2018, p. 2.
2. Schatz, 2009, p. 50.
3. Buba, interview with the author, 16 June 2016.
4. Sheridan, 2020; Berk, 2019. The impact of this interaction between a non-profit film office, public television and an independent production company is intriguing, suggesting a rich area of analysis for future research into regional filmmaking.
5. Berk, 2019.
6. Stanley, interview with the author, 12 January 2021; Stein, interview with the author, 12 January 2021.
7. Interviewed in *Light in the Darkness*, 2018.
8. The documentary *Birth of the Living Dead* (Kuhns, 2013) celebrates the making-of and cultural impact of *Night* and was executive produced by Glass Eye Pix.
9. Kohn, 2011.
10. Wissot, 2009.
11. Kohn, 2011.
12. Kohn, 2016.
13. For their part, Gerwig and Wingard seem more intent on becoming major Hollywood players. Gerwig parlayed Academy Award nominations for her films *Lady Bird* (2017) and *Little Women* (2019) into a job directing the live action adaptation of *Barbie* for Sony and toy manufacturer Mattel. Wingard is the director of Warner's shared universe epic *Godzilla vs. Kong* (2021).
14. Porterfield quoted in Hope, 2010.
15. Galin, interview with the author, 23 May 2018.
16. ViacomCBS Inc., 2020.

LAUREL MEDIOGRAPHY

Includes work produced by parent company Latent Image and successor New Amsterdam Entertainment.

Latent Image

1968	*Night of the Living Dead*, film, directed by George A. Romero. USA: Image Ten/Continental Distributing.
1971	*There's Always Vanilla*, film, directed by George A. Romero. USA: Cambist Films.
1972	*Jack's Wife*, film, directed by George A. Romero. USA: Jack H. Harris Enterprises.
1973	*The Crazies*, film, directed by George A. Romero. USA: Cambist Films.

Laurel Tape & Film

1973	*The Amusement Park*, educational film, directed by George A. Romero. USA: Film Emporium.
1973–1975	*The Winners*, television series, created by Richard P. Rubinstein and George A. Romero. USA: Laurel Tape & Film.
1976	*Magic at the Roxy*, television special, directed by Mark Gargiulo. USA: ABC.

Laurel/The Laurel Group

1977	*Martin*, film, directed by George A. Romero. USA: Libra Films.
1978	*Dawn of the Dead*, film, directed by George A. Romero. USA/IT: UFDC.
1981	*Knightriders*, film, directed by George A. Romero. USA: UFDC.

Laurel Entertainment

1982	*Creepshow*, film, directed by George A. Romero. USA: Warner Bros.
1983–1988	*Tales from the Darkside*, television series, produced by William Teitler and T. J. Castronovo. USA: LBS Communications.
1985	*Day of the Dead*, film, directed by George A. Romero. USA: UFDC.
1987	*Creepshow 2*, film, directed by Michael Gornick. USA: New World Pictures.
1988–1991	*Monsters*, television series, created by Richard P. Rubinstein and Mitchell Galin. USA: Tribune Entertainment.
1989	*Pet Sematary*, film, directed by Mary Lambert. USA: Paramount Pictures.
1990	*Tales from the Darkside: The Movie*, film, directed by John Harrison. USA: Paramount Pictures.
1991	*Golden Years*, television series, created by Stephen King. USA: Worldvision Enterprises, Inc./CBS.
1991	*The Secrets of Dick Smith*, video documentary, directed by Anne Lieres. USA: Laurel Productions/Worldvision Enterprises, Inc.
1994	*Stephen King's The Stand*, television miniseries, directed by Mick Garris. USA: Worldvision Enterprises, Inc./ABC.
1994	*The Vernon Johns Story*, movie for television, directed by Kenneth Fink. USA: Worldvision Enterprises, Inc./WGN.
1995	*Precious Victims*, movie for television, directed by Peter Levin. USA: Worldvision Enterprises, Inc./CBS.
1995	*Stephen King's The Langoliers*, miniseries, executive producers Richard P. Rubinstein and Mitchell Galin. USA: Worldvision Enterprises, Inc./ABC.

Spelling Entertainment

1996	*A Season in Purgatory*, miniseries, directed by David Greene. USA: CBS.
1996	*Stephen King's Thinner*, film, directed by Tom Holland. USA: Paramount Pictures.

New Amsterdam Entertainment

1996 *Kiss and Tell*, movie for television, directed by Andy Wolk. USA: ABC.
1997 *The Night Flier*, film, directed by Mark Pavia. USA: New Line Cinema.
2000 *Dune*, miniseries, directed by John Harrison. USA: The Sci-Fi Channel.
2003 *Children of Dune*, miniseries, directed by Greg Yaitanes. USA: The Sci-Fi Channel.
2004 *Dawn of the Dead*, film, directed by Zack Snyder: Universal Pictures.
2008 *Giving it Up*, documentary, directed by Frank Ruy. USA: Fleit/Daw/Ruy.

BIBLIOGRAPHY

Aaron Spelling Productions, Inc. (1989), *Proxy Statement*, 20 January, Washington, DC: Securities and Exchange Commission.

Abor, Joshua and Charles K. D. Adjasi (2007), 'Corporate Governance and the Small and Medium Enterprises Sector: Theory and Implications', *Corporate Governance*, 7: 2, pp. 111–22.

Abrams, Simon (2015), 'Roger Corman on Losing *Easy Rider*, Polling *Sharktopus* Fans, and the Future of Indie Film', *Vulture*, online, 27 August, <https://www.vulture.com/2015/08/roger-corman-sharktopus-easy-rider.html> (accessed 15 November 2020).

Affair of the Heart: The Making of There's Always Vanilla (2017), Blu Ray bonus material, produced by Michael Felsher, [Blu Ray], UK: Arrow Video.

Alexander, Chris (2010), 'Romero on Romero', *Fangoria*, 293, May, pp. 46–7.

Alkire, Sabina (2008), 'Concepts and Measures of Agency', *OPHI Working Paper 9*, University of Oxford, online, January, pp. 1–23 <https://ophi.org.uk/working-paper-number-09> (accessed 11 December 2020).

Allan, William (1964), 'Pittsburgh On Location for Moviemen: Latent Image Certain Industry Can Grow Here', *The Pittsburgh Press*, 2 March, p. 16.

Allan, William (1965), 'Film Firm Gets Loan, Plans Movie', *The Pittsburgh Press*, 11 April, p. 9.

Allen, Michael (2003), *Contemporary US Cinema*, Harlow: Longman.

Allen, Tom (1979), 'Knight of the Living Dead', *The Village Voice*, 23 April, pp. 1, 44–6.

Alsop, Ruth, Mette Bertelsen and Jeremy Holland (2006), *Empowerment in Practice: From Analysis to Implementation*, Washington, DC: The World Bank.

Altman, Ian (2015), 'How to Attract a Merger, or Acquisition', *Forbes*, online, 14 July, <https://www.forbes.com/sites/ianaltman/2015/07/14/how-to-attract-a-merger-or-acquisition/#67e0e760630b> (accessed 27 November 2020).

Altman, Rick (1999), *Film/Genre*, London: British Film Institute.

Alvey, Mark (1997), 'The Independents: Rethinking the Television Studio System', in Lynn Spigel and Michael Curtin (eds), *The Revolution Wasn't Televised: Sixties Television and Social Conflict*, New York: Routledge, pp. 139–60.

Amburgey, Terry L. and Anne S. Miner (1992), 'Strategic Momentum: The Effects of Repetitive, Positional, and Contextual Momentum on Merger Activity', *Strategic Management Journal*, 13: 5, pp. 335–48.

Anderson, George (1977), 'Romero's "*Martin*" in the Black Already', *Pittsburgh Post-Gazette*, 13 July, p. 14.

Anderson, George (1979), 'The Triangle Tattler', *Pittsburgh Post-Gazette*, 5 February, p. 16.

Anderson, George (1987), 'The Tattler: Strong Films Make for Hot Summer at Theaters', *Pittsburgh Post-Gazette*, 24 June, p. 30.

Argento, Dario (1996), 'Murder in the Dark', *Sight & Sound*, 6: 9, September, p. 61.

Applebome, Peter (1991), 'TV Gets a New Poltergeist: Stephen King', *New York Times*, 14 July, pp. H25, H32.

Arnold, Thomas K. (2005), 'Blockbuster's 20-Year Odyssey', *Home Media Retailing*, 27: 26, pp. 1, 14, 46.

Auty, Chris (1979), 'The Haunting of Middle America', *Time Out*, 30 November-6 December, pp. 28–9.

Axl and Jscott (2013), 'Episode 139 – Mike Gornick Interview', *Profondo Cinema*, online, 20 March <http://profondo-cinema.blogspot.com/2013/03/episode-139-mike-gornck-interview.html> (accessed 28 October 2016).

Bach, Stephen (1986), *Final Cut: Dreams and Disaster in the Making of Heaven's Gate*, London: Faber and Faber.

Badley, Linda, Claire Perkins and Michele Schreiber (eds) (2016), *Indie Reframed: Women's Filmmaking and Contemporary American Independent Cinema*, Edinburgh: Edinburgh University Press.

Balio, Tino (2009), *United Artists: The Company That Changed the Film Industry Volume 2, 1951–1978*, Madison: University of Wisconsin Press.

Ball, David (2016), Interview with the author, 25 January.

Banks, Mark, Andy Lovatt, Justin O'Connor and Carlo Raffo (2000), 'Risk and Trust in the Cultural Industries', *Geoforum*, 31: 4, pp. 453–64.

Barker, Chris and Emma A. Jane (2016), *Cultural Studies: Theory and Practice*, 5th edn, London: SAGE Publications.

Bart, Peter (1994), 'With Par Score, Redstone Barges into "The Club"', *Variety*, online, 17 February <https://variety.com/1994/voices/columns/with-par-score-redstone-barges-into-the-club-1117859445> (accessed 27 November 2020).

Beard, Steve (1993), 'No Particular Place to Go', *Sight & Sound*, 3: 4, April, pp. 30–1.

Becker, Gary S. (1962), 'Investment in Human Capital: A Theoretical Analysis', *Journal of Political Economy*, 70: 5, Pt. 2, pp. 9–49.

Belton, John (1994), *American Cinema/American Culture*, New York: McGraw-Hill.

Benson-Allott, Caetlin (2013), *Killer Tapes and Shattered Screens: Video Spectatorship From VHS to File Sharing*, Berkeley: University of California Press.

Bennyx (2016), 'Dario Argento and Nicolas Winding Refn – *Dawn of the Dead* – [*Zombi*, 1978] – George A. Romero', *YouTube*, online, 13 September <https://www.youtube.com/watch?v=tDMWyVXZ8tk> (accessed 19 May 2020).

Berk, Nancy (2019), 'Mister Rogers' Real Life Neighborhood Committed to the Film Business', *Forbes*, online, 24 July <https://www.forbes.com/sites/nancyberk/2019/07/24/mister-rogers-real-life-neighborhood-committed-to-the-film-business/?sh=1a0d638ace65> (accessed 7 January 2021).

Bernardini, Craig (2010), 'Auteurdämmerung: David Cronenberg, George A. Romero, and the Twilight of the (North) American Horror Auteur', in Steffen Hantke (ed.), *American Horror Film: The Genre at the Turn of the Millennium*, Jackson: University Press of Mississippi, pp. 161–92.

Bernardoni, James (1991), *The New Hollywood: What the Movies Did with the New Freedoms of the Seventies*, Jefferson: McFarland and Company.

Bharadwaji, Sundar G. and Anil Menon (1993), 'Determinants of Success in Service Industries: A PIMS-Based Empirical Investigation', *Journal of Services Marketing*, 7: 4, pp. 19–40.

Biodrowski, Steve (2007), '*Dawn of the Dead* (1979) – A Retrospective', *Cinefantastique*, online, 2 October <http://archive.is/NoA2#selection-709.4-709.44> (accessed 3 June 2020).

Birth of the Living Dead (2013), documentary, directed by Rob Kuhns, [DVD], USA: First Run Features.

Blackford, James (2014), 'The Interview: George A. Romero', *Sight & Sound*, 24: 2, February, pp. 50–4.

Blank, Edward L. (1976), 'Tax Reforms Threat to Local Film Production', *The Pittsburgh Press*, 13 September, p. 8.

Blank, Edward L. (1977), 'Thrilling *Martin* His Type of Film', *The Pittsburgh Press*, 18 September, p. 134.

Blank, Edward L. (1979), 'Romero Turns from "*Dawn*" to "*Knights*"', *The Pittsburgh Press*, 25 July, p. 53.

Blank, Edward L. (1980), 'No Horsing Around for These Knights', *The Pittsburgh Press*, 27 July, pp. 8–10.

Block, Alex B. (1972), 'Filming *Night of the Living Dead*', *Filmmakers Newsletter*, 5: 3, January, pp. 20–4.

Block, Alex B. (2012), 'The Real Force Behind "*Star Wars*": How George Lucas Built an Empire', *The Hollywood Reporter*, online, 9 February <https://www.hollywoodreporter.com/news/george-lucas-star-wars-288513> (accessed 22 November 2020).

Blythe, Jim (2014), *Principles and Practice of Marketing*, 3rd edn, London: SAGE Publications.

Boddy, William (1993), *Fifties Television: The Industry and its Critics*, Urbana: University of Illinois Press.

Bordwell, David (2002), 'Intensified Continuity: Visual Style in Contemporary American Film', *Film Quarterly*, 55: 3, pp. 16–28.

Bosiok, Delia (2013), 'Leadership Styles and Creativity', *Online Journal of Applied Knowledge Management*, online, 1: 2, pp. 64–77 <http://www.iiakm.org/ojakm/articles/2013/volume1_2/OJAKM_Volume1_2pp64-77.pdf> (accessed 11 November 2020).

Botti, Simona (2000), 'What Role for Marketing in the Arts? An Analysis of Arts Consumption and Artistic Value', *International Journal of Arts Management*, 2: 3, Spring, pp. 14–27.

Bourdieu, Pierre (2008), 'Introduction to Distinction', in Ernest Mathijs and Xavier Mendik (eds), *The Cult Film Reader*, Maidenhead: Open University Press, pp. 386–91.

Boyle, Charles E. (2001), 'Hollywood and the Insurance Industry', *Insurance Journal*, online, 10 September <https://www.insurancejournal.com/magazines/magfeatures/2001/09/10/21957.htm> (accessed 10 December 2020).

Bradley, John F. (1973), 'Notice of Incorporation: Laurel Productions of Pennsylvania', *Pittsburgh Post-Gazette*, 16 October, p. 24.

Bragg, Steven M. (2009), *Running a Public Company: From IPO to SEC Reporting*, Hoboken: John Wiley & Sons.

Braithwaite, John (2005), *Markets in Vice, Markets in Virtue*, Annandale, NSW: The Federation Press.

Beaupre, Lee (1977), 'How to Distribute a Film', *Film Comment*, 13: 4, p. 50.

Brown, Colin (1993), 'Chain Reaction', *Screen International*, 12–18 March, p. 1.

Bruner, Robert F. (2004), *Applied Mergers and Acquisitions*, Hoboken: John Wiley & Sons.

Brunetta, Gian Piero (2009), *The History of Italian Cinema: A Guide to Italian Films from its Origins to the Twenty-First Century*, Princeton: Princeton University Press.

Buba, Tony (2016), Interview with the author, 16 June.

Buckingham, David (2009), 'A Commonplace Art? Understanding Amateur Media Production', in Buckingham and Rebekah Willet (eds), *Video Cultures: Media Technology and Everyday Creativity*, New York: Palgrave Macmillan, pp. 23–50.

Burke-Block, Candace (1981), 'The Film Journal Interviews: George A. Romero on "Knightriders"', *Film Journal*, 84: 4, May, p. 25.

Burlingame, Russ (2014), 'Celebrated Iron Man Writer Bob Layton Shares Plans for a George Romero/Marvel Collaboration in the '80s', *comicbook*, online, 12 August <https://comicbook.com /blog/2014/08/13/NA> (accessed 15 December 2020).

Butler, Jeremy G. (2010), *Television Style*, New York: Routledge.

Caldwell, John Thornton (2008), *Production Culture: Industrial Reflexivity and Critical Practice in Film and Television*, Durham, NC: Duke University Press.

Canby, Vincent (1989), 'A Cat and a Toddler Give Reincarnation a Bad Name', *New York Times*, 22 April, p. 16.

Cannon Group, Inc. (1983), 'The Cannon Group, Inc. is Flying High with Golan-Globus 1983–84 Productions' [advertisement], *Variety 26th International Film Annual for Cannes 1983*, 4 May, pp. 17–59.

Capcom Co., Ltd., et al. v. The MKR Group, Inc. (2008), No. C 08-0904 RS, USDC N. D. California, *Loeb & Loeb LLP*, online 20 October <https://www.loeb.com/en/insights/publications/2008/10/capcom-co-ltd-et-al-v-the-mkr-group-inc> (accessed 28 December 2020).

Carney, Ray (1990), *Cassavetes on Cassavetes*, London: Faber & Faber.
Cart (1981), 'Film Reviews: *Knightriders*', *Variety*, 8 April, p. 20.
Chaillet, Jean-Paul and Elizabeth Vincent (1985), *Francis Ford Coppola*, New York: St Martin's Press.
Christopherson, Susan and Michael Storper (1989), 'The Effects of Flexible Specialization on Industrial Politics and the Labor Market: The Motion Picture Industry', *ILR Review*, 42: 3, pp. 331–47.
Chute, David (1983), 'Outlaw Cinema: Its Rise and Fall', *Film Comment*, 19: 5, pp. 9–15.
Chute, David (1986), 'Wages of Sin, II', *Film Comment*, 22: 5, pp. 56–61.
Cohen, Kris R. (n.d.), 'agent/agency', *The Chicago School of Media Theory*, online <https://lucian.uchicago.edu/blogs/mediatheory/keywords/agentagency> (accessed 3 December 2020).
Cohn, Lawrence (1989), 'Laurel Following "*Sematary*" with Another Horror Pic for Par Plus King's "*Stand*"', *Variety*, 15 November, p. 13.
'Companies, Going Public' (2014), *U.S. Securities and Exchange Commission*, 14 October, online <https://www.sec.gov/fast-answers/answers-comppublichtm.html> (accessed 22 November 2020).
Cones, John W. (2013), *Dictionary of Film Finance and Distribution: A Guide for Independent Filmmakers*, New York: Algora Publishing.
Contreras, Brian (2017), 'Adam Lowenstein Makes a Case for Horror Cinema as Racial Dialogue', *The Chautauquan Daily*, online, 10 August <http://chqdaily.com/2017/08/adam-lowenstein-makes-case-horror-cinema-racial-dialogue> (accessed 12 February 2020).
Cook, David A. (2000), *Lost Illusions: American Cinema in the Shadow of Watergate and Vietnam, 1970–1979*, Berkeley: University of California Press.
Cook, Everett (2015), 'Mogul to Mentor', *The Desert Sun*, online, 8 May <https://eu.desertsun.com/story/life/2015/04/29/digicom-film-festival-vogel-mogel-mentor/26559375> (accessed 22 November 2020).
Corman, Roger (2011), 'Working with Young Directors', in Constantine Nasr (ed.), *Roger Corman: Interviews*, Jackson: University Press of Mississippi, pp. 90–3.
Cornwell, Regina (1981), 'Cents and Sensibility, or Funding Without Tears', *American Film*, 6: 10, September, pp. 63–4, 80, 84.
Corrigan, Timothy (1990), 'The Commerce of Auteurism: A Voice Without Authority', *New German Critique*, 49, Winter, pp. 43–57.
Crawford, Travis (2017), *There's Always Vanilla*, audio commentary, [Blu Ray], UK: Arrow Video.
Crawley, Tony (1982a), '*Creepshow*', *Starburst*, 4: 8, pp. 46–50.
Crawley, Tony (1982b), 'Richard P. Rubinstein on Romero', *Starburst*, 4: 6, pp. 36–9.
Curtis, David (1992), 'A Tale of Two Co-Ops', in David E. James (ed.), *To Free the Cinema: Jonas Mekas & the New York Underground*, Princeton: Princeton University Press, pp. 255–65.
Daily, Catherine M. and Dan R. Dalton (1992), 'Financial Performance of Founder Managed Versus Professionally Managed Small Corporations', *Journal of Small Business Management*, 30: 2, pp. 25–34.

Daniel, Dennis (1988), 'Savini Speaks: Interview with a Master Illusionist', *Deep Red*, 3, June, pp. 5–18.

David, Peter (2011), 'Stan Lee & Jim Shooter Talk – Marvel Age 1983', *20th Century Danny Boy*, online, 12 November <https://ohdannyboy.blogspot.com/2011/11/stan-lee-jim-shooter-talk-marvel-age.html> (accessed 4 December 2020).

'*Dawn of the Dead* in $1,300,000 Gross at 65 N.Y. Sites' (1979), *Variety*, 9 May, p. 8.

Dawson, Nick (2008), '"A Lot of People Settle for the Vanilla": George A. Romero on *Diary of the Dead*', *Filmmaker Magazine*, online, 15 February <https://filmmakermagazine.com/1303-george-a-romero-diary-of-the-dead/#.X_N82C-Q3EM> (accessed 4 January 2021).

De Bernardis, Luigi and Luca Giustiniano (2015), 'Evolution of Multiple Organisational Identities After an M&A Event: A Case Study from Europe', *Journal of Organizational Change Management*, 28: 3, pp. 333–55.

Decherney, Peter (2005), *Hollywood and the Culture Elite: How the Movies Became American*, New York: Columbia University Press.

Dekker, Julie, Nadine Lybaert, Tensie Steijvers and Benoît Depaire (2015), 'The Effect of Family Business Professionalization as a Multidimensional Construct on Firm Performance', *Journal of Small Business Management*, 53: 2, pp. 516–38.

Dempsey, Michael (1981), 'After the Fall', *American Film*, 6: 10, pp. 52–6.

Desroches, Jocelyn J-Y. and Vijay M. Jog, with collaboration from Ghislain F. Théberge (1991), *Entrepreneurs and Initial Public Offerings: Decision-Process-Impact*, Halifax, Nova Scotia: The Institute for Research on Public Policy.

Digging up the Dead: The Lost Films of George A. Romero (2005), DVD bonus feature, directed by Gary Hertz, [DVD], USA: Anchor Bay Entertainment.

Dillard, R. H. W. (1987), '*Night of the Living Dead*: It's Not Like Just a Wind That's Passing Through', in Gregory A. Waller (ed.), *American Horrors: Essays on the Modern American Horror Film*, Urbana: University of Illinois Press, pp. 14–29.

Dixon, Wheeler Winston (2011), 'The Orson Welles of the Z Picture: An Interview with Roger Corman', in Constantine Nasr (ed.), *Roger Corman: Interviews*, Jackson: University Press of Mississippi, pp. 136–47.

Document of the Dead (1985), documentary, directed by Roy Frumkes, [DVD], USA: The School of Visual Arts/Synapse Films.

Doherty, Thomas (2002), *Teenagers and Teenpics: The Juvenilization of American Movies in the 1950s*, revised and expanded edn, Philadelphia: Temple University Press.

Doyle, Gillian (2013), *Understanding Media Economics*, 2nd edn, London: SAGE.

Drake, Philip (2013), 'Reputational Capital, Creative Conflict and Hollywood Independence: The Case of Hal Ashby', in Geoff King, Claire Molloy and Yannis Tzioumakis (eds), *American Independent Cinema: Indie, Indiewood and Beyond*, Abingdon: Routledge, pp. 140–52.

Drew, Clare L. (1990), 'The Selling of Spelling', *Channels: The Business of Communications*, 10: 7, pp. 26–30.

Drydyk, Jay (2013), 'Empowerment, Agency, and Power', *Journal of Global Ethics*, 9: 3, pp. 249–62.

Dubensky, Tom (2016), Interview with the author, 16 June.

Edgerton, Gary (1986), 'The Film Bureau Phenomenon in America and its Relationship to Independent Filmmaking', *Journal of Film and Video*, 38: 1, pp. 40–8.
Eger, Harvey J. (1975), 'Articles of Amendment', *Pittsburgh Post-Gazette*, 10 January, p. 17.
Ehrich, Thomas Lindley (1970), 'Newest New Wave?: Pittsburgh Makes Bid to be a Movie Center', *Wall Street Journal*, 12 March, pp. 1, 25.
Eisenhardt, Kathleen M. (1989), 'Agency Theory: An Assessment and Review', *The Academy of Management Review*, 14: 1, pp. 57–74.
Eller, Claudia (1993), 'Is Miramax Going the Disney Route? Well, Yes and No', *Los Angeles Times*, 2 September, pp. B8-B9.
'Executives in Turnaround' (1987), *Variety*, 29 July, p. 6.
Fabrikant, Geraldine (1987), 'Small Studios' Tough Season', *New York Times*, 6 July, pp. L37–L38.
Fabrikant, Geraldine (1994), 'Hints of Viacom-Blockbuster Union', *New York Times*, 7 January, pp. D1–D2.
Fallows, Tom (2018), '"More than Rutting Bodies": Cambist Films, Quality Independents, and the "Lost" Films of George A. Romero', *Journal of Popular Film and Television*, 46: 2, pp. 82–94.
Fama, Eugene. F. and Michael C. Jensen (1983), 'Separation of Ownership and Control', *Journal of Law & Economics*, 26: 2, pp. 301–25.
Fanning, Win (1967), 'Nixon Interviewed on Ch. 13 "Journal"', *Pittsburgh Post-Gazette*, 16 November, p. 51.
Fanning, Win (1970), '"A Word from the Sponsor" May Be the Best on the Tube', *Pittsburgh Post-Gazette*, 20 July, p. 31.
Farber, Stephen (1986), 'Success of *"Tales from the Darkside"*', *New York Times*, 9 June, p. C22.
Farber, Stephen and Estelle Changas (1972), 'Putting the Hex on "R" and "X"', *New York Times*, 9 April, pp. D1, D15.
Ferrell, O. C., Geoffrey A. Hirt and Linda Ferrell (2017), *M: Business*, 5th edn, New York: McGraw-Hill Education.
'50 Top-Grossing Films: Week Ending May 2' (1979), *Variety*, 9 May, p. 45.
Filatotchev, Igor, Steve Toms and Mike Wright (2006), 'The Firm's Strategic Dynamics and Corporate Governance Life-Cycle', *International Journal of Managerial Finance*, 2: 4, pp. 256–79.
Fillis, Ian (2006), 'Art for Art's Sake or Art for Business Sake: An Exploration of Artistic Product Orientation', *The Marketing Review*, 6: 1, pp. 29–40.
Final Cut: The Making and Unmaking of Heaven's Gate (2004), documentary, directed by Michael Epstein, USA: Specialty Films.
Finke, Nikki (1989), 'Can Spelling Cast His Spell Again?: Veteran Producer is Searching for the Magic Touch in a New Era', *Los Angeles Times*, 26 March, pp. 3, 82–3.
Fisher, Kieran (2017), 'Fade Out: George Romero, The Father of Modern Horror', *Film School Rejects*, online, 19 July <https://filmschoolrejects.com/george-romero-father-modern-horror> (accessed 13 November 2020).
Fiske, John (1992), 'The Cultural Economy of Fandom', in Lisa A. Lewis (ed.), *The Adoring Audience: Fan Culture and Popular Media*, London: Routledge, pp. 30–49.

Fitch, Alex (2014), 'Crazies, Creeps and Living Dead: Interview with George A. Romero', *Electric Sheep*, online, 30 January <http://www.electricsheepmagazine.co.uk/features/2014/01/30/night-of-the-living-dead-interview-with-george-a-romero> (accessed 23 November 2020).

Flyvbjerg, Bent (2006), 'Five Misunderstandings About Case-Study Research', *Qualitative Inquiry*, 12: 2, April, pp. 219–45

Forbes, Elliot and David Pierce (1994), 'Who Owns the Movies?', *Film Comment*, 30: 6, pp. 43–6, 48–50.

Fox v. Commissioner (1983), 80 T. C. 972, United States Tax Court, *Leagle*, online, 18 May <https://www.leagle.com/decision/1983105280aztc97211001> (accessed 19 May 2020).

Freeman, Matthew (2016), *Industrial Approaches to Media: A Methodological Gateway to Industry Studies*, Bath: Palgrave Macmillan.

Friedan, Betty (1963), *The Feminine Mystique*, New York: W. W. Norton.

Furlow, Clark W. (2009), 'Reflections on the Revlon Doctrine', *University of Pennsylvania Journal of Business Law*, 11: 3, pp. 519–72.

Fyfe, Stew (2008), '*The Crazies* (1973, USA): Average Shot Length Data', *Cinemetrics*, online, 25 February <https://www.cinemetrics.lv/movie.php?movie_ID=1175> (accessed 29 May 2020).

Gabrielsson, Jonas (2007), 'Correlates of Board Empowerment in Small Companies', *Entrepreneurship: Theory and Practice*, 31: 5, pp. 687–711.

Galin, Mitchell (2018), Interview with the author, 23 May.

Gamble, Andrew, Gavin Kelly and John Parkinson (2000), 'Introduction', in Parkinson, Gamble and Kelly (eds), *The Political Economy of the Company*, Oxford: Hart Publishing, pp. 1–20.

Gange, Paul R. (1982), '*Creepshow*: It's an $8 million Comic Book from George Romero & Friends', *Cinefantastique*, 13: 1, pp. 16–35.

Gange, Paul R. (1983), 'Trick or Treat', *Cinefantastique*, 14: 2, p. 14.

Gange, Paul R. (1987), *The Zombies That Ate Pittsburgh: The Films of George A. Romero*, New York: Dodd, Mead and Company.

Gapay, Les (1979), 'An Unauthorized Progress Report on *Heaven's Gate*', *Los Angeles Times*, 2 September, pp. M1, 6–7.

Gastil, John (1994), 'A Definition and Illustration of Democratic Leadership', *Human Relations*, 47: 8, pp. 953–75.

Gates, Richard (2013), *Production Management for Film and Video*, 3rd edn, Burlington: Focal Press.

Gedajlovic, Eric, Michael H. Lubatkin and William S. Schulze (2004), 'Crossing the Threshold from Founder Management to Professional Management: A Governance Perspective', *Journal of Management Studies*, 41: 5, pp. 899–912.

Gelmis, Joseph (1970), *The Film Director as Superstar*, New York: Doubleday.

Ghauri, Pervez, Kjell Grønhaug and Roger Strange (2020), *Research Methods in Business Studies*, 5th edn, Cambridge: Cambridge University Press.

Gibb, Cecil A. (1969), 'Leadership', in Gardner Lindzey and Elliot Aronson (eds), *The Handbook of Social Psychology: Volume Four: Group Psychology and Phenomena of Interaction*, 2nd edn, Reading: Addison-Wesley, pp. 205–82.

Gifford, Sharon (2011), 'Risk and Uncertainty', in Zoltan J. Acs and David B. Audretsch (eds), *Handbook of Entrepreneurship Research: An Interdisciplinary Survey and Introduction*, 2nd edn, New York: Springer, pp. 303–18.
Gitlin, Todd (1994), *Inside Prime Time*, 2nd edn, London: Routledge.
'Glossary: Annual Report' (n.d.), *Investor.gov: U.S. Securities and Exchange Commission*, online <https://www.investor.gov/introduction-investing/investing-basics/glossary/annual-report> (accessed 28 December 2020).
Gold, Richard (1989), 'Sony-CPE Union Reaffirms Changing Order of Intl. Showbiz', *Variety*, 27 September, p. 5.
Goldman, Kevin (1994), 'ABC Will Try to Buck a Trend with a Four-Night Miniseries', *Wall Street Journal*, 2 May, p. B1.
Goldstein, Patrick (1988), 'George Romero: Movies "Are Not Perceived as an Art Form by the Industry"', *Los Angeles Times*, online, 31 July <https://www.latimes.com/entertainment/movies/la-et-mn-george-romero-19880731-story.html> (accessed 4 January 2021).
Goleman, Daniel (2000), 'Leadership That Gets Results', *Harvard Business Review*, 78: 2, March-April, pp. 78–90.
Gomery, Douglas (2004), 'The Hollywood Studio System: 1930–49', in Thomas Schatz (ed.), *Hollywood: Critical Concepts in Media and Cultural Studies, Volume One – Historical Dimensions: The Development of the American Film Industry*, London: Routledge, pp. 107–28.
Gomery, Douglas (2013), 'The Economics of the Horror Film', in James B. Weaver III and Ron Tamborini (eds), *Horror Films: Current Research on Audience Preferences and Reactions*, New York: Routledge, pp. 49–62.
Gorfinkel, Elena (2008), 'Cult Film or Cinephilia by Any Other Name', *Cinéaste*, 34: 1, pp. 33–8.
Grint, Keith (2005), *The Sociology of Work: Introduction*, 3rd edn, Cambridge: Polity Press.
Grossman, Laurie M. and Gabriella Stern (1993), 'Blockbuster to Buy Controlling Stake in Spelling in Swap', *Wall Street Journal*, 9 March, p. B10.
'The Guardian Interview with Samuel Z Arkoff' (2003), DVD bonus material, *Blood of Dracula*, [DVD], UK: Direct Video Distribution.
Guttman, Barney C. (2017), Interview with the author, 13 January.
Handel, Leo A. (1953), 'Hollywood Market Research', *The Quarterly of Film Radio and Television*, 7: 3, Spring, pp. 304–10.
Hanners, John and Harry Kloman (1982), '"The McDonaldization of America": An Interview with George A. Romero', *Film Criticism*, 7: 1, pp. 69–81.
Harmetz, Aljean (1982), 'From the Cecil B. DeMilles of Pittsburgh: "*Creepshow*"', *New York Times*, 7 November, pp. H15, H25.
Harmetz, Aljean (1983), 'New Film-Comic-Superhero Coming', *New York Times*, 1 March, p. C11.
Harmetz, Aljean (1984), '"*Pet*" Film Rights Sold', *New York Times*, 8 June, p. C10.
Harrington, Richard (1987), 'Horror and Humor', *The Washington Post*, 6 May, p. B6.
Harrison, John (2018), Interview with the author, 22 March.

Hart, Adam (2020), 'George A. Romero Rarities with Adam Hart', *Northwest Film Forum*, online <https://nwfilmforum.org/events/george-romero-rarities-with-adam-hart-online> (accessed 25 October 2020).

Hawkins, Joan (2009), 'Culture Wars: Some New Trends in Art Horror', *Jump Cut: A Review of Contemporary Media*, online, 51, Spring 2009 <http://www.ejumpcut.org/archive/jc51.2009/artHorror> (accessed 24 March 2020).

Heffernan, Kevin (2002), 'Inner-City Exhibition and the Genre Film: Distributing *Night of the Living Dead* (1968)', *Cinema Journal*, 41: 3, pp. 59–77.

Heffernan, Kevin (2004), *Ghouls, Gimmicks, and Gold: Horror Films and the American Movie Business, 1953–1968*, Durham: Duke University Press.

Heffernan, Nick (2000), *Capital, Class & Technology in Contemporary American Culture: Projecting Post-Fordism*, London: Pluto Press.

Heffernan, Nick (2015), 'No Parents, No Church, No Authorities in Our Films: Exploitation Movies, the Youth Audience, and Roger Corman's Counterculture Trilogy', *Journal of Film and Video*, 67: 2, pp. 3–20.

Heim, Robert G. (2002), *Going Public in Good Times and Bad: A Legal and Business Guide*, New York: ALM Publishing.

Heimann, Sandra W. (1992), 'Spelling Entertainment Group Inc. Announce Agreements in Principle to Sell Remaining Oil Operations', *PR Newswire*, 12 November, p. 1.

Heimel, Cynthia (1980), 'The *Living Dead* Ride Again', *New York Magazine*, 21 July, pp. 46–8.

Henry9785 (2019), 'Unpopular Opinion: *IT 2* Was Too Mainstream', *reddit*, online, 4 September <https://www.reddit.com/r/ItTheMovie/comments/d47m92/unpopular_opinion_it_2_was_too_mainstream> (accessed 19 January 2021).

Herbert, Daniel, Amanda D. Lotz and Aswin Punathambekar (2020), *Media Industry Studies*, Cambridge: Polity Press.

Heritage Entertainment, Inc. (1989), *Proxy Statement*, 11 May, Washington, DC: Securities and Exchange Commission.

Hervey, Ben (2020), *Night of the Living Dead: BFI Film Classics*, 2nd edn, London: Bloomsbury Publishing.

Hillier, Jim and Aaron Lipstadt (1986), 'The Economics of Independence: Roger Corman and New World Pictures, 1970–80', *Movie*, 31/32, pp. 43–53.

Hills, Matt (2013), 'Cult Movies With and Without Cult Stars: Differentiating Discourses of Stardom', in Kate Egan and Sarah Thomas (eds), *Cult Film Stardom: Offbeat Attractions and Processes of Cultification*, London: Palgrave Macmillan, pp. 21–36.

Hilmes, Michele (2009), 'Nailing Mercury: The Problem of Media Industry Historiography', in Jennifer Holt and Alisa Perren (eds), *Media Industries: History, Theory, and Method*, West Sussex: Wiley-Blackwell, pp. 21–33.

Hiltzik, Michael A. (1998), 'Spidey's Movie Mess', *Los Angeles Times*, online, 29 September <http://www.teako170.com/spidey.html> (accessed 4 December 2020).

Hiltzik, Michael A. (2002), 'Untangling the Web', *Los Angeles Times*, online, 24 March <https://www.latimes.com/archives/la-xpm-2002-mar-24-tm-34460-story.html> (accessed 8 December 2020).

Hirschman, Elizabeth C. (1983), 'Aesthetics, Ideologies and the Limits of the Marketing Concept', *Journal of Marketing*, 47: 3, Summer, pp. 45–55.

Hjort, Mette (ed.) (2012), *Film and Risk*, Detroit: Wayne State University Press.
Hoberman J. and Jonathan Rosenbaum (1991), *Midnight Movies*, Boston: Da Capo Press.
Hofmeister, Sallie (1995), 'Viacom Puts its 78% Stake in Spelling Up for Sale', *Los Angeles Times*, 11 August, pp. D1, D5.
Hofmeister, Sallie (1998), 'Spelling Entertainment to Close Film Division, Parcel Out Projects', *Los Angeles Times*, online, 20 February <http://articles.latimes.com/1998/feb/20/business/fi-21020> (accessed 29 June 2020).
Holt, Jennifer (2002), 'Steven Soderbergh', in Yvonne Tasker (ed.), *Fifty Contemporary Filmmakers*, London: Routledge, pp. 303–11.
Holt, Jennifer and Alisa Perren (2009), 'Introduction: Does the World Really Need One More Field of Study?', in Holt and Perren (eds), *Media Industries: History, Theory, and Method*, West Sussex: Wiley-Blackwell, pp. 1–16.
Honeycutt, Kirk (1980), 'Mavericks of the Movies – Regional Filmmakers', *New York Times*, 9 November, pp. D19, D23.
Hope, Ted (2010), 'Matthew Porterfield on Truly Collaborative, Egalitarian & Economical Filmmaking', *Hope for Film*, online, 10 February <http://trulyfreefilm.hopeforfilm.com/2010/02/matthew-porterfield-on-truly-collaborative-egalitarian-economical-filmmaking.html/> (accessed 29 May 2020).
Horton, Adrian (2019), 'The Last Laugh: Behind the Multimillion-Dollar Deals to Buy Old Sitcoms', *The Guardian*, online, 8 October <https://www.theguardian.com/tv-and-radio/2019/oct/08/the-last-laugh-behind-the-multimillion-dollar-deals-to-buy-old-sitcoms> (accessed 1 December 2020).
'The Independent Feature Movement: Changing the Rules of the Game' (1981), *American Film*, 6: 10, September, p. 57.
Insdorf, Annette (1981), 'Ordinary People, European-Style, or How to Spot an Independent Feature', *American Film*, 6: 10, September, pp. 57–60.
An Interview with Professor Michele Hilmes (2014), online video, created by Samuel Ward, UK: University of Nottingham, online, 29 April <https://mediaspace.nottingham.ac.uk/media/An+Interview+with+Professor+Michele+Hilmes/1_5os55evn> (accessed 28 December 2020).
'Italo "*Dawn of the Dead*" Goes to United Film' (1979), *Variety*, 7 February, p. 34.
Jacobs, Diane (1979), 'Reports from the New York Film Festival', *Film Comment*, 15: 6, pp. 59–61.
Jacobs, Diane (1980), *Hollywood Renaissance*, New York: Dell Publishing.
Jain, Bharat A. and Omesh Kini (1999), 'The Life Cycle of Initial Public Offering Firms', *Journal of Business Finance & Accounting*, 26: 9/10, pp. 1281–307.
James, David E. (1989), *Allegories of Cinema: American Film in the Sixties*, Princeton: Princeton University Press.
Jancovich, Mark (2000), '"A Real Shocker": Authenticity, Genre and the Struggle for Distinction', *Continuum: Journal of Media & Cultural Studies*, 14: 1, pp. 23–35.
Jancovich, Mark (2002), 'Cult Fictions: Cult Movies, Subcultural Capital and the Production of Cultural Distinctions', *Cultural Studies*, 16: 2, pp. 306–22.
Jayaraman, Narayanan, Ajay Khorana, Edward Nelling and Jeffrey Covin (2000), 'CEO Founder Status and Firm Financial Performance', *Strategic Management Journal*, 21, pp. 1215–24.

Jenkins, Henry (2003), '*Quentin Tarantino's Star Wars?*: Digital Cinema, Media Convergence, and Participatory Culture', in David Thorburn and Jenkins (eds), *Rethinking Media Change: The Aesthetics of Transition*, Cambridge, MA: The MIT Press, pp. 281–312.

Jensen, Michael C. (1983), 'Organization Theory and Methodology', *The Accounting Review*, 58: 2, pp. 319–39.

Jensen, Michael C. and William H. Meckling (1976), 'Theory of the Firm: Managerial Behavior, Agency Costs and Ownership Structure', *Journal of Financial Economics*, 3: 4, pp. 305–60.

Jobber, David and Fiona Ellis-Chadwick (2019), *Principles and Practice of Marketing* [Kindle], 9th edn, New York: McGraw-Hill.

Jones, Alan (1982), 'George Romero Interview', *Starburst*, 4: 12, pp. 34–8.

Jones, Alan (1990), 'George A. Romero Speaks Out', *Starburst*, 12: 7, pp. 16–19.

Kael, Pauline (1963), 'Circles and Squares', *Film Quarterly*, 16: 3, pp. 12–26.

Karr, Lee (2014), *The Making of George A. Romero's Day of the Dead*, London: Plexus.

Keasey, Kevin and Mike Wright (1993), 'Issues in Corporate Accountability and Governance: An Editorial', *Accounting and Business Research*, 23: 91a, pp. 291–303.

Kehr, Dave (2011), *When Movies Mattered: Reviews from a Transformative Decade*, Chicago: University of Chicago Press.

Kellner, Douglas (2002), 'The Frankfurt School and British Cultural Studies: The Missed Articulation', in J. T. Nealon and C. Irr (eds), *Rethinking the Frankfurt School: Alternative Legacies of Cultural Critique*, New York: State University of New York Press, pp. 31–58.

Kelly, Kate (2006), 'Defying the Odds, Hedge Funds Bet Billions on Movies', *The Wall Street Journal*, online, 29 April <https://www.wsj.com/articles/SB114627404745739525> (accessed 27 November 2020).

Kiely, Kathy (1982), 'IRS Has Role in Film Investment', *The Pittsburgh Press*, 24 January, pp. 1, A-18.

King, Geoff (2005), *American Independent Cinema*, London: I. B. Tauris.

King, Geoff (2009), *Indiewood, USA: Where Hollywood Meets Independent Cinema*, London: I. B. Tauris.

King, Geoff (2013), *Indie 2.0: Change and Continuity in Contemporary American Indie Film*, London: I. B. Tauris.

King, Geoff (2017), 'Introduction: What Indie Isn't...Mapping the Indie Field', in King (ed.), *A Companion to American Indie Film*, West Sussex: John Wiley & Sons, pp. 1–21.

King, Geoff, Claire Molloy and Yannis Tzioumakis (2013), 'Introduction', in King, Molloy and Tzioumakis (eds), *American Independent Cinema: Indie, Indiewood and Beyond*, Abingdon: Routledge, pp. 1–8.

King, Stephen (1978), *The Stand*, the Complete and Uncut Edition, 2012 First Anchor Books Edition, New York: Anchor Books.

Klain, Stephen (1981), 'Laurel Ups Pic Development Lode Beyond Romero; Eyes Two Yearly', *Variety*, 3 June, pp. 6, 36.

Kleinhans, Chuck (1975), 'Reading and Thinking about the Avant-Garde', *Jump Cut*, online <https://www.ejumpcut.org/archive/onlinessays/JC06folder/AvantGdeReading.html> (accessed 5 June 2020).

Kleinhans, Chuck (1998), 'Independent Features: Hopes and Dreams', in Jon Lewis (ed.), *The New American Cinema*, Durham, NC: Duke University Press, pp. 307–27.

Kohn, Eric (2011), 'A Kingmaker in the Realm of Cheapie Horror', *New York Times*, 15 April, p. AR10.

Kohn, Eric (2016), 'Joe Swanberg's Filmmaking Factory: How the DIY Filmmaker is Supporting a Community of Directors on the Rise', *Indiewire*, online, 27 October <https://www.indiewire.com/2016/10/joe-swanberg-forager-films-support-indie-film-1201740588> (accessed 13 January 2021).

Kolbert, Elizabeth (1993), 'What's a Network TV Censor to Do?', *New York Times*, 23 May, pp. H1, 31.

Kolev, Kalin, Jerayr Haleblian and Gerry McNamara (2012), 'A Review of the Merger and Acquisition Wave Literature: History, Antecedents, Consequences, and Future Directions', in David Faulkner, Satu Teerikangas and Richard J. Joseph (eds), *The Handbook of Mergers and Acquisitions*, Oxford: Oxford University Press, pp. 19–39.

Kotler, Philip (1967), *Marketing Management: Analysis, Planning, and Control*, Englewood Cliffs: Prentice Hall.

Kotler, Philip, Gary Armstrong, Lloyd C. Harris and Hogwei He (2020), *Principles of Marketing*, 8th European edn, Harlow: Pearson Education.

Kotler, Philip, Kevin Lane Keller, Mairead Brady, Malcolm Goodman and Torben Hansen (2016), *Marketing Management*, 3rd edn, Harlow: Pearson Education.

Kouvaros, George (2004), *Where Does it Happen?: John Cassavetes and Cinema at the Breaking Point*, Minneapolis: University of Minnesota Press.

Kroll, Jack (1981), '"Heaven" Can Wait', *Film Comment*, 17: 1, pp. 58–9.

Lammi, Ed (2018), Interview with the author, 19 April.

Lamont, Austin (1981), 'Independents Day', *Film Comment*, 17: 6, pp. 15–20, 69–74, 76.

Lang, Brent (2018), 'Apple Taps A24 to Produce Slate of Films', *Variety*, online, 15 November <https://variety.com/2018/film/news/apple-a24-films-1203029800> (accessed 2 December 2020).

Larson, Magali Sarfatti (1977), *The Rise of Professionalism: A Sociological Analysis*, Berkeley: University of California Press.

Laurel Entertainment, Inc. (1980), *Form 10-K for Fiscal Year Ended 31 March 1980*, Washington, DC: Securities and Exchange Commission.

Laurel Entertainment, Inc. (1981), *Form 10-K for Fiscal Year Ended 31 March 1981*, Washington, DC: Securities and Exchange Commission.

Laurel Entertainment, Inc. (1982a), *Annual Report for Fiscal Year Ended 31 March 1982*, Washington, DC: Securities and Exchange Commission.

Laurel Entertainment, Inc. (1982b), *Form 10-K for Fiscal Year Ended 31 March 1982*, Washington, DC: Securities and Exchange Commission.

Laurel Entertainment, Inc. (1983a), 'Announcing Our Program of Theatrical Motion Pictures . . .', [advertisement], *Variety 26th International Film Annual for Cannes 1983*, 4 May, pp. 61–9.

Laurel Entertainment, Inc. (1983b), *Annual Report for Fiscal Year Ended 31 March 1983*, Washington, DC: Securities and Exchange Commission.

Laurel Entertainment, Inc. (1983c), *Form 10-K for Fiscal Year Ended 31 March 1983*, Washington, DC: Securities and Exchange Commission.

Laurel Entertainment, Inc. (1984a), *Annual Report for Fiscal Year Ended 31 March 1984*, Washington, DC: Securities and Exchange Commission.

Laurel Entertainment, Inc. (1984b), 'Exhibit 10.5: Employment Agreement with George A. Romero Dated as of June 19, 1983', *Form 8-K for Fiscal Year Ended 31 March 1984*, Washington, DC: Securities and Exchange Commission, pp. 1–19.

Laurel Entertainment, Inc. (1984c), 'Exhibit 10.6: Employment Agreement with Richard P. Rubinstein Dated as of June 19, 1983', *Form 8-K for Fiscal Year Ended 31 March 1984*, Washington, DC: Securities and Exchange Commission, pp. 1–13.

Laurel Entertainment, Inc. (1984d), 'Exhibit 10.10: Lease Agreement Concerning the Company's Pittsburgh Facility', *Form 8-K for Fiscal Year Ended 31 March 1984*, Washington, DC: Securities and Exchange Commission, 1984, pp. 1–5.

Laurel Entertainment, Inc. (1984e), *Form 10-K for Fiscal Year Ended 31 March 1984*, Washington, DC: Securities and Exchange Commission.

Laurel Entertainment, Inc. (1985a), *Annual Report for Fiscal Year Ended 31 March 1985*, Washington, DC: Securities and Exchange Commission.

Laurel Entertainment, Inc. (1985b), 'Exhibit 10.13: Memorandum of Agreement Between the Company and George A. Romero Dated 20 March 1985', *Form 8-K for Fiscal Year Ended 31 March 1985*, Washington, DC: Securities and Exchange Commission, pp. 1–3.

Laurel Entertainment, Inc. (1985c), *Form 10-K for Fiscal Year Ended 31 March 1985*, Washington, DC: Securities and Exchange Commission.

Laurel Entertainment, Inc. (1986), *Form 10-K for Fiscal Year Ended 31 March 1986*, Washington, DC: Securities and Exchange Commission.

Laurel Entertainment, Inc. (1987a), *Annual Report for Fiscal Year Ended 31 March 1987*, Washington, DC: Securities and Exchange Commission.

Laurel Entertainment, Inc. (1987b), *Form 10-K for Fiscal Year Ended 31 March 1987*, Washington, DC: Securities and Exchange Commission.

Laurel Entertainment, Inc. (1988), *Form 10-K for Fiscal Year Ended 31 March 1988*, Washington, DC: Securities and Exchange Commission.

Laurel Entertainment and LBS (1983), '*Tales from the Darkside*', [advertisement], *Variety*, 20 July, p. 97.

'Laurel Entertainment Out of Development Stage as Cash Flows' (1982), *Variety*, 7 July, p. 4.

'Laurel's First Profitable Year' (1983), *Pittsburgh Post-Gazette*, 30 June, p. 8.

Levitt, Theodore (1960), 'Marketing Myopia', *Harvard Business Review*, July-August, pp. 45–56.

Levy, Alan (1965), 'Peekaboo Sex, or How to Fill a Drive-In', *LIFE*, 59: 3, July, pp. 81–8.

Levy, Emanuel (1999), *Cinema of Outsiders: The Rise of American Independent Film*, New York: New York University Press.

Lien, Yung-Chih and Shaomin Li (2014), 'Professionalization of Family Business and Performance Effect', *Family Business Review*, 27: 4, pp. 346–64.

Light in the Darkness: The Impact of Night of the Living Dead (2018), Blu Ray bonus feature, directed by Satoko Sugiyama, [Blu Ray], USA: Criterion.

Lippe, Richard, Tony Williams and Robin Wood (1980), 'The George Romero Interview', *Cinema Spectrum*, 1: 1, pp. 4–7.

Lippman, John and James Bates (1994), 'Viacom, Blockbuster Unveil Surprise Merger', *Los Angeles Times*, online, 8 January <http://articles.latimes.com/1994-01-08/news/mn-9710_1_viacom-paramount-merger> (accessed 27 November 2020).

Little, Fred A. and Fred Drasner (1976), 'The Tax Shelter: A Reappraisal', *The John Marshall Law Review*, 10: 1, pp. 67–92.

Littleton, Cynthia (1998), 'Supplier Holds Steady Course', *Variety*, 5 January, pp. 53–4, 66.

Lotz, Amanda D. (2009), 'Industry-Level Studies and the Contributions of Gitlin's *Inside Prime Time*', in Vicki Mayer, Miranda J. Banks and John Thornton Caldwell (eds), *Production Studies: Cultural Studies of Media Industries*, New York: Routledge, pp. 25–38.

Lotz, Amanda D. (2014), *The Television Will Be Revolutionized*, 2nd edn, New York: New York University Press.

Lotz, Amanda D. and Horace Newcomb (2012), 'The Production of Entertainment Media', in Klaus Bruhn Jensen (ed.), *A Handbook of Media and Communication Research: Qualitative and Quantitative Methodologies*, 2nd edn, Abingdon: Routledge, pp. 71–86.

Loynd, Ray (1993), 'CBS Tuesday Movie *Precious Victims*', *Variety*, online, 28 September <https://variety.com/1993/tv/reviews/cbs-tuesday-movie-precious-victims-1200433153> (accessed 18 December 2020).

Lubatkin, Michael (1983), 'Mergers and the Performance of the Acquiring Firm', *The Academy of Management Review*, 8: 2, pp. 218–25.

Lubatkin, Michael (1987), 'Merger Strategies and Stockholder Value', *Strategic Management Journal*, 8: 1, pp. 39–53.

Lucas, Tim (1997), 'Dawns of the Dead', *Video Watchdog*, 38, pp. 40–9.

Lyons, James (2014), 'The American Independent Producer and the Film Value Chain', in Andrew Spicer, A. T. McKenna and Christopher Meir (eds), *Beyond the Bottom Line: The Producer in Film and Television Studies*, New York: Bloomsbury, pp. 195–212.

MacAdams, Lewis (2001), *Birth of the Cool: Beat, Bebop, and the American Avant-Garde*, New York: The Free Press.

McCarthy, Todd (1983), 'Laurel Sked Creeps Quickly', *Variety*, 23 March, pp. 6, 31.

McCarthy, Todd (1987), 'Indies Releasing Pics in a Major Way', *Variety*, 17 June, pp. 3, 34.

McClellan, Steve (1993), 'Company Finds Life Beyond the Grave', *Broadcasting & Cable*, 6 December, p. 74.

McDonald, Paul (2018), 'Introduction', *Media Industries: Current Debates and Future Directions: Conference Programme*, online, 18–20 April, King's College London <https://media-industries.org/2018-conference> (accessed 8 January 2021), pp. 1–3.

Mallin, Christine A. (2019), *Corporate Governance*, 6th edn, Oxford: Oxford University Press.

Marotta, Jenna (2018), 'Apple May Not Buy A24, But Don't Be Surprised If It Did: Silicon Valley Increasingly Defines Hollywood', *Indiewire*, online, 30 March <https://www.indiewire.com/2018/03/apple-acquisition-a24-john-hodges-1201945328> (accessed 2 December 2020).

Martin, Adrian (2004), 'Possessory Credit', *Framework: The Journal of Cinema and Media*, 45: 1, pp. 95–9.
Martin, Bob (1981a), 'George Romero: Part One', *Fangoria*, 13, June, pp. 32–6.
Martin, Bob (1981b) '*Knightriders*', *Fangoria*, 12, April, pp. 17–19, 66–7.
Martin, R. H. (1985), 'George Romero on *Day of the Dead* and *Pet Sematary*', *Fangoria*, 48, October, pp. 43–7.
Maslin, Janet (1979), '"*Dawn of the Dead*": Morning After', *New York Times*, 20 April, p. C14.
Mathijs, Ernest and Xavier Mendik (2008), 'Editorial Introduction: What is Cult Film?', in Mathijs and Mendik (eds), *The Cult Film Reader*, Maidenhead: Open University Press, pp. 1–11.
Mathijs, Ernest and Xavier Mendik (2011), *100 Cult Films*, London: Palgrave.
May, Mike (2010), 'Pittsburgh's Real '60s "Mad Men"', *Pittsburgh Magazine*, online, 26 January <https://www.pittsburghmagazine.com/pittsburghs-real-60s-mad-men> (accessed 29 May 2020).
Mekas, Jonas and J. Hoberman (2007), '*Shadows* (John Cassavetes, 1958/1959)', in Dennis Lim (ed.), *The Village Voice Film Guide: 50 Years of Movies from Classics to Cult Hits*, Hoboken: John Wiley & Sons, pp. 237–43.
Menne, Jeff (2019), *Post-Fordist Cinema: Hollywood Auteurs and the Corporate Counterculture*, New York: Columbia University Press.
Merritt, Greg (2000), *Celluloid Mavericks: A History of American Independent Film*, New York: Thunder's Mouth Press.
Micklethwait, John (1989), 'A Survey of the Entertainment Industry', *The Economist*, 23 December, pp. 3–18.
Midnight Movies: From the Margin to the Mainstream (2005), documentary, directed by Stuart Samuels, [DVD], USA: Starz Home Entertainment.
Miller, Timothy (1992), 'The Roots of the 1960s Communal Revival', *American Studies*, 33: 2, pp. 73–93.
Monaco, James (1984), *American Film Now: The People, the Power, the Money, the Movies*, 2nd edn, New York: New York Zoetrope.
Monell, Raymundo (2008), 'George Romero: Our Zombie in Havana', *Daily News*, online, 14 February <https://www.nydailynews.com/latino/george-romero-zombie-havana-article-1.309086> (accessed 1 April 2020).
Moran, James M. (2002), *There's No Place Like Home Video*, Minneapolis: University of Minnesota Press.
Morris, Meaghan (1989), 'Tooth and Claw: Tales of Survival and "*Crocodile Dundee*"', *Social Texts*, 21, pp. 105–27.
Mosco, Vincent (2009), *The Political Economy of Communication*, 2nd edn, London: SAGE Publishing.
Murphy, J. J. (2019), *Rewriting Indie Cinema: Improvisation, Psychodrama, and the Screenplay*, New York: Columbia University Press.
Naremore, James (2004), 'Authorship', in Toby Miller and Robert Stam (eds), *A Companion to Film Theory*, Malden, MA: Blackwell Publishing, pp. 9–24.
New American Cinema Group (1961a), 'Film Unions and the Low-Budget Independent Film Production – An Exploratory Discussion', *Film Culture*, 22–3, Summer, pp. 134–50.

New American Cinema Group (1961b), 'The First Statement of the New American Cinema Group', *Film Culture*, 22–3, Summer, pp. 131–3.

'New Amsterdam Riding New Dawn Project' (1996), *Variety*, 7 October, p. 4.

'Newest Fun for Kids – A "Copter Ride"' (1962), *Pittsburgh Post-Gazette*, 6 September, p. 37.

Newman, Kim (2006), 'American Horror Cinema Since 1960', in Linda Ruth Williams and Michael Hammond (eds), *Contemporary American Cinema*, Maidenhead: Open University Press, pp. 134–7.

Newman, Michael Z. (2009), 'Indie Culture: In Pursuit of the Authentic Autonomous Alternative', *Cinema Journal*, 48: 3, Spring, pp. 16–34.

Niepmann, Friederike and Tim Schmidt-Eisenlohr (2014), 'International Trade, Risk, and the Role of Banks', *Federal Reserve Bank of New York Staff Reports*, 633, September 2013; revised November 2014 <https://www.newyorkfed.org/medialibrary/media/research/staff_reports sr633.pdf> (accessed 19 November 2020).

'*Night of the Living Dead* budget breakdown' (2002), DVD bonus material, *Night of the Living Dead*, [DVD], USA: Elite Entertainment.

Nikolic, Vladan (2017), *Independent Filmmaking and Digital Convergence: Transmedia and Beyond*, New York: Routledge.

Noglows, Paul (1994), 'It's Official: Viacom Inc', *Variety*, 11 July, pp. 11, 13.

Nowell, Richard (2014), 'There's Gold in Them There Chills', in Nowell (ed.), *Merchants of Menace: The Business of Horror Cinema*, New York: Bloomsbury, pp. 1–10.

Ogrodnik, Benjamin (2019), 'Forging an Alternative Cinema: Sally Dixon, the Film Section, and the Museum-Based Media Center', *Film History: An International Journal*, 31: 2, Summer, pp. 144–78.

Ortner, Sherry B. (2012), 'Against Hollywood: American Independent Film as a Critical Cultural Movement', *HAU: Journal of Ethnographic Theory*, 2: 2, pp. 1–21.

Payne, Dinah and Cecily A. Raiborn (2018), 'Aggressive Tax Avoidance: A Conundrum for Stakeholders, Governments, and Morality', *Journal of Business Ethics*, 147: 3, pp. 469–87.

Perren, Alisa (2012), *Indie, Inc.: Miramax and the Transformation of Hollywood in the 1990s*, Austin: University of Texas Press.

Perren, Alisa (2013), 'Last Indie Standing: The Special Case of Lions Gate in the New Millennium', in Geoff King, Claire Molloy and Yannis Tzioumakis (eds), *American Independent Cinema: Indie, Indiewood and Beyond*, Abingdon: Routledge, pp. 108–20.

Perry, Simon (1979), 'Romero, Rubinstein Widen Sights as "*Dawn*" Pays Off', *Variety*, 5 December, p. 32.

Peterson, Richard A. and David G. Berger (1971), 'Entrepreneurship in Organizations: Evidence from the Popular Music Industry', *Administrative Science Quarterly*, 16: 1, pp. 97–106.

Phillips, Kendall R. (2012), *Dark Directions: Romero, Craven, Carpenter, and the Modern Horror Film*, Carbondale: Southern Illinois University Press.

Phillips, Mark C. (1992), 'The Role of Completion Bonding Companies in Independent Productions', *Loyola of Los Angeles Entertainment Law Review*, 12: 1, pp. 97–125.

Pirie, David (2001), '*Jack's Wife*', in John Pym (ed.), *Time Out Film Guide*, 9th edn, London: Penguin, p. 548.

'Pix Must "Broaden Market":18% of Public; 76% of Audience' (1968), *Variety*, 20 March, p. 1.

Plotnik, Gene (1955), 'Open-Ends Stack Up as Local Ad's Best', *The Billboard*, 17 December, p. 19.

Pokorny, Michael and John Sedgwick (1998), 'The Risk Environment of Film Making: Warner Bros in the Inter-War Years', *Explorations in Economic History*, 35, pp. 196–220.

Pokorny, Michael and John Sedgwick (2012), 'The Financial and Economic Risks of Film Production', in Mette Hjort (ed.), *Film and Risk*, Detroit: Wayne State University Press, 2012, pp. 181–96.

Poll (1979), '*Martin*', *Variety*, 10 January, p. 27.

Porton, Richard (2002), 'Blue Collar Monsters: An Interview with George Romero', *Filmhäftet*, 119: 1, pp. 1–6.

Prince, Stephen (2002), *A New Pot of Gold: Hollywood Under the Electronic Rainbow, 1980–1989*, Berkeley: University of California Press.

Quint, Michael (1993), 'M.& A. Redux, With a Difference', *New York Times*, 19 September, p. 112.

Raphael, Melissa (1999), *Introducing Thealogy: Discourse on the Goddess*, Sheffield: Sheffield Academic Press.

Rappaport, Alfred and Mark L. Sirower (1999), 'Stock or Cash?: The Trade-Offs for Buyers and Sellers in Mergers and Acquisitions', *Harvard Business Review*, 77: 6, pp. 147–58.

Reed, Cara (2018), 'Professionalizing Corporate Professions: Professionalization as Identity Project', *Management Learning*, 49: 1, pp. 1–17.

Reflections on the Living Dead (2005), documentary, directed by Thomas Brown. USA: Tempe Entertainment.

Revokcom (2010), 'Umberto Lenzi – Interview (Part 2) Discussing the Making of *SPASMO*', *YouTube*, online, 27 April <https://www.youtube.com/watch?v=aE4kp5c8Mhs> (accessed 12 May 2020).

'Richard P. Rubinstein: Breathe Deep NYC No Charge' (2006), *Art Cat*, online <http://calendar.artcat.com/exhibits/2246> (accessed 5 May 2020).

Rigoletto, Sergio (2014), *Masculinity and Italian Cinema: Sexual Politics, Social Conflict and Male Crisis in the 1970s*, Edinburgh: Edinburgh University Press.

Rielly, Edward J. (2003), *The 1960s: American Popular Culture Through History*, Westport: Greenwood Press.

Romero, George A. (1983), *Copperhead Conquers the Warhawks*, based on a story by Romero and Jim Shooter, second draft, October, unproduced screenplay.

Romero, George A. (1984), *Day of the Dead*, third version, second draft, 21 September, unproduced screenplay.

Romero, George A. (2013), 'In Conversation with Alan Jones', *BFI*, online, 8 November <https://player.bfi.org.uk/film-george-romero-in-conversation-2013> (accessed 22 March 2016).

Romero, George A. (2016), Interview with the author, 7 April.

Romero, George A., Tom Savini, John Amplas and Christine Romero (2013), *Knightriders*, audio commentary, [Blu Ray], UK: Arrow Films.

'Romero and Argento Aim Ghoul Tale for Exposure at Cannes Marketplace' (1978), *The Independent Film Journal*, 81: 4, p. 12.

'Romero's "*Dawn of the Dead*" Non-Theatrically to C5' (1979), *Variety*, 12 September, p. 36.

'Romero-Rubinstein "*Knights*" for UA-Overseas; Producers Detail Other Deals, Viewpoint' (1979), *Variety*, 27 June, pp. 6, 26.

Rosen, David with Peter Hamilton (1990), *Off-Hollywood: The Making and Marketing of Independent Films*, New York: Grove Weidenfeld.

Rosenkrantz, Ehrenkrantz, Lyon & Ross, Inc. (1980), *Laurel Entertainment, Inc. Sale of Common Stock Prospectus*, 24 April, New York.

Ross, Stephen A. (1973), 'The Economic Theory of Agency: The Principal's Problem', *The American Economic Review*, 63: 2, pp. 134–9.

Rountree, Kathryn (1999), 'The Politics of the Goddess: Feminist Spirituality and the Essentialism Debate', *Social Analysis: The International Journal of Anthropology*, 43: 2, pp. 138–65.

Rowney, Mark (2015), 'What's Wrong with Tax Avoidance?', *New Statesman*, online, 20 April <https://www.newstatesman.com/politics/2015/04/whats-wrong-tax-avoidance> (accessed 7 May 2020).

Rubinstein, Richard (1973), 'Update on George ("*Night of the Living Dead*") Romero: Or, What Happens After Your First Successful Film?', *Filmmakers Newsletter*, 6: 8, pp. 22–4.

Rubinstein, Richard P. (1975), 'The Selling of O. J. Simpson: Independent Production for Television', *Filmmakers Newsletter*, 8: 6, pp. 28–30.

Rubinstein, Richard P (1989), '"*Pet Sematary*": Know Where Your Children Are', *New York Times*, 21 May, p. H3.

Rubinstein, Richard P. and Perry Martin (2004), *Dawn of the Dead*, audio commentary, [DVD], USA: Anchor Bay, 2004.

Rundle, Rhonda L. (1988), 'Spelling Agrees to Join with Unit of Great American', *Wall Street Journal*, 26 July, p. 1.

Russell, Bob (1999), *More with Less: Work Reorganization in the Canadian Mining Industry*, Toronto, University of Toronto Press.

Russo, John (2012), *The Complete Night of the Living Dead Filmbook*, Glassport: CreateSpace.

Russo, John (2016), Interview with the author, 30 June, email communication.

Rutenberg, Jim (2000), 'Miniseries King Robert Halmi Guards His Throne . . . Judge Judy Is Huge. . .Alison Stewart Resurfaces', *Observer*, online, 28 February <https://observer.com/2000/02/miniseries-king-robert-halmi-guards-his-throne-judge-judy-is-huge-alison-stewart-resurfaces> (accessed 16 May 2018).

Sarris, Andrew (1962–3), 'Notes on the Auteur Theory in 1962', *Film Culture*, 27, Winter, pp. 1–8.

Sarris, Andrew (2007), 'Kevin Smith', *Esquire*, online, 29 January <https://www.esquire.com/entertainment/movies/a1580/kevin-smith-0300> (accessed 22 November 2020).

Schatz, Thomas (2004), 'General Introduction', in Schatz (ed.), *Hollywood: Critical Concepts in Media and Cultural Studies, Volume One – Historical Dimensions: The Development of the American Film Industry*, London: Routledge, pp. 1–22.

Schatz, Thomas (2008), 'The Studio System and Conglomerate Hollywood', in Paul McDonald and Janet Wasko (eds), *The Contemporary Hollywood Film Industry*, Malden, MA: Blackwell, pp. 13–42.

Schatz, Thomas (2009), 'Film Industry Studies and Hollywood History', in Jennifer Holt and Alisa Perren (eds), *Media Industries: History, Theory, and Method*, West Sussex: Wiley-Blackwell, pp. 45–56.

Schatz, Thomas (2014), 'Film Studies, Cultural Studies, and Media Industries Studies', *Media Industries Journal*, 1: 1, pp. 39–43.

Schein, Edgar H. (1983), 'The Role of the Founder in Creating Organizational Culture', *Organizational Dynamics*, 12: 1, pp. 13–28.

Schuyten, Peter J. (1978), 'United Artists' Script Calls for Divorce', *Fortune*, 97, 16 January, pp. 130–7.

Sconce, Jeffrey (1995), '"Trashing" the Academy: Taste, Excess, and an Emerging Politics of Cinematic Style', *Screen*, 36: 4, pp. 371–93.

Scott, Tony (1973), 'Romero: An Interview with the Director of *Night of the Living Dead*', *Cinefantastique*, 2: 3, winter, pp. 8–15.

The Secret Life of Jack's Wife (2005), DVD bonus feature, directed by Gary Hertz, [DVD], USA: Anchor Bay Entertainment.

Segal, Hillel (1988), 'Spelling Unit Devours Laurel Entertainment', *Pittsburgh Post-Gazette*, 20 September, p. 26.

Segrave, Kerry (2004), *Foreign Films in America: A History*, Jefferson: McFarland and Company.

Seligson, Tom (2011), 'George Romero: Revealing the Monsters Within Us', in Tony Williams (ed.), *George A. Romero: Interviews*, Jackson: University Press of Mississippi, pp. 74–87.

Sexton, Jamie (2012), 'US "Indie-Horror": Critical Reception, Genre Construction, and Suspect Hybridity', *Cinema Journal*, 51: 2, pp. 67–86.

Sharkey, Betsy and Michael Freeman (1998), 'It's Great to be a King Again', *Mediaweek*, 8: 3, pp. 18–21.

Sheridan, Patricia (2020), 'PFO's Lights! Glamour! Action!' *Pittsburgh Post-Gazette*, online, 10 February <https://www.post-gazette.com/life/seen/2020/02/10/Lights-Glamour-Action-benefit-PIttsburgh-Film-Office-Oscar-Party/stories/202002100002> (accessed 7 January 2021).

Sherman, Stratford P. (1980), 'The Empire Pays Off', *Fortune*, October 6, pp. 52–5.

Shipka, Danny (2011), *Perverse Titillation: The Exploitation Cinema of Italy, Spain and France, 1960–1980*, Jefferson: McFarland.

Shleifer, Andrei and Robert W. Vishny (1991), 'Takeovers in the '60s and the '80s: Evidence and Implications', *Strategic Management Journal*, 12, Winter, pp. 51–9.

Sikov, Ed (1981), 'Review: *Knightriders*', *Cinéaste*, 11: 3, pp. 31–3.

Simões, Cláudia, Sally Dibb and Raymond P. Fisk (2005), 'Managing Corporate Identity: An Internal Perspective', *Journal of the Academy of Marketing Science*, 33: 2, pp. 153–68.

Singh, Harbir and Cynthia A. Montgomery (1987), 'Corporate Acquisition Strategies and Economic Performance', *Strategic Management Journal*, 8: 4, pp. 377–86.

Sitney, P. Adams (2000), 'The New American Cinema', in Sitney (ed.), *Film Culture Reader*, New York: Cooper Square Press, pp. 71–2.

'Six Big Ideas: Gary Becker's Concept of Human Capital' (2017), *The Economist*, online, 5 August <https://www.economist.com/schools-brief/2017/08/05/gary-beckers-concept-of-human-capital> (accessed 6 May 2020).

Spainhower, Mark (1986), 'George Romero', in V. Vale and Andrea Juno (eds), *Incredibly Strange Films*, London: Plexus, pp. 182–4.

Spelling Entertainment, Inc. (1989a), *Form 10-K for Fiscal Year Ended 31 July 1989*, Washington, DC: Securities and Exchange Commission.

Spelling Entertainment, Inc. (1989b), *Form 10-Q for 31 January 1989*, Washington, DC: Securities and Exchange Commission.

Spelling Entertainment, Inc. (1989c), *Form 10-Q for 30 April 1989*, Washington, DC: Securities and Exchange Commission.

Spelling Entertainment, Inc. (1990), *Annual Report for Fiscal Year Ended 31 July 1990*, Washington, DC: Securities and Exchange Commission.

Spelling Entertainment, Inc. (1991), *Form 10-K for Fiscal Year Ended 31 July 1991*, Washington, DC: Securities and Exchange Commission.

Spelling Entertainment, Inc. (1992), *Annual Report for Fiscal Year Ended 31 December 1992*, Washington, DC: Securities and Exchange Commission.

Spelling Entertainment, Inc. (1993), *Form 10-K for Fiscal Year Ended 31 December 1993*, Washington, DC: Securities and Exchange Commission.

'Spelling Ent. Forms Intl. Subsidiary' (1990), *Variety*, 26 November, p. 50.

Spicer, Andrew, A. T. McKenna and Christopher Meir (2014), 'Introduction', in Spicer, McKenna and Meir (eds), *Beyond the Bottom Line: The Producer in Film and Television Studies*, New York: Bloomsbury, pp. 1–24.

Spretnak, Charlene (1982), 'Introduction', in Charlene Spretnak (ed.), *The Politics of Women's Spirituality: Essays by Founding Mothers of the Movement*, New York: Doubleday, pp. xi-xxx.

Staiger, Janet (2013), 'Independent of What? Sorting Out Differences from Hollywood', in Geoff King, Claire Molloy and Yannis Tzioumakis (eds), *American Independent Cinema: Indie, Indiewood and Beyond*, Abingdon: Routledge, pp. 15–27.

Staiger, Janet (2017), 'Proto-Indie: 1960s "Half-Way" Cinema', in Geoff King (ed.), *A Companion to American Indie Film*, Malden, MA: Wiley-Blackwell pp. 209–32.

Stanley, Jeffrey (2021), Interview with the author, 12 January, email communication.

Stanton, William J., Kenneth E. Miller and Roger A. Layton (1994), *Fundamentals of Marketing*, 3rd Australian edn, Roseville, NSW: McGraw-Hill.

Stein, Andrew (2021), Interview with the author, 12 January, email communication.

Stevens, Brad (2013), 'The Knights of King George', *George A. Romero's Knightriders*, Collectors Booklet, UK: Arrow Films, pp. 7–14.

Surmacz, Gary Anthony (1975), 'Anatomy of a Horror Film', *Cinefantastique*, 4: 1, pp. 14–27.

Swires, Steve (1983), 'Aliens Invade New York! On the Set of "Strange Invaders"', *Starlog*, 67, February, pp. 42–4.

Szebin, Frederick C. (1996), 'Lean and Mean', *American Cinematographer*, 77: 4, pp. 30–2, 34.

Teitler, William (2018), Interview with the author, 21 April.
Thomas, Bob (1979), 'An X Rated Movie Without Even a Kiss', *The Anniston Star*, 7 July, p. 40.
Thomas, Paulette (1995), 'Lindner Empire Starts to Evolve from Junk Age', *Wall Street Journal*, 6 July, p. B1.
Titanus (1978), '*Dawn of the Dead*', [advertisement], *Variety*, 18 October, pp. 14–15.
Tobias, Scott (2004), 'Jim Jarmusch', *The AV Club*, online, 19 May <https://www.avclub.com/jim-jarmusch-1798208341> (accessed 22 November 2020).
Tomkins, Calvin (1973), 'All Pockets Open', *The New Yorker*, online, 6 January <http://jonasmekas.com/images/new-yorker-profile.pdf> (accessed 19 January 2021).
Tompkins, Joe (2014), 'Bids for Distinction: The Critical-Industrial Function of the Horror Auteur', in Richard Nowell (ed.), *Merchants of Menace: The Business of Horror Cinema*, New York: Bloomsbury, pp. 203–14.
'Top Rental Features of 1963' (1964), *Variety*, 8 January, p. 71.
Torres, Craig (1991), 'Momentum Investors Hit the Skids on Blockbuster's Blow Out', *Wall Street Journal*, 4 March, p. C1.
'Types of Mergers: Different Types of M&A in the Corporate World' (n.d.), *CFI*, online <https://corporatefinanceinstitute.com/resources/knowledge/deals/types-of-mergers> (accessed 31 August 2020).
Tzioumakis, Yannis (2013a), *Hollywood's Indies: Classics Divisions, Specialty Labels and the American Film Market*, Edinburgh: Edinburgh University Press.
Tzioumakis, Yannis (2013b), 'American Independent Cinema in the Age of Convergence', *Revue française d'études américaines*, 2: 136, pp. 52–66.
Tzioumakis, Yannis (2017), *American Independent Cinema: An Introduction*, 2nd edn, Edinburgh: Edinburgh University Press.
'UA Argues X, Stigma of Porno, Ought Apply to No Other Types' (1979), *Variety*, 20 June, p. 26.
'UFD's Hassamein [sic] "Interested only in Commercial Feature Films"' (1985), *Screen International*, 493: 20, April, p. 172.
Ulin, Jeffrey C. (2019), *The Business of Media Distribution: Monetizing Film, TV, and Video Content in an Online World*, 3rd edn, New York: Routledge.
United States, Joint Committee on Internal Revenue Taxation (1975), *JCS-26-75 Tax Shelters: Movie Films*, online, 10 September, Washington: JCT <https://www.jct.gov/publications/1975/jcs-26-75> (accessed 11 May 2020).
Vale, Vivian and Andrea Juno (1986), 'Introduction', in Vale and Juno (eds), *Incredibly Strange Films*, London: Plexus, pp. 4–6.
Vallan, Giulia D'Agnolo (2006), 'A Pinewood Dialogue with George A. Romero', *Museum of the Moving Image*, Pannonia Foundation, online <http://www.movingimagesource.us/files/dialogues/2/42571_programs_transcript_html_244.htm> (accessed 27 May 2020).
Vella, Kevin James and T. C. Melewar (2008), 'Explicating the Relationship Between Identity and Culture: A Multi-Perspective Conceptual Model', in T. C Melewar (ed.), *Facets of Corporate Identity, Communication and Reputation*, Abingdon: Routledge, pp. 3–34.
ViacomCBS Inc. (2020), 'Exhibit 21: Subsidiaries of ViacomCBS Inc. as of January 1, 2020', *Form 10-K for Period Ending 31 December 2019*, Washington, DC:

Securities and Exchange Commission, online, 20 February <https://sec.report/Document/0000813828-20-000013> (accessed 13 January 2021).
'Viacom-Par Merger: What's in It' (1994), *Variety*, 21 February, p. 185.
Vogel, Harold L. (2020), *Entertainment Industry Economics: A Guide for Financial Analysis*, 10th edn, Cambridge: Cambridge University Press.
'VT Program Guide' (1973), *Radical Software*, 2: 5, pp. 46–51.
Warren, Bill (1994a), 'The Long Road to *The Stand*', *Fangoria*, 132, May, pp. 28–33.
Warren, Bill (1994b), 'Stephen King takes *The Stand*', *Fangoria*, 133, June, pp. 40–5, 82.
Wasko, Janet (2003), *How Hollywood Works*, London: SAGE Publications.
Waters, John (2005), *Shock Value: A Tasteful Book About Bad Taste*, New York: Thunder's Mouth Press.
'WB Has Domestic "*Creepshow*" Rights' (1982), *Variety*, 23 June, pp. 3, 32.
Weiskind, Ron (1984), 'Scare Shows', *Pittsburgh Post-Gazette*, 5 October, p. W28.
Werba, Hank (1978), '"Creative Co-Prod." Test Pays Off for Filmmakers Romero, Argento', *Variety*, 29 November, p. 40.
When Romero Met Del Toro (2017), Blu Ray bonus feature, directed by Chris Alexander, [Blu Ray], UK: Arrow Films.
Whetten, David A. (2006), 'Albert and Whetten Revisited: Strengthening the Concept of Organizational Identity', *Journal of Management Inquiry*, 15: 3, pp. 219–34.
Williams, Linda (1991), 'Film Bodies: Gender, Genre, and Excess', *Film Quarterly*, 44: 4, pp. 2–13.
Williams, Tony (2001), 'An Interview with George and Christine Romero', *Quarterly Review of Film & Video*, 18: 4, pp. 397–411.
Williams, Tony (2015), *The Cinema of George A. Romero: Knight of the Living Dead*, 2nd edn, New York: Wallflower Press.
Williams, Jr, B. John (2003), 'Resolving Tax Shelters: By Settlement or Litigation', *Chicago Bar Association Federal Taxation Committee*, online, 25 February <https://www.irs.gov/pub/irs-utl/shelters-feb25.pdf> (accessed 10 May 2020).
Wissot, Lauren (2009), 'Community of Fear', *Filmmaker Magazine*, online, Fall <https://www.filmmakermagazine.com/archives/issues/fall2009/glass-eye.php> (accessed 9 January 2021).
Witt, Ulrich (1998), 'Imagination and Leadership: The Neglected Dimension of an Evolutionary Theory of the Firm', *Journal of Economic Behavior and Organization*, 35, pp. 161–77.
Wood, Gary L. (1991), 'King in Development: *The Stand*', *Cinefantastique*, 21: 4, February, pp. 28–9.
Wood, Gary L. (1994), 'Development Movie Hell', *Cinefantastique*, 25: 2, April, pp. 19–21.
Wood, Robin (1980), 'Neglected Nightmares', *Film Comment*, 16: 2, March–April, pp. 24–32.
Wu, Harmony H. (2003), 'Trading in Horror, Cult and Matricide: Peter Jackson's Phenomenal Bad Taste and New Zealand Fantasies of Inter/National Cinematic Success', in Mark Jancovich, Antonio Lázaro Reboll, Julian Stringer and Andy Willis (eds), *Defining Cult Movies: The Cultural Politics of Oppositional Tastes*, Manchester: Manchester University Press, pp. 84–108.

Wyatt, Justin (1998), 'The Formation of the "Major Independent": Miramax, New Line and the New Hollywood', in Stephen Neale and Murray Smith (eds), *Contemporary Hollywood Cinema*, London: Routledge, pp. 74–90.

Wyatt, Justin (2000), 'The Stigma of X: Adult Cinema and the Institution of the MPAA Ratings System', in Matthew Bernstein (ed.), *Controlling Hollywood: Censorship and Regulation in the Studio Era*, London: Athlone Press, pp. 238–63.

Wylie, William H. (1972), 'Pittsburghers Steal a Scene from Hollywood Movie Moguls', *The Pittsburgh Press*, 12 March, p. D-12.

Yakir, Dan (1979), 'Morning Becomes Romero: An Interview with George Romero', *Film Comment*, 15: 3, pp. 60–5.

Yakir, Dan (1981), 'Knight After Night with George Romero', *American Film*, 6: 7, May, pp. 42–5, 69.

Zahra, Shaker A. and Igor Filatotchev (2004), 'Governance of the Entrepreneurial Threshold Firm: A Knowledge-based Perspective', *Journal of Management Studies*, 41: 5, pp. 885–97.

Zimmerman, Paul D. (1971), 'We Killed 'em in Pittsburgh', *Newsweek*, 8 November, p. 118.

INDEX

ABC (television network), 22, 56, 60, 145, 148–9, 151, 154, 159, 163n
À bout de souffle, 62
advertising sector, 3, 8, 19–20, 28–9, 31, 34, 37–8, 40, 48, 56, 69, 126, 149–50; *see also* television
agency theory, 22, 108, 124–5, 127, 130–1
Alambrista!, 8, 109
Alfred Hitchcock Presents, 126
Allen, Tom, 55, 64, 77, 79n, 80n, 127
Allen, Woody, 92, 118
Allied Artists, 36, 61
Altman, Robert, 52n, 147
Amazing Stories, 126–7
AMC, 166
American International Pictures (AIP), 35–6, 48–9, 61, 144; *see also* Arkoff, Samuel Z.
American Playhouse, 7
American Zoetrope, 94, 106n; *see also* Coppola, Francis Ford
Amusement Park, The, 170
An Occult Guide to South America, 63

Anders, Allison, 4
Anderson, Lawrence J., 29
Angeles Cinema Investors, 140–1
Anticipation of the Night, 6
Arabian Nights, 77
Argento, Claudio, 72, 74
Argento, Dario, 11, 21, 62, 72–5; *see also* Seda Spettacoli
Argento, Salvatore, 72
Arkoff, Samuel Z., 35; *see also* American International Pictures (AIP)
Atlantic Releasing, 114, 142
A24, 162n
auteur theory, 2, 3, 5–6, 11, 14, 20, 31–2, 39–40, 51, 69–70, 75, 86, 116, 137
Autoerotic, 168
Avellán, Elizabeth, 167; *see also* Troublemaker Studios

Bachman, Richard *see* King, Stephen
Ball, David, 19, 120–1, 137
Ballie, Bruce *see* Canyon Cinema
Barbie, 169n

197

Barenholtz, Ben, 65–6, 71; *see also* Libra Films
Barker, Clive, 126
Basic Instinct, 147
Battle Beyond the Stars, 113
Battleship Potemkin, 62
Bava, Mario, 62
Beastmaster, The, 113
Beetlejuice, 110
Bell, Book and Candle, 5
Benji, 46
Beverly Hills, 90210, 149, 157
Billy Jack, 46
Bird with the Crystal Plumage, The, 62, 72
Blackboard Jungle, 35
Blazing Stewardesses, 49
Bleier, Rocky, 61, 88
Bloch, Robert, 126
Blockbuster Entertainment, 18, 154–7, 160, 163n; *see also* Huizenga, Wayne
Blood and Black Lace, 62
Blow Job, 32
Blue Skies Again, 140–1
Blumhouse Productions, 12, 168
Bogdanovich, Peter, 5
Booby Hatch, The, 45
Boorman, John, 94, 148
Boy and His Dog, A 25n
Braddock, 66–7, 109, 131n, 166; *see also* Pittsburgh, PA
Brakhage, Stan, 6, 38
branding, 1, 12, 21, 65–6, 69–71, 74–5, 77, 79, 83, 86, 91–3, 96–8, 105, 121–2, 127, 136, 146, 149–50, 167
Breathe Deep NYC No Charge, 57
Bresson, Robert, 6
Bruiser, 166
Buba, Pasquale, 89, 166
Buba, Tony, 18, 64, 89, 166
Buffalo '66, 15
business orientation, 48–51, 54n, 168

Caiman, Charles Jeffrey, 138
Calley, John, 93–4
Cambist Films, 9, 46–7, 49–51; *see also* Hessel, Lee
Cannes Film Festival, 4, 71, 77, 111, 114–15, 122
Cannon Group, the, 111, 113–15, 142
Canterbury Tales, The, 77
Canyon Cinema, 7
CARA ratings system, 52n
Carelli, Joann, 119
Carnegie Museum of Art, 38
Carolco Pictures, 114–15, 147
Carpenter, John, 4, 9, 39, 69
Carrie, 94
Cassavetes, John, 5–6, 8, 39, 45–6, 93, 114
Castle, William, 37
Castronovo, T. J., 126
Cat People (1942), 94
Cat People (unproduced), 85, 94–5, 106–7n, 110
Cattle Annie and Little Britches, 120
CBS, 2, 18, 56, 94, 138, 148, 151, 169
Chan is Missing, 113
Charlie's Angels, 139
Chase, Chevy, 92
Cheever, John, 126
Chelsea Girls, 6
Children of Dune, 159, 172
China Rose, 138
Cimino, Michael, 118–19, 133n
Cinecom, 142
Cinema 16, 6–7
Coen brothers, 4
Color of Money, The, 116
Columbia Pictures, 5, 36–7, 61, 65, 112–13, 143–4
Columbia University, 7, 17, 57, 89, 167
completion guarantor, 19, 118–21
Concorde Pictures, 114
Condon, Bill, 94, 106–7n
Connection, The, 44
Constellation Films, 45–6

Continental Releasing, 37, 41; see also Walter Reade Organization
Conversation, The, 116
Cook, the Thief, His Wife & Her Lover, The, 77
Copperhead, 21, 111–15, 122, 131
Coppola, Francis Ford, 39, 94, 106n, 116; see also American Zoetrope
Corman, Roger, 47–8, 50, 112, 136; see also New World Pictures
corporate governance, 2, 17, 21, 84, 87, 89, 91, 104, 124–5, 129, 140, 152, 160
corporate identity, 17, 21, 22, 57, 71, 83, 91–2, 97–8, 104, 109, 127, 130, 135, 140, 146–7, 150–4, 160
Craven, Wes, 4, 69
Crazies, The, 30, 46–7, 50–1, 56, 62, 66, 69, 85, 107n, 149, 170
Creepshow, 1, 2, 85–6, 89, 94–6, 110, 115, 119–20, 122–3, 126–8, 137, 171
Creepshow (TV show), 2, 166
Creepshow 2, 111, 115, 121, 127, 135–7, 140, 171
Croft, Alvin C., 40, 46, 50, 56
Cronenberg, David, 9, 11
Crown International Pictures, 36
cult cinema, 1–3, 10–13, 15, 17, 21, 22, 24n, 51, 55, 65–6, 68–71, 75, 77, 79, 81n, 92–3, 97–8, 101, 105, 109, 121, 123, 135, 146, 148
Cuomo, Alfredo, 72

Daly, Robert A., 94
Dark Knight Rises, The, 166
Daughters of Satan, 43
David and Lisa, 41, 44
David Holzman's Diary, 44
Dawn of the Dead, 1, 3–4, 9, 21, 37, 45, 55, 69, 72–9, 80n, 83–6, 88, 91–2, 94, 107n, 116, 121–3, 127, 171
Dawn of the Dead (2004), 172

Day of the Dead, 19, 21–2, 85, 90, 111, 115–16, 120–4, 128, 133n, 149–50, 166, 171
Dead Don't Die, The, 12
Deep Red, 72, 74
De Laurentiis Entertainment Group, 142
democratic leadership, 30–2, 40, 51
Depraved, 168
Dick Cavett Show, The, 70
Diller, Barry, 156; see also QVC
Dirty Dancing, 15
Disney, 90, 111, 152–3, 155, 157, 166
Dolls (1987), 111
Dolls (unproduced), 111
Dracula, 68
Dubensky, Tom, 18, 62, 74, 88–9, 121, 166
Dune (2000), 159, 172
Dune (2021), 19
Dynasty, 139, 154
Dziga Vertov Group, 32, 34; see also Godard, Jean-Luc; Gorin, Jean-Pierre

Eastman, Marilyn, 34
Eastwood, Clint, 94
Easy Rider, 39
Eat, 32
EC Comics, 74
Ellison, Harlan, 126
El Mariachi, 13
El Topo, 24n, 65
Emmanuel, 114
Empire International Pictures, 114, 142
English Patient, The, 153
Entertainment industry unions, 8, 27, 29, 74, 90, 118–20, 140; see also Screen Actors Guild (SAG)
entrepreneurism, 17, 55, 58–9, 71, 78–9, 83, 85, 87, 126, 129, 155
Excalibur, 148
Exorcist, The, 94
Expostulations, 34
Exterminator 2, 114

Fantastic Voyage, The, 30
Fellini, Federico, 94
Feminine Mystique, The, 41–2
Fences, 166
Fessenden, Larry, 167–8; *see also* Glass Eye Pix
Film Fund, The, 7
Film-Makers' Cooperative, 6–7, 43, 49; *see also* Mekas, Jonas; New American Cinema Group
Film Section, the, 38–9, 53n
Filmways, 56, 76, 78, 144
flexible specialisation *see* post-Fordism
Forager Film, 168; *see also* Swanberg, Joe
Ford Foundation, 7
Forrest, Christine, 67, 90, 107n, 166
40 Acres and a Mule, 86 *see also* Lee, Spike
Frankfurt School, 16, 38
Free Voice of Labor: The Jewish Anarchists, 109
Friday the 13th, 70
Fritz the Cat, 76

Gal Young 'Un, 8, 109
Galin, Mitchell, 19, 136–9, 142, 146–7, 149, 151–2, 157, 159
Game Show Models, 45
Garris, Mick, 2, 149
Gerwig, Greta, 168, 169n
Get Out, 12
giallo films, 62–3, 66, 80n
Gilliam, Terry, 11
Girl Who Loved Tom Gordon, The, 166
Goblin, 74–5, 80n
Godard, Jean-Luc, 32, 62; *see also* Dziga Vertov Group
Godfather, The, 116
Godzilla vs. Kong, 169n
Golden Years, 148–9, 151, 171
Golod, Jerry, 126
Goodbye, Columbus, 39
Gordy, 153

Gorin, Jean-Pierre, 32; *see also* Dziga Vertov Group
Gornick, Michael, 67, 74, 87–9, 97, 115, 119, 121, 128–9, 136–8
Graduate, The, 39, 53n
Great American Communications Company (GACC), 145
Greenwood, L. C., 61
Grunwald, Peter, 166
Gulf and Western, 143; *see also* Paramount Pictures
Gunperson, 85

Habit, 167
Haimovitz, Jules, 142, 146
Hallmark, 138
Halloween, 69
Halmi, Robert *see* Robert Halmi, Inc.
Hanna-Barbera, 145
Hanson, John, 8, 44, 93
Hardman, Karl, 31, 34, 40
Harlan County U.S.A., 8, 109
Harris, Franco, 60–1
Harris, Jack H. *see* Jack H. Harris Enterprises
Harrison, John, 18, 89, 107n, 111, 116, 120, 128, 137, 139, 159, 166
Hassanein, Richard, 76, 78, 91, 95, 120, 122; *see also* United Film Distribution Company (UFDC)
Hassanein, Salah M., 58, 76, 78, 95, 120, 123; *see also* United Film Distribution Company (UFDC)
Heartbeat, 154
Heat, 89
Heaven's Gate, 118–19
Hemdale Film Corporation, 114
Hercules, 113–14
Heritage Entertainment, 144–5
Hessel, Lee, 46–7, 50; *see also* Cambist Films
Hitchcock, Alfred, 5–6, 27–8, 68, 69, 139
Hooper, Tobe, 4, 9, 94

INDEX

House of the Long Shadows, 114
Huizenga, Wayne, 155; *see also* Blockbuster Entertainment
human capital, 59–60, 64, 78, 79n, 125, 128, 151–3

Image Ten, 34, 36–7, 66
Independent Feature Project (IFP), 7
Independent-International Pictures *see* Constellation Films
indiewood, 5, 153
initial public offering (IPO), 84–7, 89, 91–2, 96, 98–9, 103–4, 105n, 110, 140
Into the West, 153
Intruder, The, 47
Investigation of a Citizen Above Suspicion, 65
Irreconcilable Differences, 140
It Happened to Jane, 5
It, 148

Jack H. Harris Enterprises, 36, 45–6, 49
Jack's Wife, 11, 20, 41–7, 49–51, 56, 170
Jackson, Peter, 11
Jarmusch, Jim, 4, 12, 93
Jaygee Productions, 142
Jerome Foundation, 7, 23n
Jodorowsky, Alejandro, 11, 24n, 65
Jones, Duane, 3, 37
Joseph Brenner Associates, 66
Jumanji (franchise), 166

Kentucky Fried Movie, The, 77
Kesey, Ken, 31
Killing of a Chinese Bookie, The, 8
King, Stephen, 1, 70, 85–6, 94–6, 111, 116–18, 122, 126–8, 130, 136–7, 146–52, 154, 159, 163n, 166, 169
Kiss and Tell, 159, 172
KNB EFX Group *see* Nicotero, Greg
Knightriders, 1, 17, 21, 83, 85, 89–91, 98–105, 109, 115, 116, 118–21, 128, 171

Krull, 113
Kubrick, Stanley, 94

Ladd Company, The, 94
Lady Bird, 169n
Lambert, Mary, 136–7
Lammi, Ed, 19, 90, 116, 120, 122–3, 166
Last Starfighter, The, 113
Last Temptation of Christ, The, 116
La Superstar International, 80n
Latent Image, 2, 3, 7, 20, 27–32, 34–41, 44–7, 50–1, 55–7, 59, 62, 66, 69, 80n, 83, 88, 89, 101, 129, 140, 168, 170
Laughlin, Michael, 94, 106n
Laurel, 1–4, 7, 12–13, 15–22, 28, 34, 55–66, 69–79, 80n, 81n, 83–99, 103–5, 108–16, 118–30, 133n, 135–42, 145–57, 159–60, 165–9
  assets, 19, 140–2, 154
  closure, 2, 22, 147, 151, 154, 157–60, 169
  employment and staffing, 18–19, 56, 59, 62, 87–90, 107n, 118, 124, 127–30, 137–8, 140, 142, 157, 159, 169
  expansion and growth, 59, 64, 71, 78, 83–8, 90–2, 95–6, 98–9, 103–5, 109–10, 114, 124, 128–31, 135, 140, 142, 146, 151–2, 154, 160
  facilities, 29, 56, 58, 106n, 140
  formation, 3, 7, 20, 55–6
  Laurel Productions of Pennsylvania, 3, 56, 124
  offices and studio space, 29, 56, 59, 62, 88, 98, 106n, 107n, 138–40, 151–2, 159, 169
  merger with Spelling, 18, 22, 135, 142, 145–7, 151–4, 160
  revenue, 86, 95–6, 121, 129, 138–40, 145, 154
  subsidiaries, 89, 120, 148–9
Lee, Spike, 4, 13, 86

Legend of Cherry Jankowski, The see *Booby Hatch, The*
Lenzi, Umberto, 62–3
Le Secret, 62, 65
Le Vent d'Est, 32
Levin, Ira, 70
Lexington Broadcast Services (LBS), 126–7, 129, 139
Libra Films, 62, 65, 68; see also Barenholtz, Ben
Lindner Jr, Carl, 145, 154
Lion of the Desert, 121
Little Women, 169n
Little World of Humongo Bongo, The, 166
Living Dead at the Manchester Morgue, The, 72
Lombardo, Goffredo, 75
Lord of the Rings, The, 148, 153
Lorimar-Telepictures Corporation see Lorimar
Lorimar, 113–14, 147–8
Love Streams, 114
Lucas, George, 39, 86, 94, 112–13
Lumet, Sidney, 52n
Lynch, David, 147–8

Ma Rainey's Black Bottom, 166
Macabre, 37, 53n
McDowell, Michael, 110
McGuire, Virginia M., 138
McLuhan, Marshall, 56, 79n
Magic at the Roxy, 170
Maîtresse, 65
Mark of the Witch, 43
marketing concept, 17, 20, 35–6, 48–51
marketing philosophy see marketing concept
Married . . . With Children, 163n
Martin, 1, 12, 17, 21, 65–71, 74, 79, 80n, 85, 86, 88, 95, 121, 131n, 150, 167, 171
Marvel, 21, 111–12, 114–15, 132n
Mastandrea, Nicholas, 166
Matta-Clark, Gordon, 57

Medium Cool, 79n
Mekas, Adolfas, 6; see also New American Cinema Group
Mekas, Jonas, 6, 8, 27, 30, 32, 38, 43; see also Film-Makers' Cooperative; New American Cinema Group
MGM, 5, 27, 35, 110, 113, 141
Midnight, 31
Midnight movies, 44, 65–6, 71
Miramax, 5, 15, 77, 152–3, 155, 167
Mister Rogers' Neighborhood, 28
Moment of Fear, 139
Mongrel: The Legend of Copperhead see *Copperhead*
Monkey Shines, 11, 136
Monsters, 139, 142, 151, 152, 159, 171
Motion Picture Association of America (MPAA), 35–6, 76, 118
MPI Media Group, 167
Murdoch, Rupert, 143
My Dinner with Andre, 113

National Endowment for the Arts (NEA), 7–8, 38, 44
Naughty Stewardesses, The, 45
NBC, 56, 126, 161n
Necronomicon, 85, 110
Nelson, Dusty, 89
Neon Demon, The, 75
Neverending Story III: Escape from Fantasia, The, 153
New American Cinema Group, 6–7, 12, 27, 39; see also Film-Makers' Cooperative; Mekas, Adolfas; Mekas, Jonas
New American Films, 40, 45–6
New Amsterdam Entertainment, 159–60, 170, 172
New Line Cinema, 5, 152–3, 155, 159
New World Pictures, 48–50, 113–15, 136; see also Corman, Roger

New York, 1, 5–8, 27, 29–30, 32, 34–5, 39, 42, 44, 49, 50–1, 56–7, 63, 65, 71, 74, 97–8, 111, 118, 126, 138–40, 159, 167–8
New York Film Festival, 7, 109
Nicotero, Greg, 166
Night Call Nurses, 48
Night Flier, The, 159, 172
Night of the Living Dead, 1, 3–4, 12, 15, 18, 20, 31–4, 36–8, 40–1, 45, 47, 51, 53n, 65–6, 69, 71–2, 75–6, 107n, 127, 166–7, 169n, 170
Nightmare on Elm Street, A, 69
Night Rose, 139
Nights and Weekends, 168
Nilsson, Rob, 8, 44, 93
Nobel, George, 57
North by Northwest, 5, 27
Northern Lights, 8, 44, 109
Nuñez, Victor, 8, 44, 93
NYPD Blue, 163n

Ophuls, Max, 6
opportunity structures, 13, 17, 22, 115, 125, 128, 130, 132n, 147, 168
Orion Pictures, 94, 136, 142, 144
  Orion Classics, 113
Out of This Furnace, 85, 109–10, 113, 131n
Outer Limits, The, 126

Pallenberg, Rospo, 148
Paramount Consent Decrees, the, 27, 30
Paramount Pictures, 61, 95, 113, 136, 143, 144, 147, 155–60
  Paramount Vantage, 5
PBS, 7, 70
Peckinpah, Sam, 52n
Penn, Arthur, 52n
Pet Sematary, 116–17, 130, 136–7, 146, 171
Peyton Place, 5

Phantom of the Opera, The, 138
Pink Flamingos, 24n, 65–6
Pittsburgh Film Office (PFO), 166
Pittsburgh, PA, 1, 2, 4, 7, 28–9, 34–8, 40–1, 46–7, 61, 64–5, 97, 135, 140, 146, 166, 168
Pittsburgh Steelers, 60
Player, The, 147
PMK, 70, 92–3
Pohl, Frederik, 126
Polar Express, The, 166
Porterfield, Matthew, 168
post-Fordism, 20, 30–1, 34, 37, 51
Precious Victims, 151, 171
professionalisation, 21, 83–5, 91–2, 97–9, 104–5, 123
proto-indies, 41–5, 51
Pulp Fiction, 153
Putney Swope, 44
Putty Hill, 168

QVC, 156; see also Diller, Barry

Rambo (franchise), 147
Rascoe, Judith, 148
Redford, Robert, 8, 15, 92; see also Sundance Institute
Redstone, Sumner, 155–6, 159–60; see also Viacom
regional filmmaking, 1–3, 7–8, 15, 34–6, 38–9, 41, 44–5, 59, 61–2, 64, 66–7, 74, 89, 93, 129, 139–40, 166–8, 169
Regional Industrial Development Company (RIDC), 29, 38–9, 46
Republic Pictures, 155–6
Return of the Jedi, 112–13
Return of the Secaucus Seven, 113
Ricci, Richard, 31
Ricci, Rudolph J., 28, 34, 40, 85
risk, 17, 21, 39, 46, 49, 55–6, 58–62, 64, 66, 69–73, 77–9, 84–5, 89, 91, 97, 110, 114, 119, 124, 133n, 141–2, 156, 168
Robert Halmi, Inc., 138, 151

203

Robocop, 112, 132n
Rocky Horror Picture Show, The, 65
Rodriguez, Robert, 13, 167; *see also* Troublemaker Studios
Romero, George A., 1–5, 7, 9–13, 16, 18–22, 25n, 27–32, 34, 36–8, 40–1, 43, 45–8, 50–1, 54n, 55–66, 68–79, 80n, 83–4, 86–8, 90–105, 107n, 108–16, 118, 120–31, 135–7, 140–1, 146, 148–51, 160, 166–7
  as auteur, 1–4, 11–12, 18, 20–2, 31–2, 34, 40, 47–8, 50–1, 55, 62–5, 68–70, 74–5, 77–8, 79, 83, 97–8, 108–9, 116–21, 125, 130–1, 135–7, 140, 146, 167–8
  corporate responsibilities, 40, 46, 63–4, 87–8, 90, 92, 97–8, 107n, 109, 124, 127, 130
  cult filmmaker, 1–3, 10–13, 21, 65–6, 69–71, 75, 79, 92–3, 97–8, 101, 104–5, 109, 121, 123, 135, 146
  departure from Laurel, 21, 22, 103, 108, 115, 123–4, 130, 135–7, 140, 153, 160, 167
  employment agreement, 88, 127
  family and upbringing, 7
  filmmaking style, 29–30, 32, 60, 73–5, 120
  Hollywood internship and early career, 5, 27–8
  leadership, 20, 28, 30–2, 34, 40–1, 46, 50, 55, 59, 97, 101–2, 109–10, 114, 125, 129, 151
  novels and books by, 86, 166
  partnership with Rubinstein, 1, 3, 12, 16, 22, 51, 56–60, 62, 64, 69, 71, 78, 88, 91, 97–8, 107n, 108–9, 116, 123–5, 127–30, 135–6
  unproduced projects, 21, 34–5, 85–6, 94–5, 106n, 107n, 108–17, 121–3, 130–1, 136, 148
  views on Hollywood, 4, 22, 27–8, 30, 50, 57, 92–3, 95–6, 100, 102–4

Rubinstein, Richard P., 1, 3, 11–13, 16–20, 22, 51, 55–64, 69, 71, 73, 76–8, 81n, 83–5, 87–91, 96–8, 103, 107n, 108–10, 113–16, 120–31, 135–40, 142, 146–50, 153, 157, 159–60, 166–7
  education and background, 1, 17, 51, 56–7, 59, 62, 89, 97
  employment agreements, 18, 88, 91, 127–8, 146, 159–60
  entrepreneurism, 55, 58–9, 71, 78–9, 83, 85, 126
  funding, 64, 66, 73, 76, 77–8, 95–6, 110–11, 121–3, 126, 129, 149; *see also* tax shelters
  journalism, 51, 56, 60
  leadership, 59, 87–90, 97–8, 116, 120–1, 125, 127–31, 135, 138, 146, 157, 159
  media engagement, 19, 86, 97–8, 108–9, 136–7, 150
  partnership with Romero, 1, 3, 12, 16, 22, 51, 56–60, 62, 64, 69, 71, 78, 88, 91, 97–8, 107n, 108–9, 116, 123–5, 127–30, 135–6
  producer, 1, 3, 19, 56, 64, 90–1, 136, 147–9, 159
  risk, 55, 58–60, 64, 73, 77–9, 85, 89, 97, 114
  television, 3, 56–7, 59–61, 89, 125–8, 138–9, 153, 159
Russo, John A., 18, 31, 40, 45, 56, 72

Salem's Lot, 94–5
Saturday Night and Sunday Morning, 37
Savini, Tom, 67, 100, 107n, 122, 128, 166
Saw, 15
Scandalous, 140
Sci-Fi Channel, 159
Scorsese, Martin, 39, 116
Screen Actors Guild (SAG), 90, 118; *see also* Entertainment industry unions

Season of the Witch see Jack's Wife
Sebastiane, 65
Seda Spettacoli, 72–4; *see also* Argento, Dario
Seinfeld, 161n
Semel, Terry, 94
sex, lies, and videotape, 4, 44
Shadows, 5–6
Shapiro Entertainment, 114
Shapiro, Irvin, 62, 64, 72
Sherman, Sam, 45
She's Gotta Have It, 13, 86
Shining, The, 94
Shoo-Be-Doo-Be-Moon, 85, 89, 121–2, 133n
Shook, Warner, 128
Shooter, Jim, 111–12
Shudder, 2, 166
Simpson, O. J., 60
Sinful Bed, The, 77
Singleton, Ralph S., 136
Sleepwalkers, 149
Smith, Kevin, 86
Soderbergh, Steven, 4, 44
Sparrow, Susanna, 86
Spasmo, 62–3, 65
Spelling, Aaron, 139, 145–6, 154
  Aaron Spelling Productions, 22, 142, 145, 147, 152, 154, 160
  Spelling Entertainment, 18, 22, 145–7, 149, 151–2, 154–7, 159, 169, 171–2
  Spelling Films International 146–7, 157
Stake Land, 167
Star Trek, 10
Star Trek III: The Search for Spock, 113
Stargell, Willie, 61
Star Wars, 86, 112–13
Stein & Day, 63–4
Stephen King's The Langoliers, 151, 171
Stephen King's The Stand, 2, 17, 22, 85–6, 96, 111, 115, 147–51, 160, 163n, 171

  original novel, 85, 111, 148–50
  CBS remake, 2, 169
Stephen King's Thinner, 146–7, 159, 171
Storyville, 147
Straub, Peter, 70
Streiner, Gary, 40, 56
Streiner, Russell, 28–9, 31–3, 36, 40, 45, 56
Struggles in Steel: The Fight for Equal Opportunity, 166
Sundance Institute, 8, 44; *see also* Redford, Robert
Sundance-Miramax era, 5
Superman: The Movie, 112
Superman II, 112
Superman IV: The Quest for Peace, 115
Survinski, Vincent D., 28, 33
Survival of the Dead, 3
Suspiria, 72, 74
Swanberg, Joe, 168; *see also* Forager Film
Swing Shift, 140
Syfy *see* Sci-Fi Channel

Tales from the Darkside, 19, 79n, 110, 126–9, 136, 138–42, 149, 159, 166, 169, 171
Tales from the Darkside: The Movie, 116, 126–7, 135–7, 142, 146–7, 171
Tax Reform Act, 61–3
tax shelters, 16, 59–66, 80n, 126, 140–1
Technicolor, 4, 74
Teitler, William, 19, 110, 126–7, 138–9, 166
television, 3, 8, 16–17, 20, 22, 27–9, 31, 52n, 55–7, 59–62, 64, 72, 76, 86, 89, 92, 94, 96, 109, 113, 125–9, 136–42, 144–55, 157, 159, 161n, 163n, 166, 169; *see also* advertising sector
Ten Little Indians, 62

Terminator 2: Judgement Day, 147
Texas Chain Saw Massacre, The, 94
There's Always Vanilla, 11, 31, 38–41, 44–7, 49, 55–6, 170
Thing About Sculpture, The, 57
THX 1138, 94
Time, Inc., 143
Timeline, The, 60
Tintorera: Killer Shark, 77
Titanus, 75
Tombs of the Blind Dead, 72
Tonight Show, The, 29
Torso, 66
Total Recall, 147
Tribune Broadcasting Company, 126, 139
Troublemaker Studios, 167–8
Truffaut, François, 5
Turner, Ted, 141, 152, 155
20th Century Fox, 5, 143, 155, 163n
  Fox Searchlight, 5
Twilight Zone, The, 126
Twin Peaks, 148
Twin Peaks: Fire Walk with Me, 147

Ultimate Mirror, 56–7, 59, 63, 81n, 126
United Artists (UA), 61, 76–7, 85, 94, 118–19, 141
  United Artists Theatre Circuit (UATC), 76, 78
  UA Classics, 65, 113
United Film Distribution Company (UFDC), 21, 76–8, 90–1, 95, 99, 108, 115, 118–24, 126, 133n, 167; *see also* Hassanein, Richard; Hassanein Salah M.
Universal Pictures, 15, 95, 113
  Universal Classics, 113

Van Sant, Gus, 4
Varèse Sarabande Records, 86
Vernon Johns Story, The, 151, 171
Vestron Pictures, 114, 142

Viacom, 18, 22, 144, 146, 155–60, 169; *see also* Redstone, Sumner
ViacomCBS, 18, 169
View Askew *see* Smith, Kevin
Vilagi, Diane, 138
Virgin Witch, 66
Visconti, Luchino, 94
Vogel, Amos, 6, 8
Vogel, David E., 87–90, 116, 126–7, 137, 165–6
Vogel, Marcia, 6, 8

Walking Dead, The, 166
Walt Disney Motion Picture Group *see* Disney
Walter Reade Organization, 36–7, 76; *see also* Continental Releasing
Warhol, Andy, 6, 7, 32
Warner Bros., 19, 61, 76, 78, 93–9, 104, 108, 110–11, 126, 136, 138, 143, 148, 157, 169n
  Time-Warner, 157
  Warner Home Video, 149
WBTV, 94, 148
Waters, John, 24n, 66
WDTV, 28
We Are Alive! The Fight to Save Braddock Hospital, 166
Weintraub Entertainment Group, 142
Where There's Smoke, 62, 65
Wingard, Adam, 168, 169n
Winners, The, 60–2, 88, 126, 170
Witch, The, 12
Woman Under the Influence, A, 8, 45–6
Wood, Robin, 4, 9, 46
Worldvision Enterprises, 142, 145, 147–9, 151–2, 154–5

X-rating, 71, 76–7

Young, Robert M., 93

Zola, Émile, 11